CRAIG BROWN

Ma'am Darling

99 Glimpses of
Princess Margaret

4th ESTATE · London

For my mother, Jennifer, born five days later; with love

4th Estate
An imprint of HarperCollins*Publishers*
1 London Bridge Street
London SE1 9GF
www.4thEstate.co.uk

First published in Great Britain in 2017 by 4th Estate
This 4th Estate paperback edition published in 2018

1

A catalogue record for this book is
available from the British Library

ISBN 978-0-00-820363-4

Printed and bound in Great Britain by
CPI Group (UK) Ltd, Croydon, CR0 4YY

MIX
Paper from
responsible sources
FSC® C007454

This book is produced from independently certified FSC paper
to ensure responsible forest management.

For more information visit: www.harpercollins.co.uk/green

My dreams
Watching me said
One to the other:
'This life has let us down.'
Paul Potts

Boredom: the desire for desires.
Leo Tolstoy

The love of place, and precedency, it rocks us in our cradles,
it lies down with us in our graves.
John Donne

1

21 August 1930
'Her Royal Highness The Duchess of York gave birth to a daughter this evening. Both Her Royal Highness and the infant Princess are making very satisfactory progress.'

31 October 1955
'I would like it to be known that I have decided not to marry Group Captain Peter Townsend. I have been aware that, subject to my renouncing my rights of succession, it might have been possible for me to contract a civil marriage. But mindful of the Church's teachings that Christian marriage is indissoluble, and conscious of my duty to the Commonwealth, I have resolved to put these considerations before others. I have reached this decision entirely alone, and in doing so I have been strengthened by the unfailing support and devotion of Group Captain Townsend. I am deeply grateful for the concern of all those who have constantly prayed for my happiness.'

21 May 1958
'The Press Secretary to the Queen is authorised to say that the report in the *Tribune de Genève* concerning a possible engagement between Princess Margaret and Group Captain Peter Townsend is entirely untrue. Her Royal Highness's statement of 1955 remains unaltered.'

26 February 1960
'It is with the greatest pleasure that Queen Elizabeth the Queen Mother announces the betrothal of her beloved daughter The Princess Margaret to Mr Antony Charles Robert Armstrong-Jones, son of Mr R.O.L. Armstrong-Jones Q.C., and the Countess of Rosse, to which union the Queen has gladly given her consent.'

19 March 1976
'HRH The Princess Margaret, Countess of Snowdon, and the Earl of Snowdon have mutually agreed to live apart. The Princess will carry out her public duties and functions unaccompanied by Lord Snowdon. There are no plans for divorce proceedings.'

10 May 1978
'Her Royal Highness The Princess Margaret, Countess of Snowdon, and the Earl of Snowdon, after two years of separation have agreed that their marriage should formally be ended. Accordingly Her Royal Highness will start the necessary legal proceedings.'

9 February 2002
'The Queen, with great sadness, has asked for the following announcement to be made immediately. Her beloved sister, Princess Margaret, died peacefully in her sleep this morning at 6.30 in the King Edward VII Hospital. Her children, Lord Linley and Lady Sarah Chatto, were at her side. Princess Margaret suffered a further stroke yesterday afternoon. She developed cardiac problems during the night and was taken from Kensington Palace to the King Edward VII Hospital at 2.30 a.m. Lord Linley and Lady Sarah were with her and the Queen was kept fully informed throughout the night. Queen Elizabeth, the Queen Mother, and other members of the Royal Family are being informed.'

For Immediate Release
Monday, 10 April 2006
London – Christie's announces that jewellery and works of art from the Collection of Her Royal Highness The Princess Margaret, Countess of Snowdon, will be sold in London on 13 and 14 June 2006. This important and unparalleled historic sale will celebrate and pay tribute to Princess Margaret's renowned beauty, style and taste. Comprising over eight hundred items, with estimates ranging from under £100 to over £500,000, the auction will feature a superb selection of jewellery and Fabergé as well as a broad range of furniture, silver, works of art and decorative objects.

2

Yet, perhaps, in the secret chambers of consciousness, she had her thoughts, too. Perhaps her fading mind called up once more the shadows of the past to float before it, and retraced, for the last time, the vanished visions of that long history – passing back and back, through the cloud of years, to older and even older memories – to the warm clasp of Crawfie, so full of do's and don'ts; to Sir Roy Strong's strange clothes and high demeanour; and her last afternoon tea with Peter; and Tony dancing attendance on her mother; and Roddy emerging from the sea at Mustique in his brand-new trunks; and the audience hooting with laughter at Dusty Springfield's impertinent aside; and President Johnson steering her into dinner in the White House, his right palm lingering perhaps a little too long on her royal behind; and the old Queen, her grandmother, reprimanding her for erratic behaviour with a bouncing ball; and Lilibet's voice down the telephone reassuring her once more that no harm had been done; and her mother laughing and saying 'Such fun!' before giving her that pitying look, and her father on his final evening bidding her good night, and see you in the morning.

3

Yoo-hoo!

Coo-EEEE!

She shows up without warning, popping her head around the door of every other memoir, biography and diary written in the second half of the twentieth century. Everyone seems to have met her at least once or twice, even those who did their best to avoid her.

I first noticed her ubiquity when I was researching another book. Wherever I looked, up she popped. Can you spot her here, in the index to Andy Warhol's diaries?

Mansfield, Jayne
Manson, Charles
Mao Zedong
Mao Zedong, Mrs *see* Chiang Ching
Mapplethorpe, Robert
Marciano, Sal
Marcos, Ferdinand
Marcos, Imelda
Marcovicci, Andrea
Marcus, Stanley
Margaret, Princess
Marianne (*Interview* staff)
Marilyn (Boy George's friend)

Or here, in the diaries of Richard Crossman?

It is like playing 'Where's Wally?', or staring at clouds in search of a face. Leave it long enough, and she'll be there, rubbing shoulders with philosophers, film stars, novelists, politicians.

I spy with my little eye, something beginning with M!

Here she is, sitting above Marie Antoinette in Margaret Drabble's biography of Angus Wilson:

And here, in the diaries of Kenneth Williams:

Would she rather have been sandwiched for eternity between Maresfield Park and Marie Antoinette, or Elspeth March and Margate? I'd guess the latter was more her cup of tea, though as luck would have it, there is a Princess Margaret Avenue in Margate,* named in celebration of her birth in 1930, so, like it or not, her name, rendered both topographical and tongue-twisting, will be forever linked to Margate.

Why is she in all these diaries and memoirs? What is she *doing* there? In terms of sheer quantity, she could never hope to compete with her sister, HM Queen Elizabeth II, who for getting on for a century of brief encounters ('Where have you come from?' 'How long have you been waiting?') must surely have met more people than anyone else who ever lived. Yet, miraculously, the Queen has managed to avoid saying anything striking or memorable to anyone. This is an achievement, not a failing: it was her duty and destiny to be dull, to be as useful and undemonstrative as a postage stamp, her life dedicated to the near-impossible task of saying nothing of interest. Once, when Gore Vidal was gossiping with Princess Margaret, he told her that Jackie Kennedy had found the Queen 'pretty heavy going'.

'But that's what she's there for,' explained the Princess.

---

* At present the headquarters of the mobile hairdresser 'Haircare at Home by Sharon'. As it happens, HRH Princess Margaret was fond of visiting her own hairdresser, almost to the point of addiction, often popping in twice in one day.

4

In her distrust of the unexpected, the Queen has taken a leaf from her grandfather's book. King George V liked only what was predictable, regarding everything else as an infernal nuisance. A typical diary entry begins with an account of the weather ('a nice bright morning, but strong wind'), accompanied, where appropriate, by a frost report ('seven degrees frost this morning'). It then chronicles the exact time he had breakfast ('up at 6.45, breakfast at eight with May'), and briefly mentions anyone notable he has encountered, and any advances he has made with his 325 stamp albums ('The Prime Minister came to see me and we had a long talk. Spent the afternoon with Bacon choosing more stamps'). And that's it. He disdains any sort of detail, telling or otherwise, about people and places. World events play second fiddle to stamps, clocks, barometers and bedtime. 'The poor archduke and his wife were assassinated this morning in Serbia. They were in a motorcar. Terrible shock for the Emperor …' he writes on the evening of 28 June 1914. He then adds: 'Stamps after lunch, bed at 11.30.'

Few people have ever transcribed a conversation with his eldest granddaughter. Some remember what they said to the Queen, but have no memory of what she said to them, or indeed if she said anything at all. Gyles Brandreth is one of the few exceptions. At a drinks party in 1990, he found himself alone with her in a corner of the room. 'There was no obvious means of escape for either of us, and neither of us could think of anything very interesting to say.'

But he didn't leave it there. When he got home, he recorded their exchange in his diary:

GB (GETTING THE BALL ROLLING): Had a busy day, Ma'am?

HM (WITH A SMALL SIGH): Yes, very.

GB: At the Palace?

HM (SUCKING IN HER LIPS): Yes.

GB: A lot of visitors?

HM (APPARENTLY BITING THE INSIDE OF HER LOWER LIP): Yes. (PAUSE)

GB (BRIGHTLY): The Prime Minister? (John Major)

HM: Yes. (PAUSE)

GB: He's very nice.

HM (NODDING): Yes, very. (LONG PAUSE)

GB (STRUGGLING): The recession's bad.

HM (LOOKING GRAVE): Yes.

GB (TRYING TO JOLLY THINGS ALONG): I think this must be my third recession.

HM (NODDING): We do seem to get them every few years … and none of my governments seems to know what to do about them.

(A MOMENT OF TINKLY LAUGHTER FROM HM, A HUGE GUFFAW FROM GB, THEN TOTAL SILENCE)

GB (SUDDENLY FRANTIC): I've been to Wimbledon today.

HM (BRIGHTENING BRIEFLY): Oh, yes?

GB (DETERMINED): Yes.

HM: I've been to Wimbledon, too.

GB (NOW WE'RE GETTING SOMEWHERE): Today?

HM: No.

GB (OH WELL, WE TRIED): No, of course not. (PAUSE) I wasn't at the tennis.

HM: No?

GB: No, I was at the theatre. (LONG PAUSE) Have you been to the theatre in Wimbledon?

(PAUSE)

HM: I imagine so.

(INTERMINABLE PAUSE)

GB (A LAST, DESPERATE ATTEMPT): You know, Ma'am, my wife's a vegetarian.

HM (WHAT WILL SHE SAY?): That must be very dull.

GB (WHAT NEXT?): And one of my daughters is a vegetarian, too.

HM (OH NO!): Oh, dear.

Her technique is to let others do the talking. Often – perhaps more often than not – the dizzying experience of talking to a stranger more instantly recognisable than your own mother, a stranger the back of whose miniaturised face you have licked countless times, is enough to start you spouting a stream of gibberish. While you do so, Her Majesty may occasionally say, 'Oh, really?' or 'That must be interesting,' but most of the time she says nothing at all.

As a drama student in the mid-seventies, I found myself presented to her at a party, quite unexpectedly. Our host – who later explained that he thought she might want to meet one of the younger generation – told Her Majesty that I had recently had an article published in *Punch*, and then left us to it. 'That must be interesting,' she said. This was more than enough to convince me of her thirst to know more. Within seconds I was regaling her with my various complex and no doubt impenetrable theories of humour, while every now and then she was urging me on with an 'Oh, really?' or a 'That must be interesting,' and from there I proceeded to remind her of Bertolt Brecht's theories of alienation ('Oh, really?'), with particular reference to their application to comedy ('That must be interesting').

I have learned since that the way the Queen signals the end of a conversation is to take one step backwards, but I did not know this at the time. Friends who witnessed our meeting from the other side of the room told me that, during the final half of my discourse on Brecht, Her Majesty took first one step back, then another, then another, then another, but still found herself trapped: for each of her steps back I took a step forward.

Throughout her life, the Queen's technique of giving nothing away has paid dividends. Nowadays, everyone seems content to interpret her silence as wisdom. The less she says, the more we believe she has something to say. Peter Morgan's play *The Audience* and his film *The Queen* are both predicated on this paradox: her advisers and her prime ministers may prattle away, but, Buddha-like, it is Her Majesty the Queen, with her How long have you been heres? and her Have you come fars?, who remains the still, small voice of calm, radiating common sense.

But her younger sister was another matter. As the second-born, the also-ran, she was denied the Chauncey Gardiner option. She could never have been another whitewashed wall, there for people to see in her whatever they chose to see. To impress on people that she was royal, Princess Margaret had to take the only other path available to her: to act imperiously, to make her presence felt, to pull well-wishers up short, to set strangers at their unease. If I had tried to tell Margaret about Bertolt Brecht she would have interrupted me – '*Too* tiresome!' – before I had got to the end of the 'Bert –'. Like a *grand guignol* version of her elder sister, she took a perverse pleasure in saying the wrong thing, ruffling feathers, disarming, disdaining, making her displeasure felt. One socialite remembers seeing her at a party at Sotheby's in 1997. By that stage, people were so reluctant to be snapped at by her that there was a sort of compulsory rota system in operation. A senior Sotheby's figure told the socialite that he would guarantee him an invitation to every future Sotheby's party attended by Princess Margaret if he would promise to talk to her for five minutes on each occasion.

Compare the Queen's conversation with Brandreth to Princess Margaret's dinner-party conversation, as witnessed by Edward St Aubyn and recreated in his wonderfully beady novel, *Some Hope*.

As the main course arrives, the Princess asks her host, Sonny, 'Is it venison? It's hard to tell under this murky sauce.' A few minutes later, the French ambassador, sitting next to her, accidentally flicks globules of the sauce over the front of the Princess's blue tulle dress.

'The Princess compressed her lips and turned down the corners of her mouth, but said nothing. Putting down the cigarette holder into which she had been screwing a cigarette, she pinched her napkin between her fingers and handed it to Monsieur d'Alantour.

'"Wipe!" she said with terrifying simplicity.'

While the ambassador is on his knees, dipping his napkin in a glass of water and rubbing the spots of sauce on her dress, the Princess lights a cigarette and turns back to her host.

'I thought I couldn't dislike the sauce more when it was on my plate.'

The ambassador's wife offers to help.

'He spilled it, he should wipe it up!' replies the Princess. She points to a spot the ambassador has missed. 'Go on, wipe it up!' She then complains about 'being showered in this revolting sauce'. At this point, the table falls silent.

'"Oh, a silence," declared Princess Margaret. "I don't approve of silences. If Noël were here," she said, turning to Sonny, "he'd have us all in stitches."'

Before long, Sonny's seven-year-old daughter appears, having found it hard to get to sleep. Her mother asks the Princess if she may present her.

'"No, not now, I don't think it's right," said the Princess. "She ought to be in bed, and she'll just get overexcited."'

5

More often than not, the presence of

Margaret, HRH the Princess

in an index signals yet another tale of haughty behaviour. In the autobiography of Cherie Blair she comes between Mandela, Nelson and May, Brian. The brittle wife of the former prime minister recalls the occasion she was talking to Princess Margaret at a gala performance at the Royal Opera House when the secretary of state for culture came over.

'Have you met Chris Smith, our culture secretary, Ma'am?' asked Mrs Blair. 'And this is his partner ...'

'Partner for *what*?' said the Princess.

At this point, writes Cherie Blair, 'I took a breath.'

'Sex, Ma'am.'

This reply proved unwelcome. 'She stalked off.' But Mrs Blair remains unapologetic. 'She knew exactly what kind of partner I meant. She was just trying to catch me out.'

Most of the stories follow another arc: the Princess arrives late, delaying dinner to catch up with her punishing schedule of drinking and smoking. At the table, she grows more and more relaxed; by midnight, it dawns on the assembled company that she is in it for the long haul, which means that they will be too, since protocol dictates that no one can leave before she does. Then, just as everyone else is growing more chatty and carefree, the Princess abruptly remounts her high horse and upbraids a hapless guest for over-familiarity: 'When you say my sister, I imagine you are referring to Her Majesty the Queen?'

At such moments it is as though she has been released by alcohol from the constrictions of informality. After a succession of drinks she is able to enter a stiffer, grander, more subservient world, a world in which people still know their place: the world as it used to be.

She had a thirst for the putdown, particularly where food and drink were concerned. Kenneth Rose,* the biographer of King George V, recorded her curt response when Lord Carnarvon offered her a glass of his very rare and precious 1836 Madeira: 'Exactly like petrol.' The author and photographer Christopher Simon Sykes remembers her arrival at his parents' house one teatime. Full of excitement, the staff had prepared a scrumptious array of cakes, scones and sandwiches. The Princess glanced at this magnificent spread, said 'I HATE tea!' and swanned past.

In the 1980s she paid an official visit to Derbyshire in order to open the new district council offices in Matlock. Among those on hand to receive her was Matthew Parris, at that time the local Conservative MP. 'It was 10 a.m.,' he recalled. 'I drank instant coffee. She drank gin and tonic.'

Having opened the offices, she was driven to the north of the constituency to open some sheltered bungalows for old people. A dish of coronation chicken had been specially cooked for her. 'This looks like sick,' she said.

The mighty and the glamorous were by no means excluded from these rebuffs. In 1970 the producer of *Love Story*, Robert Evans, and its star, his wife Ali MacGraw, flew to London to attend the Royal Command Performance in the presence of HM Queen Elizabeth the Queen Mother and HRH the Princess Margaret.

---

* Often known as 'The Climbing Rose'.

'All of us stood in a receiving line as Lord Somebody introduced us, one by one, to Her Majesty and her younger daughter. It was a hell of a thrill, abruptly ending when the lovely princess shook my hand.

'"Tony saw *Love Story* in New York. Hated it."

'"Fuck you too," I said to myself, smiling back.'

It was almost as though, early in life, she had contracted a peculiarly royal form of Tourette's Syndrome, causing the sufferer to be seized by the unstoppable urge to say the wrong thing. When the model Twiggy and her then boyfriend, Justin de Villeneuve, were invited to dinner by the Marquis and Marchioness of Dufferin in the 1960s, their hostess warned them that Princess Margaret would be among the guests. Before the royal arrival, the marquis instructed them in royal protocol. 'We were tipped off to stand if she stood, and to call her Ma'am. Fine, no probs,' recalled de Villeneuve.

Sitting close to the Princess, de Villeneuve was shocked to find that her smoking was seamless. 'When we started to eat, she lit a ciggie and then continued to chainsmoke, lighting one ciggie off another, throughout the meal. Where's the protocol in that?'

The Princess ignored Twiggy – at that time one of the most famous women in Britain – until the very last moment. She then turned and asked her what her name was.

'Lesley, Ma'am. But my friends call me Twiggy.'

'How unfortunate,' replied the Princess, and turned her back on her once more.

At this point, Lord Snowdon, never the most loyal husband, leaned over towards de Villeneuve. 'You will get this with the upper classes,' he sighed.

'Well, I think it's a *charming* name,' chipped in the Marquis of Dufferin.

6

The Princess liked to one-up. I have heard from a variety of people that she would engineer the conversation around to the subject of children's first words, asking each of her fellow guests what their own child's first words had been. Having listened to responses like 'Mama' and 'doggy', she would say, '*My* boy's first word was "*chandelier*".'

But her strong competitive streak was not always matched by ability. A regular fellow guest recalled one particular fit of bad sportsmanship. 'We were playing Trivial Pursuit, and the question was the name of a curried soup. She said, "It's just called curried soup. There isn't any other name for it. It's curried soup!" Our host said, "No, Ma'am – the answer is 'Mulligatawny'." And she said, "No – it's *curried soup*!" And she got so furious that she tossed the whole board in the air, sending all the pieces flying everywhere.'

Her snappiness was instinctive and unstoppable, like a nervous twitch. 'I hear you've completely ruined my mother's old home,' she said to the architect husband of an old friend who had been working on Glamis Castle. To the same man, who had been disabled since childhood, she said, 'Have you ever looked at yourself in the mirror and seen the way you walk?' Her more sympathetic friends managed to overlook such cruel remarks, believing them to be almost involuntary, or at least misguided. 'I think she was trying to be cheeky. She thought she was trying to reach a kind of intimacy,' says one. 'But she suffered from a perpetual identity crisis. She didn't know who she was.

She never knew whether she was meant to be posh or to be matey, and so she swung between the two, and it was a disaster.'

In the 1990s, two senior representatives from Sotheby's, one tall and thin, the other rather more portly, came to Kensington Palace to assess her valuables. The Princess asked them what they thought.

'Well –' began the tall man.

'No, not you – the fat one,' snapped the Princess.

The rebuke became her calling card, like Frank Ifield's yodel or Tommy Cooper's fez. Who wanted to sit through her analysis of current affairs, or her views on twentieth-century literature? No one: the connoisseurs wanted to see her getting uppity; it was what she did best. If you were after perfect manners, an early night and everything running like clockwork, then her sister would oblige. But if you were in search of an amusing tale with which to entertain your friends, you'd opt for the immersive Margaret experience: a late night and a show of stroppiness, all ready to jot down in your diary the moment she left, her high-handedness transformed, as if by magic, into anecdote.

Hoity-toity is what was wanted. For most recipients, hosts and guests alike, it was part of a package deal: once she had finally gone and the dust had settled, they were left with a suitably outrageous story – the ungracious royal! the bad Princess! – to last a lifetime. She had a small circle of lifelong friends, loyal to the last. Though they forgave her faults, they also liked to store them up, ready for repetition to others less loyal. 'Princess Margaret's friends are devoted to her,' wrote A.N. Wilson in 1993. 'But one seldom meets any of them after they have had the Princess to stay, without hearing a tale of woe – how she has kept the company up until four in the morning (it is supposedly not allowed to withdraw from a room until a royal personage has done so); or insisted on winning at parlour games, even those such as Trivial Pursuit which require a degree of knowledge which she simply did not possess; how she has expected her hostess to act as a lady-in-waiting, drawing back the curtains in the morning, and so forth.'

Ever discreet, Kenneth Rose would amuse his friends with the tale of the vintage Madeira ('Exactly like petrol!'), but would bide his time before putting it into print, for fear of losing his friendship with the Princess. His oleaginous discretion was assured, and this was how he remained a frequent visitor to Kensington Palace. This discretion extended to the moment of Princess Margaret's death, at which point he employed the anecdote to lend spice to her obituary in the *Sunday Telegraph*. Her death unleashed many such tales, rising like so many phoenixes from the ashes. For instance, in a diary for the *New Statesman*, the comedian John Fortune recalled an encounter with her at the BBC Television Centre in the early seventies.

First, he introduced her to his producer, Denis Main Wilson. 'She asked him what he did. He stood up very straight and said: "Ma'am, I have the honour to produce a little show called *Till Death Us Do Part*." The Princess replied: "Isn't that that frightfully dreary thing in the East End?"

'After a few more minutes of conversation, I found myself saying: "Well, it was a pleasure to meet you, Princess Margaret, but I have someone waiting for me downstairs and I have to go."

'She fixed me with a beady look. "No you don't," she said. "No one leaves my presence until I give them permission to do so."'

But, for all her haughtiness, Fortune detected 'a look of mischief in her eyes'. 'At that moment, I knew she didn't mean it. Had she, perhaps, been waiting all her life for someone to tell her they had to go?'

Fortune felt that if he had replied, 'Well, that's too bad, I'm off anyway,' then nothing would have happened. But he wasn't prepared to take the risk. A formal conversation continued for a few more minutes, and then she said, 'I'm very bored here. Isn't there somewhere else in this place we can go and have a drink?'

He knew of a bar in Light Entertainment that stayed open late, so he raced down two floors, only to find the barman pulling the metal grille down. "'Stop, stop," I cried, "open up again. Quick, Princess Margaret is coming."'

'Pull the other one …' said the sceptical barman.

At that moment they saw what Fortune described as 'the pocket battleship' bearing down on them.

Fortune ordered two gin and tonics, one for himself and one for Princess Margaret. He then spotted a director of *The Old Grey Whistle Test* slumped against the bar, so he presented him to the Princess. 'I think he must have been Australian, because within minutes the talk was of Sydney Harbour, convicts and the penalties for stealing a loaf of bread in the eighteenth century.

'And what made it perfect,' enthused the Princess, not getting the point of the story, 'was that it was STALE bread!' Within minutes, Fortune had made his excuses and left.

7

Throughout her adult life, Princess Margaret was happy to be tempted away from her solid bedrock of tweedy friends towards the more glittering world of bohemia. She leaned towards the artistic, the camp and the modish, even going so far as to marry a man at the centre of that particular Venn diagram. Her royal presence was enough to gratify the snobbish tendencies of the bohemians, while her snooty behaviour let them laugh at her behind her back, thus exonerating themselves from

the charge of social climbing. Hers was a name to drop, generally to the sound of a tut-tut or a titter.

The Princess was drawn to theatrical types, and they to her; they detected something camp in her, something of the pantomime dame, some element of irony in the way she adopted her royal airs, as though with a wink and a nudge she might at any moment reveal her haughty persona to have been no more than a theatrical tease. She enjoyed playing with the boundaries of being royal, popping out from under the red silk rope, and then, just as abruptly, popping back beneath it, returning to her familiar world of starch and vinegar. The Princess would draw bohemians to her with a smoky, nightclub worldliness, mischievously at odds with her position. Then, having enticed them in and helped them loosen up, she would suddenly and without warning snap at them, making it clear that by attempting to engage with her on equal terms they were guilty of a monstrous presumption.

A keen theatregoer, she went to see Derek Jacobi as Richard II at the Phoenix Theatre in 1988, sending word asking him to remain onstage at the end of the performance, so that she could meet him.

'I did, and she kept me waiting,' he remembered. 'She had gone to hospitality, had a couple of whiskies, and then tottered through to say hello onstage half an hour later.'

After another show, she invited him to dine with her and some ballet friends at Joe Allen's restaurant in Covent Garden. 'There were eight of us and I sat next to her. She smoked continuously, not even putting out her cigarette when the soup arrived, but instead leaning it up against the ashtray. We got on terribly well, very chummy, talking about her mum and her sister, and she really made me feel like I was a friend, until she got a cigarette out and I picked up a lighter and she snatched it out of my hand and gave it to a ballet dancer called David Wall.

'"You don't light my cigarette, dear. Oh no, you're not that close."'

Bohemian society in sixties London was formed of an unresolved mix of egalitarianism and snobbery. Kenneth Tynan was as devoted to

Princess Margaret as he was to the British working class, though he took care to keep the two enthusiasms separate. Tracy Tynan remembers her father arguing that her birthday party should be postponed because Princess Margaret would be out of town. But her presence at his arty get-togethers was unsettling. An actress who was sometimes a guest told me that the assembled iconoclasts – actors, writers, artists, musicians – would kowtow to Her Royal Highness while she was present, only to make fun of her the moment she left, imitating her squeaky, high-pitched voice, her general ignorance, her cackhanded opinions, her lofty putdowns, her air of entitlement. If a fellow guest's over-familiarity had prompted her to execute one of her 'Off with his head!' reprimands, then they would have something extra to giggle about. The presence of the Princess would endow a party with grandeur; her departure would be the signal for mimicry to commence. Beside these laughing sophisticates, the Princess could often appear an innocent.

8

The baby had been expected any time between 6 and 12 August 1930. The mother, HRH the Duchess of York, planned to give birth to this, her second child, at her family seat, Glamis Castle. This was disappointing news for the home secretary, J.R. Clynes, who had been looking forward to a family holiday in Brighton in the first weeks of August. A socialist who had started work in a cotton mill at the age of ten, Clynes now found himself bound by law to be at hand for the royal birth.

Some had suggested that Clynes could make a last-minute dash from London to Scotland the moment news of the first contractions came through, but his stuffy ceremonial secretary, Harry Boyd, was having none of it: if the birth was not properly witnessed by the home secretary, then the baby's relatively high place in the line of succession – third for a boy, fourth for a girl – would be placed in jeopardy. Nothing should be left to chance.

So, like it or not, Boyd and Clynes boarded the train to Scotland in good time, arriving at Cortachy Castle, where they would be staying, promptly on the morning of 5 August. A special telephone wire had been installed from Glamis to Cortachy, with a dispatch rider at hand in case the wire broke down.

The two men were to have a long wait. Clynes, quiet and retiring, occupied his time with long walks, sometimes in the company of his hostess, Lady Airlie. Boyd, on the other hand, was more worked-up;

he preferred to stay indoors, fearful lest he miss the vital phone call. Nor did he rule out the possibility of an accident, or some sort of muddle-up, or even sabotage. Had he spent too long out East? 'I could not help feeling that his long residence in China was inclining him to view the situation in too oriental a light,' Lady Airlie recalled in her memoirs.

On the 11th, the three of them – the home secretary, the countess, the civil servant – were on red alert, sitting up all night, 'sustained by frequent cups of coffee', but it was a false alarm. On the 14th, Boyd lost his temper when Clynes said he was thinking of going sightseeing with Lady Airlie; on the morning of the 21st, 'wild-eyed and haggard after sitting up all night', Boyd telephoned Glamis for any news, and was told there was none. Unable to contain his nerves, he stomped out into the garden and started kicking stones.

That same evening, just as they were dressing for dinner, the call from Glamis at last came through. Boyd, wearing only a blue kimono, a souvenir from his China days, was caught on the hop. 'What? In an hour? We must start at once!' With that, he leapt into his suit and rushed downstairs, where he found Clynes already waiting in his coat and Homburg. 'Just look at that, Boyd!' said Clynes, pointing to the sunset. 'In such a night stood Dido …' But Boyd was in no mood for an impromptu Shakespeare recital, and pushed Clynes headlong into the waiting car.

They arrived at Glamis with barely half an hour to spare. At 9.22 p.m., attended by her three doctors, the Duchess gave birth to a baby girl. Once the baby had been weighed (6lbs 3oz), the home secretary was ushered into the bedroom to bear witness. 'I found crowded round the baby's cot the Duke of York, Lord and Lady Strathmore and Lady Rose Leveson-Gower, the Duchess's sister. They at once made way for me, and I went to the cot and peeping in saw a fine chubby-faced little girl lying wide awake.'

The news that the King had another grandchild – his fourth – was greeted with forty-one-gun salutes from the Royal Horse Artillery in both Hyde Park and the Tower of London, together with the ringing of the bells of St Paul's Cathedral and Westminster Abbey. The following evening, 4,000 people gathered in the Glamis village square and followed the Glamis Pipe Band up Hunter's Hill as it played boisterous renditions of 'The Duke of York's Welcome', 'Highland Laddie' and 'The Earl of Strathmore's Welcome'. With everyone gathered at the summit, two young villagers lit a six-hundred-foot-high brushwood beacon. Within minutes, its flames could be seen from miles around.

9

Princess Margaret was born in 1930, the same year as *air hostess* and *newscaster* entered the language, and died in 2002, when *googling*, *selfie*, *blogger* and *weapons of mass destruction* first appeared.

Is it just me, or do a remarkably high proportion of the words that share her birthday also reflect something of her character? *Blasé* first made the Channel crossing in 1930, subtly altering its meaning on the way: in its home country of France, it meant 'sated by enjoyment', while here in Britain it meant something closer to 'bored or unimpressed through over-familiarity'. Also from France, or eighteenth-century France, came *negligée*, with that extra 'e' to show that it now meant a lacy, sexy dressing gown rather than an informal gown worn by men and women alike.

Inventions that first came on the market in 1930, thus introducing new words to the language, included *bulldozer*, *electric blanket* and *jingle*, all of which have a faint echo of Margaret about them. The *Gibson* – a martini-like cocktail consisting of gin and vermouth with a cocktail onion – was introduced to fashionable society. In *All About Eve* (1950), Bette Davis serves her guests Gibsons, saying, 'Fasten your seatbelts. It's going to be a bumpy night.'

Then again, *learner-driver*, *washing-up machine* and *snack bar* also came into being in 1930, yet it's hard to relate any of them to Princess Margaret, who never learned to drive, nor to operate a washing-up machine. And, as far as I know, she never entered a snack bar.

Also making their first entries that year were *to bale out*, meaning to make an emergency parachute jump, *to feel up*, meaning to grope or fondle, and *sick-making*, meaning to make one either feel queasy, or vomit, depending on the force of one's reaction. Each of these three has something Margaret-ish about it, as do *crooner* and *eye shadow* and the adjective *luxury*.

Two concepts dear to any biographer, but perhaps particularly dear to biographers of Princess Margaret, entered the language in the year of her birth: *guesstimate* and *whodunnit*.

There also came a word that had been around for several centuries, but which, as a direct result of the birth of the little Princess in 1930, was to take on a life of its own.

Horoscope.

10

At his office in Fleet Street, John Gordon, the editor of the *Sunday Express*, was struggling to come up with a fresh angle on the news of another royal birth. Then it came to him: why not ask Cheiro,* the most famous astrologer of the day, to predict what life might have in store for her? Cheiro had, in his time, given personal readings to, among others, Oscar Wilde, General Kitchener, Mark Twain and King Edward VII. The little Princess would surely be a doddle.

Gordon telephoned Cheiro's office, only to be informed by his assistant, R.H. Naylor, that the great man was unavailable. Instead, Naylor put himself forward for the task. His article, 'What the Stars Foretell for the New Princess', duly appeared the following Sunday.

Naylor foretold that Princess Margaret Rose would have 'an eventful life', a prediction that was possibly on the safe side, since few lives are without any event whatsoever. Moreover, it would be decades before anyone could confidently declare it to have been entirely uneventful, and by that time people's minds would have been distracted by other, more eventful, things. More particularly, Naylor predicted that 'events of tremendous importance to the Royal Family and the nation will come about near her seventh year'.

---

* Born William John Warner (1866–1936), he also went by the name of Count Louis Hamon. Cheiro combined his careers as a clairvoyant, numerologist and palmist with running both a champagne business and a chemical factory, though not from the same premises.

The article proved a huge success, so much so that Gordon proceeded to commission Naylor to write forecasts for the months ahead. As luck – or chance, or fate – would have it, one of his predictions was that 'a British aircraft will be in danger between October 8th and 15th'. He was just three days out: on 5 October, on its maiden overseas flight, the passenger airship *R101* crashed in Beauvais, France, killing forty-eight of the fifty-four people on board.

Naylor's reputation was made. John Gordon now hit on the idea of asking him to write a weekly column making predictions for all *Sunday Express* readers according to their birthdays. Naylor puzzled for some time over how to incorporate 365 different forecasts into a single column, and eventually devised a more off-the-peg system by dividing the sun's 360-degree transit into twelve zones, each of them spanning thirty degrees. He then named each of the twelve zones after a different celestial constellation, and offered blocks of predictions for each birth sign. This was how the modern horoscope came into being.

In the Princess's seventh year, 1936, a series of events of tremendous significance to the Royal Family did indeed come about, exactly as predicted: the death of King George V, the abdication of King Edward VIII, and the accession of King George VI. Small wonder that Naylor was now regarded as something of a genius; before long he was receiving up to 28,000 letters a week from his bedazzled readers, anxious to know what fate had up its sleeve for them.

By now, every other popular newspaper had taken to employing a resident astrologer; according to Mass-Observation, 'nearly two-thirds of the adult population glance at or read some astrological feature more or less regularly'.

One of the beauties of the horoscope, from the point of view of the astrologer, is that its followers are more than willing to forget or ignore any prediction that turns out to be wrong. In future, Naylor would be the beneficiary of this impulse to turn a blind eye. At the beginning of 1939, for instance, he confidently declared that 'Hitler's horoscope is not a war horoscope ... if and when war comes, not he but others will strike the first blow.' He also pinpointed the likely danger areas as 'the Mediterranean, the Near East and Ireland'. Furthermore, he declared that the causes of any potential conflict would be: '1) The childless marriage; 2) The failure of agriculturalists ... to understand the ways of nature and conserve the fertility of the soil.'

Within months, all these predictions had gone awry, but Naylor's reputation remained rock-solid. Nearly ninety years on, the horoscope is quite possibly the most formidable legacy of HRH the Princess Margaret, who shared her birthday, 21 August, and her star sign Leo, with a varied list of famous characters, including Count Basie, King William IV, Kenny Rogers, Aubrey Beardsley, Dame Janet Baker and Joe Strummer of the Clash.

11

In my biographer's delirium, as I looked at the list of Princess Margaret's fellow 21 August Leos I began to notice spooky similarities, and then to think that, actually, she was just like them in every way: after all, King William IV was family, and Dame Janet Baker looked a bit like her, as well as being a near-contemporary (b.1933). The two of them were chummy, too: Dame Janet remembers the Princess saying, 'Good luck, Janet – be an angel,' to her before she sang the part of the Angel in Elgar's *The Dream of Gerontius* in Westminster Abbey. Moreover, the Princess was a great fan of Count Basie, and vice versa: in 1957 Basie and his orchestra recorded 'H.R.H.', a song dedicated to her. Margaret also shared a louche, camp, decadent streak with Aubrey Beardsley, and might have identified with Kenny Rogers' songs about being disappointed by love: 'You picked a fine time to leave me, Tony'. And as for Joe Strummer, if the Margaret/Townsend romance were to be set to music, could there ever be a more perfect keynote duet than this?

PETER TOWNSEND: Darling, you got to let me know
Should I stay or should I go?
PRINCESS MARGARET: If you say that you are mine
I'll be here 'til the end of time
BOTH: So you got to let me know
Should I stay or should I go?

By now I was hallucinating. The Princess was everywhere and nowhere. It seemed as though everyone I bumped into had met her at one time or another, and had a story to tell, generally about her saying something untoward and an uneasy atmosphere ensuing. At the same time my brain was becoming entangled with the spaghetti-like argy-bargy of the Townsend affair, as knotted and impenetrable as the causes of the First World War.

I would spend hours puzzling over the same not-very-interesting anecdote told about her by different people, each contradicting the other. Should I go for the most likely, the funniest, the most interesting, or even, as part of my noble effort to write a serious book, the dullest? And which was which? I found it increasingly hard to judge. Should I favour one version of events over the other, or should I risk boring the reader by doggedly relaying every variant?

Just as the writers of the four gospels of the New Testament offer contrasting views of the same event, so do those who bear witness to the life and times of Princess Margaret. To pick just one example, here are two different versions of a quite humdrum little story about Lord Snowdon, Princess Margaret, a cigarette and a cushion. I have put them side by side, for the purposes of compare and contrast.

The first is from *Of Kings and Cabbages* (1984), a memoir by Peter Coats, former ADC to General Wavell,* boyfriend of Chips Channon, and editor of *House and Garden* magazine, widely known by the nickname 'Petti-Coats':

> Tony Snowdon was having a mild argument with his wife, Princess
> Margaret, and, having lit a cigarette, flicked the match towards an
> ashtray and it fell into Princess Margaret's brocaded lap. HRH

---

* Field Marshal Wavell (1883–1950) once sat next to Princess Margaret over lunch. Tongue-tied at the best of times, he struggled to think of something to say. At last, he was seized by an idea!

'Do you like *Alice in Wonderland*, Ma'am?'

'No.'

brushed it off quickly and, rather annoyed, said, 'Really, Tony, you might have burned my dress.' To which came the reply, 'I don't care. I never did like that material.' The princess drew herself up and said very grandly, 'Material is a word we do not use.'

I admit to having told this story several times, and it always arouses a storm-in-a-cocktail-glass of discussion. What other word? Stuff, perhaps?

So there we are. Now take a look at this second version of the same event, which comes from *Redeeming Features* (2009), an enjoyably baroque memoir by the interior decorator and socialite Nicky Haslam:

> We joined a party at Kate and Ivan Moffat's, where the growing distance and determined one-upmanship between Princess Margaret and Tony Snowdon was all too evident. Bored, Tony played with a box of matches, flicking them, lit, at his wife. 'Oh, do stop,' she said. 'You'll set fire to my dress.' Tony glowered. 'Good thing too. I hate that material.' Princess Margaret stiffened. 'We call it stuff.'

Which to pick? The Coats version is milder, the Haslam version more extreme. Coats has Snowdon lighting a cigarette and flicking a single match with the intention of making it land in an ashtray; Haslam has him playing with an entire box of matches out of boredom, and aiming and flicking the lit matches, one by one, at Princess Margaret. According to Coats, the Princess says,

> 'Material is a word we do not use.'

Coats then speculates about a feasible substitute. But Haslam makes no mention of her declaring 'Material is a word we do not use'; he simply has her observing,

> 'We call it stuff.'

We will never know which version is true, or truer, or if both are false, or half-true and half-false. If you could whizz back in time and corner both men as they left the Moffats' house, I imagine that each would swear by his own story, and someone else emerging from the same party – Lord Snowdon, or Princess Margaret, or one of the Moffats, for instance – would say that both of them had got it wrong, and the truth was more mundane, or more civilised, or more outrageous. To me, as the self-appointed theologian of that particular contretemps, Coats' version sounds marginally the more probable. A succession of lit matches flicked across a sofa strikes me as a little too chancy and hazardous, particularly if flicked in someone else's house. Moreover, 'Material is a word we do not use' sounds more imperiously Princess Margaret than 'We call it stuff.' On the other hand, Nicky Haslam is a keen observer of human behaviour, and has a knack for detail.

Even if we agree to settle for a judicious mish-mash of the two accounts, we are still obliged to embark on a discussion of late-twentieth-century royal linguistics. Both accounts agree that 'material' was a word offensive to Princess Margaret, and perhaps even to the entire ('we') Royal Family. But why? As words go, it has a perfectly good pedigree: it dates back to 1380, and was employed by Geoffrey Chaucer. On the other hand, though 'stuff' may sound more aggressively modern, coarse and general, it in fact predates 'material' by forty years. 'Stuff' originally meant fabric – in particular the quilted fabric worn under chain mail. It was centuries before it was demoted into a catch-all term applied to anything you couldn't quite remember the right name for. So the Princess's etymological instinct turns out to have been spot-on.

Or – forgive me – was her preference for 'stuff' over 'material' an unconscious throwback to her family's Germanic roots? The German for material is 'stoff', so it's possible the Royal Family's liking for 'stoff' has been handed down from generation to generation, its basis lost in time.

So much for that. As you can see, when push comes to shove, even the most humdrum royal anecdote can open up any number of different avenues of enquiry. For instance, who on earth were the Moffats? It would be easy to find out, and a true scholar would probably include their CVs either in the text itself or in a learned footnote. But there is only so much a reader can take. Does anyone really need to know?*

And what about all the other words Princess Margaret didn't like? Should I squeeze them in too? After all, she could take fierce exception to words she considered common – but she chose those words pretty much at random, so that people who weren't on the alert would utter one of them, and set off a booby trap, with the shrapnel of indignation flying all over the place. The Princess strongly objected to the word 'placement', for example, yet it's just the kind of word her friends and acquaintances would have instinctively used while dithering over who to place where around a dining table, probably thinking the word was rather classy. But no! The moment anyone said 'placement' – ka-boom! – all hell would break loose. 'Placement is what maids have when they are engaged in a household!' Princess Margaret would snap, insisting on the expression '*place à table*' instead. And the nightmare wouldn't end there. Even those who had managed to shuffle to their allocated seats without uttering the dread word were liable to be caught out the next morning, at breakfast time, when the Princess would reel back in horror if she heard the phrase 'scrambled eggs', declaring irritably, '*WE* call them "buttered eggs"!'

And so a biography of Princess Margaret is always set to expand, like the universe itself, or, in more graspable terms, a cheese soufflé, every reference breeding a hundred more references, every story a

---

* Oddly enough, the answer is probably yes. As it happens, Ivan Moffat was a film producer and screenwriter (*A Place in the Sun*, *The Great Escape*, *Giant*). Born in Cuba in 1918, he was the son of the actor-manager Sir Herbert Beerbohm Tree, the nephew of Sir Max Beerbohm, and the uncle of Oliver Reed. In Paris in the forties, Moffat was friends with Sartre and de Beauvoir, and he had affairs with two notable women who appear elsewhere in this book – Lady Caroline Blackwood and Elizabeth Taylor. Kate, his second wife, was a direct descendant of the founder of W.H. Smith, and a lady-in-waiting to the Queen Mother. So now you know.

thousand more stories, each with its own galaxy of additions, contradictions and embellishments. You try to make a haybale, but you end up with a haystack. And the needle is nowhere to be seen.

12

In 1993, the sixty-two-year-old Princess Margaret stood by a dustbin piled with letters and documents, while her chauffeur put a match to them.

David Griffin had been a professional driver for many years – double-decker buses, lorries, the 3 a.m. coach for Harrow Underground workers – before, one day in 1976, spotting a newspaper advertisement for a royal chauffeur. He leapt at it. 'I wouldn't say I was an absolute royalist. I just thought they were the ultimate people to work for, the pinnacle of the chauffeur world.'

He was to spend most of the next twenty-six years driving Princess Margaret around. He once calculated that he spent more time with her than with his own mother, though he spoke to her very rarely. 'She was part of the old school and she never changed from day one. She was very starchy, no jokey conversation. She called me Griffin and I called her Your Royal Highness.' By the end of a typical trip to Sandringham, she would have uttered a total of two words: 'Good' and 'morning'.

'There was no need to say more, she knew I knew the way. I saw myself as part of the car, an extension of the steering wheel. A proper royal servant is never seen and never heard. We preferred to work in total silence, so we didn't have to be friendly. We never used to try and chat. They used to say Princess Margaret could freeze a daisy at four feet by just looking at it.'

During this time, the Princess owned a Rolls-Royce Silver Wraith (fitted with a specially raised floor to make her look taller), a Mercedes Benz 320 for private use, a small Daihatsu runabout, and a Ford Transit minibus for ferrying friends around. As Griffin describes it, 'Six or seven people would pile in and shout: "Orf we go on our outing."' The Princess herself had never taken a driving test. Why bother?

Griffin's day began at 8 a.m., when he gave the cars a thorough polish, inside and out. He then collected any letters to be delivered, a category that included anything of the slightest importance and quite a few of no importance at all. These would be handed to him by the Princess's private secretary or a lady-in-waiting, or, every now and then, by Her Royal Highness in person. Occasionally he had to take a letter to her former husband, Lord Snowdon ('very pleasant and nice with impeccable manners'), who would invariably ask him to wait while he composed a reply. But if Snowdon telephoned Kensington Palace to ask whether Griffin could collect a message for Princess Margaret, the Princess would usually reply, 'No, he's got other things to do.'

As long as she had no official duties, her daily routine remained unvaried. Shortly after 11 a.m., Griffin would drive her to her hairdresser, latterly David and Joseph in South Audley Street. 'Then she would go out for lunch at a nice restaurant. Then she'd come back to the palace and have a rest.' Around 4.30 p.m. he would drive her to Buckingham Palace for a swim in the pool. 'Then she'd go to the hairdresser's for the second time in one day. Then I'd drive her to pre-theatre drinks, then to the theatre, then a post-theatre dinner. And I'd finish about 3 a.m. Sometimes this would happen every night. And I'd always be up at 8 a.m. At the weekend, I'd drive her to the country. If she travelled to Europe, I'd get there first and pick her up at the airport in Prague, for example, so she never thought anything was different.'

On a number of occasions, the Princess asked Griffin to drive her to Clarence House. After a couple of hours she would emerge with a large binbag filled with letters, which she would hand to him. Back at

Kensington Palace, she would put on a pair of yellow rubber gloves and help him bundle the letters, still in their bags, into a metal garden dustbin in the garage before ordering him to set light to them. 'We did it several times over a period of years,' says Griffin. 'A lot of it was old, going back donkeys' years, but I saw letters from Diana among them. We must have destroyed thousands of letters. I could see what it was we were burning. She made it very clear it was the highly confidential stuff that we burned. The rest was shredded in her office.'

13

Where memoirs of servants are concerned, it suits those upstairs to pooh-pooh them. Their authors are embittered, they say, and wrote them for money, or to settle a score. Biographers of the Royal Family tend to follow suit, turning up their noses at the reminiscences of a butler or footman, while devoting page upon page to the unreliable gush of a distant relative. But even William Shawcross, the Queen Mother's treacly biographer, acknowledges that, when it came to her mother's correspondence, Princess Margaret had a touch of the pyromaniac about her.

In the preface to his 666*-page doorstopper *Counting One's Blessings: The Selected Letters of Queen Elizabeth the Queen Mother*, Shawcross acknowledges that 'Princess Margaret … made little secret of the fact that in the 1990s she "tidied" her mother's papers and consigned many of them to black bin-bags for burning.' In his companion biography, Shawcross states that, around the time of Lord Linley's wedding in 1993, 'Princess Margaret was now engaged on one of her periodic "sortings" of her mother's papers, which were still filed haphazardly in various drawers and bags and pieces of furniture in her rooms at Clarence House and at Royal Lodge.† She wrote to her mother at Birkhall, "I am going back today to clear up some more of your room.

---

* A coincidence.

† Her house in Windsor Great Park.

Keeping the letters for you to sort later." Next day, she wrote, "Darling Mummy, I am sitting in your sitting room 'doing a bit of sorting' … I've nearly cleared the chaise longue and made an attack on the fire stool.'"

Naturally, Shawcross does his loyal best to make Margaret's little fires appear perfectly respectable, even caring: 'No doubt Princess Margaret felt that she was protecting her mother and other members of the family. It was understandable, although regrettable from a historical viewpoint.'

Shawcross writes of 'large black bags … taken away for destruction'. He acknowledges that no one will ever know what went up in flames, 'but Princess Margaret later told Lady Penn that among the papers she had destroyed were letters from the Princess of Wales to Queen Elizabeth – because they were so private, she said'.

It's likely that quite a few letters incinerated by Margaret were those she herself had written. Her relationship with her mother was often stormy, particularly in the years 1952–1960, after the death of King George VI and the accession of Queen Elizabeth II, when she was in her twenties. The two of them were living in separate apartments in Clarence House, one above the other. As the Queen Mother's authorised biographer, Shawcross is generally the smoothest of courtiers, tiptoeing around any unpleasantness with his forefinger pressed to his lips, yet he makes little attempt to conceal Margaret's prickliness towards her mother. 'Even her closest friends could not predict when her mood might change from gaiety to hauteur. Although she loved her mother, she was not always kind to her – indeed she could be rude,' he writes. 'On one occasion Lady Penn … said to Queen Elizabeth, "I can't bear to see the way Princess Margaret treats you." To which Queen Elizabeth replied, "Oh, you mustn't worry about that. I'm quite used to it."'

The household staff at Clarence House were also struck by Margaret's shirtiness towards her mother. 'Why do you dress in those ridiculous clothes?' she once asked in passing, as the Queen Mother stood chatting to a lady-in-waiting. If her mother was watching a television programme she didn't like, Princess Margaret would offhandedly switch channels without asking.

Their preferred method of communication during these years was by letter, even though, most of the time, there was only a ceiling between them. A footman doubled as a postman, taking letters upstairs and downstairs, from one to the other, on an almost daily basis. Yet in his voluminous collection, Shawcross includes just twelve letters from the Queen Mother to Margaret, as opposed to seventy to her elder daughter, Elizabeth. Judging by their tone and content, most of them were written in response to heated accusations,* perhaps after a telephone had been hung up, or flung down.

'My Darling Margaret,' the Queen Mother writes from Birkhall on 9 September 1955, at the height of the Townsend crisis:

> I sometimes wonder whether you quite realise how much I hate having to point out the more difficult and occasionally horrid problems which arise when discussing your future.
>
> It would be so much easier to gloss them over, but I feel such a deep sense of responsibility as your only living parent, and I seem to be the only person who *can* point them out, and you can imagine what anguish it causes.
>
> I suppose that every mother wants her child to be happy, and I know what a miserable & worrying time you are having, torn by so many difficult constitutional & moral problems.
>
> I think about it and you all the time, and because I have to talk over the horrid things does not mean that I don't suffer *with* you, or that one's love is any less.
>
> I have wanted to write this for a long time, as it is a thing which might sound embarrassing if said. Your very loving Mummy.

---

* Princess Margaret could be frosty with servants. Princess Diana's butler, Paul Burrell, claims that, on returning from an engagement, she would touch the television, testing it for warmth, just in case the servants had been watching when her back was turned.

Margaret's response, contained in a footnote, seems to acknowledge her own explosive nature: 'Please don't think that because I have blown up at intervals when we've discussed the situation, that I didn't *know* how you felt.'

Their relationship remained tricky right to the end. In his less dewy-eyed biography of the Queen Mother, Hugo Vickers states that 'There were those who were depressed by the way she [Margaret] could be openly rude to her mother when groups were about, though when alone with her, perhaps without an audience, she tended to be more sympathetic. But there was clearly some residual bitterness, and the Queen Mother did not always have an easy time with her younger daughter.'

For his biography *Princess Margaret: A Life of Contrasts*, Christopher Warwick was helped by the Princess herself, and was duly grateful: 'I am, of course, greatly indebted to Princess Margaret, to whom ... I offer my warmest and best thanks; not only for her time and co-operation, but also for asking some of her closest friends ... to see me.' But even this most tactful of biographers says that 'It had to be admitted ... that the Queen Mother was closer to her first-born, whose character was more like her own ... The relationship between Queen Elizabeth [the Queen Mother] and Princess Margaret was almost stereotypically mother-and-daughter: each guaranteed at times to bait and irritate the other.'

Warwick points out that it took Princess Margaret thirty years to visit the castle her mother had bought in the early days of her widowhood. Following this one and only visit, Margaret concluded, 'I can't think why you have such a horrible place as the Castle of Mey.'

'Well, darling,' replied her mother, 'you needn't come again.' And she did not.

So we leave the Princess, for the moment, in her garage at Kensington Palace, resplendent – a word much-loved by royal biographers – in her yellow rubber gloves, her eyes aglow from the blaze of her mother's letters. 'The smoke was so thick it made her eyes water and she had to leave,' recalls Griffin. 'We went back to Clarence House several times over a period after that to collect more letters and papers, and burned them all. I saw Diana's name on a few, and even her crest and handwriting, and there were lots of others addressed to the King and Queen, so they were quite old. The Princess never said why she was doing it, but she was very determined that they should all be destroyed, thousands of them. I remember thinking we were putting a match to history.'*

---

* Following Margaret's death in 2002, Griffin was made redundant, and ordered out of his Kensington Palace tied cottage within forty-two days. Until that point he had been earning £1,500 a month. There had been no shift system, and he was never paid overtime. Furious at his forced redundancy, he refused a Royal Service Medal. He now lives in a flat on the Isle of Wight, decorated with a mixture of reclining semi-nudes, press cuttings about Princess Margaret's cars and a large photograph of a Rolls-Royce Silver Shadow he bought for himself from the royal fleet. He fitted it with the numberplate HRH 8N, which he bought from a dealer. He financed these purchases by selling a bundle of cards and notes from Princess Diana for £10,500, among them a cartoon of two sperm declaring that they were swimming down someone's throat. 'Di and I used to compete to send the sauciest cards to each other, you see.'

14

'We are born in a clear field, and we die in a dark forest,' goes the Russian proverb. For fifteen years – from the age of two to seventeen – Princess Margaret was looked after by a governess, Marion Crawford; for both of them, this was their clear field.

Marion Crawford – always known to the Royal Family as 'Crawfie' – was born in Ayrshire in 1909. She studied to be a teacher, with the aim of becoming a child psychologist. She wanted to help the poorest members of society, and 'to do something about the misery and unhappiness I saw all around me'.

But a chance meeting diverted her from this calling. The Countess of Elgin asked her to teach history to her seven-year-old son, Andrew. Crawfie became the victim of her own success: impressed by her teaching skills, the Countess persuaded her to stay on to teach her other three children, and then recommended her to Lady Rose Leveson-Gower, who was after a tutor for her daughter Mary. Mary later remembered Crawfie as 'a lovely country girl, who was a very good teacher'.

And so the ball was set rolling. In turn, Lady Rose recommended her to the then Duchess of York, who needed a governess for her little daughters Princess Elizabeth, aged five, and Princess Margaret Rose, aged two.

The interview went swimmingly. Crawfie found the Duchess of York the homeliest of women. 'There was nothing alarmingly fashionable about her,' she recalled. 'Her hair was done in a way that suited her admirably, with a little fringe over her forehead.' Royal historians have credited, or discredited, Marion Crawford with obsequious, saccharine observations, but that initial view of her future employer surely has a sharp edge to it, with its needle-like suggestion of frumpiness.

The Duchess sat plumply by the window at that first meeting: 'The blue of her dress, I remember, exactly matched the sky behind her that morning and the blue of her eyes.' It's an eerie image, suggesting a disembodied royal, her dress merging into the sky, and with holes where her eyes should have been.

So Crawfie was taken on as governess, and moved into 145 Piccadilly, the London residence of the Duke and Duchess of York and their two little Princesses. After a day or two, she was presented to His Majesty King George V. In a loud booming voice – 'rather terrifying to children and young ladies' – the King barked, 'For goodness sake, teach Margaret and Lilibet to write a decent hand, that's all I ask you. Not one

of my children can write properly. They all do it exactly the same way. I like a hand with character in it.'

On her arrival, Crawfie had been aware of a widespread rumour that little Princess Margaret Rose was rarely seen in public because there was something wrong with her. 'One school of thought had it that she was deaf and dumb, a notion not without its humour to those who knew her.'* The rumour was eventually dispelled by news of a bright remark the little Princess had made over tea at Glamis Castle with the playwright J.M. Barrie. Barrie had asked Margaret if a last biscuit was his or hers. 'It is yours *and* mine,' replied Margaret. Barrie inserted the line into his play *The Boy David*, and rewarded Margaret with a penny for each time it was spoken onstage.

From the start, Crawfie found her two charges very different. Elizabeth was organised, Margaret artistic; Elizabeth discreet, Margaret attention-seeking; Elizabeth dutiful, Margaret disobedient; Elizabeth disciplined, Margaret wild. 'Margaret was a great joy and a diversion, but Lilibet had a natural grace of her own … Lilibet was the one with the temper, but it was under control. Margaret was often naughty, but she had a gay bouncing way with her which was hard to deal with. She would often defy me with a sidelong look, make a scene and kiss and be friends and all forgiven and forgotten. Lilibet took longer to recover, but she had always the more dignity of the two.'

The relationship between the two little Princesses was already set. 'Lilibet was very motherly with her younger sister. I used to think at one time she gave in to her rather more than was good for Margaret. Sometimes she would say to me, in her funny responsible

---

* Late in life, Jessica Mitford admitted that as a young woman she had tried to spread the rumour that both the Queen and Princess Margaret had been born with webbed feet, which was why nobody had ever seen them with their shoes off. Auberon Waugh attempted to play a similar trick with the children of Princess Anne and Captain Mark Phillips, noting in his *Private Eye* diary that young Peter Phillips had four legs, and 'the mysterious Baby Susan … is said to have grown a long yellow beak, black feathers and to croak like a raven'.

manner, "I really don't know what we are going to do with Margaret, Crawfie."

Margaret's Christmas present list for 1936 – their first Christmas in Buckingham Palace – shows how the elder sister took the younger in hand. Lilibet, aged ten, wrote it to remind Margaret, aged six, who would be expecting Thank You letters from her, and for what.

See-saw – Mummie
Dolls with dresses – Mummie
Umbrella – Papa
Teniquoit – Papa
Brooch – Mummie
Calendar – Grannie
Silver Coffee Pot, Clock, Puzzle – *Lilibet to Margaret*
Pen and Pencil – Equerry
China Field Mice – M.E.
Bag and Cricket Set – Boforts
China lamb – Linda

Far from being wholly anodyne, Crawfie's memoir, *The Little Princesses*, is peppered with intimations of a perilous future for Margaret. Did Lilibet also sense that her younger sister might be in for a bumpy ride? 'All her feeling for her pretty sister was motherly and protective. She hated Margaret to be left out; she hated her antics to be misunderstood. In her own intuitive fashion I think she saw ahead how later on Margaret was bound to be misrepresented and misunderstood. How often in early days have I heard her cry in real anguish, "Stop her, Mummie. Oh, please stop her," when Margaret was being more than usually preposterous and amusing and outrageous. Though Lilibet, with the rest of us, laughed at Margaret's antics – and indeed it was impossible not to – I think they often made her uneasy and filled her with foreboding.'

Of course, prescience benefits greatly from hindsight. By the time she wrote her book, Crawfie knew how the story was developing.

Nevertheless, Margaret was only nineteen when *The Little Princesses* was first published; the dark forest lay ahead.

Across fifteen years, Crawfie chronicles Margaret's progression. A keen reader, she goes from *The Little Red Hen* to *Black Beauty*, and from *Doctor Dolittle* to *The Rose and the Ring*. The young Margaret proves an obsessive chronicler of her own dreams. For many of us, this is the hallmark of a bore, but apparently not for Crawfie or Lilibet. 'She would say, "Crawfie, I must tell you an amazing dream I had last night," and Lilibet would listen with me, enthralled, as the account of green horses, wild-elephant stampedes, talking cats and other remarkable manifestations went into two or three instalments.'

Margaret used her imagination in more pragmatic ways, too, employing an imaginary friend called Cousin Halifax, 'of whom she made every use when she wanted to be tiresome. Nothing was Margaret's fault; Cousin Halifax was entirely to blame for tasks undone and things forgotten. "I was busy with Cousin Halifax," she would say haughtily, watching me out of the corner of her eye to see if I looked like swallowing that excuse.'

Little Margaret was also 'a great one for practical jokes'. Like most, hers contained an element of sadism, particularly when perpetrated on those who couldn't answer back. 'More than once I have seen an equerry put his hand into his pocket, and find it, to his amazement, full of sticky lime balls … Shoes left outside doors would become inexplicably filled with acorns.' Later, she was to marry a fellow practical joker, one of whose pranks was to secrete dead fish in women's beds.

For now, Margaret was developing a talent for mimicry, generally sharpened on her elder sister. Lilibet was, at that time, afflicted with a condition which these days would probably be diagnosed as obsessive-compulsive disorder. In later life she could channel it into waving, cutting ribbons, asking strangers how far they had travelled, and so on and so forth, but in those early years it was more of a problem than a solution. 'At one time I got quite anxious about Lilibet and her fads,' wrote Crawfie. 'She became almost too methodical and tidy. She would hop out of bed several times a night to get her shoes quite straight, her clothes arranged just so.'

Crawfie was convinced that the best cure lay not in sympathy, but mockery. 'We soon laughed her out of this. I remember one hilarious session we had with Margaret imitating her sister going to bed. It was not the first occasion, or the last, on which Margaret's gift of caricature came in very handy.'

For all Margaret's *joie de vivre* – perhaps because of it – people felt more comfortable with Lilibet than with her little sister. One elderly man in Scotland was devoted to Lilibet, but, says Crawfie, 'he was frightened of Margaret. Old men often were. She had too witty a tongue and too sharp a way with her, and I think they one and all felt they would probably be the next on her list of caricatures! Poor little Margaret! This misunderstanding of her light-hearted fun and frolics was often to get her into trouble long after schoolroom days were done.'

Her lifelong love of keeping others waiting was already evident in adolescence; so was her easy, almost eager, acceptance of the privilege bestowed upon her at birth. 'Like all young girls, she went through a phase when she could be extremely tiresome. She would dawdle over her dressing, pleased to know she kept us waiting.' Crawfie hoped she had cured this shortcoming, but evidently not. On one occasion, 'at adolescence's most tiresome stage', when Margaret was 'apt at times to be comically regal and overgracious', Lilibet's suitor Philip, nine years Margaret's senior, decided to take her down a peg or two. 'Philip wasn't having any. She would dilly-dally outside the lift, keeping everyone waiting, until Philip, losing patience, would give her a good push that settled the question of precedence quite simply.' Crawfie makes free with the adjectives 'tiresome' and 'regal', but she only ever applies them to Margaret, never Lilibet. For Lilibet, life was all about doing the right thing. For Margaret it was, and would always be, much more of a performance.

15

December 1941

The two Princesses, Elizabeth and Margaret, stage a Nativity play in St George's Hall at Windsor Castle. Elizabeth, in a gold crown and velvet tunic, is one of the Three Kings. The other two are played by evacuees; one of them has cocoa rubbed all over his face for his role as the Black King. The eleven-year-old Margaret plays the Little Child in the shepherd's hut. She sings 'Gentle Jesus, Meek and Mild' in what her governess describes as 'a most beautifully clear voice'.

December 1942

Prompted by last year's success, the Princesses decide to stage a pantomime, *Cinderella*. The two girls argue about the price of admission. 'You can't ask people to pay seven and sixpence … No one will pay that to look at *us*!' says Elizabeth.

'Nonsense!' counters Margaret. 'They'll pay anything to see us.'

Margaret grabs the title role for herself. 'Margaret had long since made up her mind she would be Cinderella. Lilibet was principal boy,' notes Crawfie. During rehearsals, the King complains that he can't hear a word anyone is saying. He also complains that Elizabeth's tunic is too short. 'Lilibet cannot possibly wear that.'

But it is a great success on the night, with the younger sister the star of the show. 'Margaret brought the house down,' notes Crawfie.

1 June 1954

Denied by protocol the chance to tread the boards in public, the twenty-three-year-old Princess Margaret accepts the position of assistant director for a production of Edgar Wallace's thriller *The Frog*. It is performed for charity for three nights at the Scala Theatre* in Charlotte Street, W1, by thirty young amateurs drawn from the upper classes, and stars Maureen, Marchioness of Dufferin and Ava, as a lavatory attendant, the Duke of Devonshire as a prison governor, the Hon. Colin Tennant† in the title role (a serial killer), Billy Wallace as a police sergeant, Henry Porchester as a Cockney detective, and Mrs Gerald Legge as the heroine. Experts in these matters estimate that ten members of the company are titled, and a further ten are the children of peers.

The first-night audience is very nearly as grand, and includes Baroness Alix de Rothschild, Prince Aly Khan, Noël Coward, the Duke and Duchess of Argyll, Professor Isaiah Berlin and Sir Bernard and Lady Docker, whose famous gold-plated Daimler is parked in a side street, guarded by a policeman. At the close of the show Princess Margaret makes a brief speech, telling the audience that they ought to give the cast 'a jolly good round of applause'.

Backstage, the cast consider the play a whopping success, and reminisce among themselves about the hilarious moments when lines were

---

* The concert sequences in the Beatles' film *A Hard Day's Night* were filmed in the Scala Theatre. After a fire in 1969 it was demolished. An apartment block – Scala House – now stands in its place.

† To defend this book from a marauding army of footnotes, I am not offering dates, jobs, pen-portraits, etc., for every single person mentioned. As I will be going back and forth in time, I also intend to stick to one name per person throughout, regardless of any transformations owing to deaths, marriages or elevations. This means that, for instance, Colin Tennant will remain Colin Tennant throughout, even though, from 1983, he was Lord Glenconner. The same applies to his wife, who was born Lady Anne Coke, then became Lady Anne Tennant, and then Lady Glenconner. From now on she will be Anne Tennant, for no reason other than simplicity. As you may already have noticed, I call the heroine of this book Princess Margaret, HRH the Princess Margaret, Margaret, or the Princess, according to whim.

fluffed and cues forgotten. They remain unaware that some members of the audience are less amused, among them Noël Coward. 'The whole evening was one of the most fascinating exhibitions of incompetence, conceit and bloody impertinence I have ever seen in my life ... the entire cast displayed no talent whatsoever,' he confides to his diary. 'It was certainly a strong moral lesson for all of us never to be nervous again on opening nights. Those high-born characters we watched mumbling and stumbling about the stage are the ones who come to our productions and criticise us! They at least displayed no signs of nervousness; they were unequivocally delighted with themselves from the first scene to the last, which, I may add, was a very long time indeed.'

After the show, Coward goes backstage to shower the cast and its assistant director with unheartfelt praise. To his diary, he confides that he found Princess Margaret tucking into foie gras sandwiches and sipping champagne. *The Noël Coward Diaries* are published in 1982, nine years after his death. Margaret buys a copy, and finally gets to read what he actually thought of her show. Next to his comments, the Princess writes crossly in the margin: 'I don't like foie gras.'

22 June 1984

Princess Margaret makes an appearance on Radio 4's long-running soap opera *The Archers*. By mutual agreement, she plays herself in her real-life role as president of the National Society for the Prevention of Cruelty to Children. The script dictates that she will be gracing the audience of a charity fashion show at the Grey Gables hotel in Borsetshire, with the equally real-life Duke of Westminster in attendance.

The recording takes place earlier in the month. The Duke of Westminster travels to the BBC Pebble Mill studio in Birmingham to make his recording, but Princess Margaret prefers to be recorded in her small library in Kensington Palace. The Duke's words and the Princess's words will be spliced together later.

When the small team from the BBC arrive – among them the actors playing the rustic entrepreneur Jack Woolley and his well-connected associate Caroline Sterling – the Princess expresses concern about the noise of plumbers elsewhere in her apartment, and the ticking of a clock. But the BBC engineer assures her it will be fine.

In their short scene, Jack Woolley is overawed by the presence of the Princess at the Borsetshire fashion show. Playing herself, Princess Margaret sounds curiously flat and uninvolved, almost as though she can't get to grips with her character; it takes quite a leap of the imagination to believe that she is not simply reading from a script.

DUKE OF WESTMINSTER: Have you met Princess Margaret?

JACK WOOLLEY: Me? Er, no, I don't believe I …

CAROLINE STERLING: She's coming this way. Gerald – if you could –

DUKE OF WESTMINSTER: Yes, of course. Ma'am, have you a moment? There's somebody I'd very much like you to meet.

PRINCESS MARGARET: Good evening.

CAROLINE STERLING: Ma'am.

JACK WOOLLEY: Your Royal Highness.

PRINCESS MARGARET: It seems to be geng terribly well, doesn't et? What a lahvely place this es. Hev you lived here long?

JACK WOOLLEY: Have I … er … I er?

CAROLINE STERLING: About 1965, wasn't it Mr Woolley?

JACK WOOLLEY: Was it?

PRINCESS MARGARET: It rilly is a beautiful part of the weld.

JACK WOOLLEY: Oh, oh yes indeed. I was born in Sturtchley you know.

PRINCESS MARGARET: Well, it's been very good of you to let us tek over your hertel.

CAROLINE STERLING: It's been our privilege, hasn't it Mr Woolley?

JACK WOOLLEY: Yes, yes I should say so.

PRINCESS MARGARET: I think you've been very generous, but is the Duke was saying, we do need all the help we can get to mek this a viry special year for the NSPCC.

JACK WOOLLEY: Well, if there's anything else we can do, anything at all, you have only to get in touch.

PRINCESS MARGARET: Careful, we might tek you up on thet.

JACK WOOLLEY: Oh, but you can, you must. In fact I was saying that very thing to er Gerald here a moment ago. Hur! Wasn't I Gerald? Hur! Hur! Hur!

After their first run-through, the producer, William Smethurst, says, 'That's very good, Ma'am, but do you think you could sound as if you were enjoying yourself a little more?'

'Well, I wouldn't be, would I?' replies the Princess.

16

The death of their grandfather, the abdication of their uncle, the accession of their father, the start of the Second World War: all these disruptions made it vital to offer the Little Princesses a sense of security, and all the harder for Marion Crawford to move on. But in 1947, at the age of thirty-seven, she finally resolved to marry her long-standing suitor, a fellow Scot called George Buthlay. How to break the news to Their Majesties? While they were away with their daughters on a tour of southern Africa, Crawfie seized the opportunity to broach the subject with old Queen Mary.

'I made my deep curtsy and kissed the Queen's hand. She then raised me, and kissed me on both cheeks.

'"Come now, Crawfie, sit down and tell me all about it," said Queen Mary in her kind way, meantime spearing for me a muffin on a small silver fork. Her Majesty never touches any food with her fingers.'

She had, she said, come to ask Her Majesty's advice, as she was planning to get married. Her Majesty's response was immediate and unequivocal.

'My dear child. You can't leave them!'

At this time, the Little Princesses were respectively sixteen and twenty years old.

Crawfie tried to explain that she had, as she put it, 'shelved the matter during the war years, feeling it was my duty then to stay'. But now the time had come to forge a life of her own.

A life of her own! Queen Mary wouldn't countenance such a thing. 'I don't see how they could manage without you. I don't think they could spare you now.' Reading their conversation today, it is striking that at no point does Queen Mary bother to enquire about Crawfie's fiancé.

On the return of Their Majesties, Crawfie sent a note to Queen Elizabeth asking to see her on 'a very urgent and important matter of a personal nature'. She was duly summoned to the Queen's sitting room, taking with her a photograph of her husband-to-be tucked cautiously under her arm. After making 'my usual deep curtsy', she presented the photograph to the Queen. 'This, Ma'am, is the urgent personal matter I have come to see you about.'

The Queen perused the photograph. 'She was obviously very surprised and somewhat disconcerted. She asked me his name, and I told her that it was George Buthlay and that he came from Aberdeen. She stood for a long time saying nothing whatever. I broke this uncomfortable silence presently and told her how at the start of the war I had wanted very much to marry, and had not done so because I felt I had a duty to Their Majesties, and considered it would be unfair of me to leave the Princesses when they most needed me. But now, I said, the time had come when I wanted a life of my own.'

'Why, Crawfie, that was a great sacrifice you made,' said the Queen. All very sensitive, but her sympathy swiftly dispersed, leaving the path clear for a stubborn counter-offensive. 'Does this mean you are going to leave us? You must see, Crawfie, that it would not be at all convenient just now. A change at this stage for Margaret is not at all desirable.'

Crawfie saw no escape. 'I assured the Queen the last thing George and I wanted to do was upset Their Majesties' plans in any way.'

In the end, having delayed for sixteen years, Crawfie married George 'very quietly' in Dunfermline 'without any fuss' the following year, just a couple of months before Lilibet married Prince Philip. Lilibet gave them a coffee set as a wedding present, and Margaret gave them three bedside lamps. But Crawfie's job was not yet done: leaving her new husband behind in Scotland, she returned briefly to her position at the Palace, alone now with Margaret.

The final pages of *The Little Princesses* are devoted to a portrait of Margaret at seventeen. Though sugar-coated, they leave a slightly bitter after-taste. 'She is learning with the years to control her sharp tongue' … 'It is a grief to her that she is so small, and she wears shoes and hats that give her an extra inch or so' … 'Margaret is more exacting to work for than Lilibet ever was' …

At one point, Crawfie grows worried about Margaret and speaks to the Queen 'quite openly' about her socialising: 'I can do nothing with

her. She is tired out and absolutely exhausted with all these late nights.' Between the two of them, the Queen and the governess agree that in future Margaret must spend one or two nights a week quietly at home, rather than out gallivanting.

The memoir ends, rather abruptly, with the birth of Prince Charles in November 1948. At the end of the year, Marion Crawford was finally permitted to retire. By now Princess Margaret was eighteen years old, pert, wilful, and intent on pursuing a life unsupervised.

17

On 22 March 1949, the Conservative MP David Eccles was sitting in the chamber of the House of Commons, listening to a speech 'so excessively boring' that, for want of anything better to do, he suggested to a neighbouring MP that they should ogle a pretty girl who had come to hear the debate from the Speaker's Gallery. The two made flirtatious signs to her, to which she was quick to respond. The next day, Eccles was surprised to hear that he had been flirting with the eighteen-year-old Princess Margaret. He was both annoyed with himself for having made such a mistake, and surprised she had responded so readily.

By the following year, Margaret's adoption as a sort of national sex symbol had gathered pace. 'Is it her sparkle, her youthfulness, her small stature, or the sense of fun she conveys, that makes Her Royal Highness Princess Margaret the most sought-after girl in England?' asked *Picture Post* in the summer of 1950. 'And this not only amongst her own set of young people but amongst all the teenagers who rush to see her in Norfolk and Cornwall, or wherever she goes.'

Though her face and her figure were similar to her elder sister's, it was generally agreed that it was Princess Margaret who had that certain something. Was this because even the most hot-blooded British male felt that his future monarch existed on a plane beyond lust, while the younger sister was still flesh and blood? Or was Margaret blessed with more S.A., as it was known at the time? Did men detect a sparkle in her eyes which suggested that she, unlike her sister, might, just possibly, be tempted? In later life, Margaret could be surprisingly candid about her youthful impulses. She once told the actor Terence Stamp that as a teenager she entertained sexual fantasies about the workmen she could see out of the Buckingham Palace windows. It is hard to imagine the Queen ever sharing such secrets.

Nearly ten years after the Eccles incident, on 18 December 1958, the publisher Rupert Hart-Davis gazed moonily as the Princess presented the Duff Cooper Prize to the fifty-two-year-old John Betjeman. Hart-Davis confessed to his old friend George Lyttelton that he had 'completely lost my heart' to her: 'My dear George, she is exquisitely beautiful, very small and neat and shapely, with a lovely skin and staggering blue eyes. I shook hands with her coming and going, and couldn't take my eyes off her in between.'

According to his friend Lady Diana Cooper, Betjeman himself was so overwhelmed by the presence of the young Princess that he was 'crying and too moved to find an apology for words'. Looking on with the doubly hard heart of the academic and the satirist, his waspish friend Maurice Bowra, the chairman of the judges, penned 'Prize Song', a parody of Betjeman's poem 'In Westminster Abbey':

Green with lust and sick with shyness,
Let me lick your lacquered toes.
Gosh, O gosh, your Royal Highness,
Put your finger up my nose,
Pin my teeth upon your dress,
Plant my head with watercress.
Only you can make me happy
Tuck me tight beneath your arm.
Wrap me in a woollen nappy;
Let me wet it till it's warm
In a plush and plated pram
Wheel me round St James's Ma'am …
Lightly plant your plimsolled heel
Where my privy parts congeal.

Bowra circulated this poem among friends, one of whom, Evelyn Waugh, pronounced it 'excellent'.

Another poet, Philip Larkin, eight years her senior, continued to nurture a private passion for the Princess well into her middle age. 'Nice photo of Princess Margaret in the S. Times this week wearing a La Lollo Waspie, in an article on corsets. See what you miss by being abroad!' he wrote to the distinguished historian Robert Conquest in June 1981, when the Princess was fifty years old, and Larkin fifty-eight.

Alas, Larkin's lust for Margaret never blossomed into verse, though he was once almost moved to employ her as a symbol of his perennial theme, deprivation. On 15 September 1984 he wrote to his fellow poet Blake Morrison that though the birth of Prince Harry had done nothing for him – 'these bloody babies leave me cold' – he had nonetheless 'been meditating a poem on Princess Margaret, having to knock off first the booze and now the fags – now that's the kind of royal poem I could write with feeling'. Stephen Spender, too, recognised a kindred spirit in the Princess. At the age of seventy he reflected that 'being a minor poet is like being minor royalty, and no one, as a former lady-in-waiting to Princess Margaret once explained to me, is happy as that'.

Her admirers came from less rarefied circles too. Ralph Ellison, author of *The Invisible Man*, a novel about the struggles of a young African-American man in a hostile society, was presented to her on a trip to Europe in 1956. He described his encounter in a letter to his friend and fellow novelist Albert Murray.

'I was one of the lucky ones who were received by the Queen Mother and Princess Margaret, two very charming ladies indeed.' The Princess was, he added, 'the kind of little hot looking pretty girl … who could upset most campuses, dances, clubs, bull fights, and three day picnics even if she had no title'. At that time, the Princess had just turned twenty-six.

18

It was in the early 1950s that Pablo Picasso first began to have erotic dreams about Princess Margaret. Occasionally he would throw her elder sister in for good measure. From time to time Picasso shared these fantasies with his friend the art historian and collector Roland Penrose, once even confiding in him that he could picture the colour of their pubic hair.

Picasso often had dreams about celebrities. In the past, both de Gaulle and Franco had popped up in them, though, mercifully, never in a sexual context. But the two royal sisters were another matter. 'If they knew what I had done in my dreams with your royal ladies, they would take me to the Tower of London and chop off my head!' Picasso told Penrose with pride.

Having moved into his vast villa, La Californie, in 1955, he set his sights on marrying the only young lady he deemed smart enough for it. There was, he said, just one possible bride for him: Princess Margaret. Not only was she a leading member of the British Royal Family, but she was also his physical type: shorter than him (at five foot four inches, he towered over her), with beautiful skin and good strong teeth. In pursuit of this fantasy, he ordered the waspish British art dealer Douglas Cooper to drop in on Her Majesty the Queen and request her younger sister's hand in marriage. Picasso made it clear that this was more than a whimsy. He would not let the matter drop, growing more and more absorbed in plotting the right strategy. He would draw up a formal document on parchment, in French, Spanish or Latin, for Cooper to present to Her Majesty on a red velvet cushion. Cooper would be accompanied by Picasso's future biographer John Richardson, who would arrive dressed as a page or herald, complete with trumpet.

'If we didn't have the right clothes, Picasso would make them for us: cardboard top hats – or would we prefer crowns?' recalled Richardson. 'He called for stiff paper and hat elastic and proceeded to make a couple of prototypes. His tailor, Sapone, would help him cut a morning coat out of paper.'

There would be no place in Picasso's married life for his current girlfriend, Jacqueline: she would have to go to a nunnery. Picasso turned to Jacqueline. 'You'd like that, wouldn't you?' 'No Monseigneur, I wouldn't. I belong to you.'

By the end of their day of planning, the artist dressed Cooper and Richardson in the ties and paper crowns he had made for them, emblazoned with colourful arabesques. 'Now you look ready to be received by the Queen,' he declared, before checking that they knew how to bow with the appropriate panache.

Picasso's fascination with Princess Margaret stayed close to fever pitch for a decade or more. In June 1960, he missed meeting her when she paid a surprise visit to his Tate Gallery exhibition. Never again would he be offered a better opportunity for saying, 'Come upstairs and let me show you my etchings.' But he was stuck in France, which meant that Roland Penrose, the exhibition's curator, was obliged to convey the Princess's reactions by post.

'My dear Pablo,' wrote Penrose, giddy with excitement, '… on Thursday, a friend of the Duke informed me – in the greatest secrecy so as to avoid a stampede to the Tate of all the journalists in the world – that the Queen wanted to come in the evening with a dozen friends to see the show. I wasn't to say a word to anyone and no official was to be present to show them the pictures, only me. And that's exactly what happened. The Queen and the Duke arrived first and later the Queen Mother joined them.'

The Royal Family, he informed the great painter, 'has never shone in their appreciation of the arts ... your work really did seem to touch them, perhaps for the first time at the depths of their being'.

Everyone had been bowled over by Picasso's brilliance: '... yet again I must thank you – your superb presence surrounding us everywhere gave me confidence, and the eyes of the Queen lit up with enthusiasm – with genuine interest and admiration ... I'd been advised not to insist on the difficult pictures and to avoid going into the cubist room – but I wasn't happy about that and to my delight she went in with an enthusiasm that increased with each step – stopping in front of each picture – "Picture of Uhde", which she thought magnificent, "Girl with a Mandolin", "Still Life with Chair Caning", which she really liked, the collages, the little construction with gruyere and sausage in front of which she stopped and said, "Oh, how lovely that is! How I should like to make something of that myself!"'

Penrose injected a note of suspense into his account by leaving until the very last moment the surprise entrance of Picasso's intended. After the rest of the royal party had made appropriate noises about the great still life of 1931 ('very enthusiastic') and the paintings of the *Guernica* period ('very disquieted'), 'at last we reached the Bay of Cannes, which the Queen Mother found superb, when someone else joined us – and turning to me the Queen said, "May I introduce my sister Margaret?" And there she was, the beautiful princess of our dreams with her photographer husband ...'

The Queen then said she would have to leave shortly, and asked Penrose to show her sister the entire exhibition all over again. Tactfully, he drew a veil over the persistent presence of Snowdon, scrubbing out 'her photographer husband' from the rest of his account, and focusing solely on the Princess: 'When she asked me whether you were going to come I said I thought that, even though you had expressed no desire to come, you would be sad not to have been there to meet her this evening. And she smiled enchantingly and I think I glimpsed a blush spreading beneath her tan.'

Once the royal party had finally departed, Penrose scribbled a few notes, solely for his own consumption. These suggest that all the various members of the Royal Family – Princess Margaret being the last to arrive – were far more slothful in their appreciation of the artworks than he suggested in his letter to Picasso. In these jottings, 'M' is Margaret, 'P' is Philip, 'Q' is the Queen, and 'QM' the Queen Mother:

Great interest in Uhde. Q.

'I can see character in it.' Q.

'I like letting my eyes wander from surface to surface without worrying about what it means.' M

P coming in: 'DO realise, darling, there are 270 pictures to see and we have hardly begun.'

'Why does he use so many different styles?' Q.

'These are the ones that make me feel a bit drunk, I'm afraid.' P. La Muse, etc.

'Why does he want to put 2 eyes on same side of face?' Q

'Did he love her v. much?' M (Portrait of Dora)

Bay at Cannes greatly appreciated by QM and Q.

Meninas subtlety of colour, restraint and feeling of texture noticed & enjoyed by QM.

Pigeons much admired.

Portrait of Jacqueline noticed by M.

'What a tremendous output! He is the greatest of our time' QM.

Some of Penrose's more radical surrealist friends refused to stomach his sycophancy to royalty, but then they knew nothing of his role as the go-between for Pablo Picasso and the young Princess. One of the most indignant, the jazz singer and surrealist collector George Melly, wrote him a particularly huffy letter:

What are you up to? I hope you will enjoy the little jokes HRH will presumably make in front of the pictures. Perhaps he will suggest that Prince Charles could do better. Honestly, I find the whole concept an insult to a great painter. What are you after? A title? An invitation to lunch at the palace? A ticket for the Royal enclosure?

I wish to put it on record now that I shall lend no picture to an exhibition in the future under the aegis of yourself or the ICA.

Melly signed the letter to his old friend 'Yours disgustedly'. Perhaps if he had known of the great painter's sexual obsession with the Queen and Princess Margaret, he might have been more supportive.*

Five years later, Picasso was still nursing his unrequited love. On 28 April 1965, 'with his wild, staring eyes', he told Cecil Beaton, who had come to photograph him, that he was 'a great admirer of Princess Margaret, with her long face', but swore Beaton to silence, 'otherwise someone will write a book about it'.

As for Penrose, Melly's snub left him undaunted. In June 1967, now Sir Roland Penrose CBE, he organised another Picasso exhibition at the Tate, this time of the sculptures. There was to be a dinner at the gallery on the evening before the private view, and furthermore, he told Picasso, 'we have invited the girlfriend of your dreams, her Royal Highness the Princess Margaret, to preside, and she has graciously agreed, and tra! la! la!'

The day after conducting Princess Margaret and Lord Snowdon around the exhibition, Penrose sent a telegram to Picasso. Once again, he cut the unnecessary photographer husband clean out of the picture:

---

* In a review of David Sylvester's book *Magritte* (1992), Melly pointed out that Sylvester 'is not … particularly impressed by those pictures in which related objects merge to create a new object, though he acknowledges *The Rape*, where the woman's body replaces the face, as one of the great icons of the century. He sees it as both horrifying and comic and, citing several people's reaction to it, includes the unnerving observation that the navel suggests a nose eaten away by tertiary syphilis. I seem to remember, although he doesn't confirm it here, that he once told me the originator of this alarming notion was Princess Margaret.'

LONDON VANQUISHED STOP ARE COMPLETELY INVOLVED
WITH YOUR SCULPTURES STOP PRINCESS CAPTIVATED STOP
PUBLIC FILLED WITH WONDER LOVE LEE ROLAND

Two days later, on 11 June, he joined Picasso for lunch, and made a
note of their meeting: 'Gave Picasso catalogues of sculpture show. He
was very keen to hear how it all went and what Margaret thought ...'

Despite the persistent efforts of Richardson, Cooper and Penrose,
Picasso's passionate yearning for Princess Margaret was never reciprocated. In fact, quite the opposite. 'Many years later, I told Princess
Margaret the story of Picasso's quest for her hand,' recalled Richardson.
'Like her great-great-great* grandmother Queen Victoria, she was not
amused; she was outraged. She said she thought it the most disgusting
thing she had ever heard.'

But what if fate had dictated otherwise?

---

* One great too many.

19

From *Pablo Picasso: Memoir of a Friendship*, by John Richardson (Jonathan Cape, 1998)

Pablo's greatest mistake was to marry HRH the Princess Margaret. It was a decision that was to have the most atrocious consequences for his art, and was, I fear, to leave his reputation within the art world forever sullied.

He had, of course, lusted after the Princess for a decade or more, but only from a distance. Despite a number of opportunities, he failed to meet her – whether through bashfulness or accident I know not – until 4 June 1967, when he insisted upon escorting her around his first major exhibition of sculptures at the Tate Gallery, with the sole proviso that no one else should be present.

Aged eighty-five, he was over twice the age of the thirty-six-year-old Princess; in fact, he was a good deal older than HM the Queen Mother. But, sexually speaking, he was well up to scratch – he had married his thirty-four-year-old mistress Jacqueline Roque, just three years Margaret's senior, in 1961 – and his worldwide fame, bullish charisma and dark, penetrating eyes continue to attract many female admirers.

For her part, the Princess was undergoing one of the rockiest times in her somewhat restless marriage to Tony Armstrong-Jones. The pair of them were getting on each other's nerves; each had begun to seek solace elsewhere. Increasingly exasperated by her husband's vanity, it may have amused Margaret to taunt him by flirting with the man universally acknowledged as the greatest artist of the twentieth century.

At 10.30 p.m., under a cloak of secrecy, the exhibition's curator, Roland Penrose, met Princess Margaret at a side entrance of the Tate, and took her through the deserted gallery to the doorway to the Picasso exhibition, where she found the artist standing, legs apart, hands on hips, ready to greet her.

From the moment they set eyes on one another, their mutual attraction was overwhelming. 'I had never seen Picasso like it,' remembered Penrose. 'He simply couldn't take his eyes off her, even when he was attempting to point out specific details in the sculptures.' Penrose felt duty-bound to accompany the Princess and the artist around the first two or three exhibits, but the couple soon made it clear that they wished to be left alone: 'If I remember rightly, the Princess turned to me and pointedly asked me if I had nothing better to do. Accordingly, I made my excuses, and retired to the hallway.'

It was well past midnight before Picasso and Princess were to emerge from the exhibition. 'I couldn't help but notice that the Princess's hair had lost a little of its shape,' reported Penrose. 'And Pablo was not even bothering to conceal that look of triumph with which I was so familiar.' The two of them left together in the Princess's car. As he went around the gallery, turning off the lights, Penrose noticed a discarded pearl earring on the floor alongside what many regard as Picasso's most singularly erotic sculpture, *Woman in the Garden*.

Over the next fortnight, while Lord Snowdon was away photographing Sir Noël Coward at his home in Jamaica, Picasso made repeated clandestine visits to Kensington Palace, often sporting a false-nose-specs-and-whiskers mask. He brought a large sketchbook with him, and as they entered her private apartment, Princess Margaret was insistent that no staff should disturb them. It is widely believed that Picasso's late series of erotic drawings, *The Kiss*, springs from this period.

The consequences of their liaison are now too well-known to require detailed repetition. On his return to Paris, Picasso informed his wife

Jacqueline that he had no further use for her. When Lord Snowdon returned to his and Princess Margaret's apartment in Kensington Palace in late June, he found all the locks changed. For a short time he stayed with the Queen Mother at Clarence House, before moving to what the press described as a 'fashionable bachelor pad' in South Kensington.

Senior members of the Royal Family were outraged on Snowdon's behalf, but there was nothing they could do. Princess Margaret was determined to marry Picasso at her earliest convenience. 'Yes, I'm sure he's awfully sweet, darling, and you know how much I love pictures – but they tell me he's desperately Spanish, and one can't help but worry that he simply won't *fit in*,' protested the Queen Mother.

Determined not to repeat her mistake of twelve years previously, on 12 September the wilful Princess applied for an uncontested divorce, and on 15 December 1967 Kensington Palace issued this brief announcement:

> Yesterday, HRH The Princess Margaret married Mr Pablo Picasso in a
> civil ceremony. Representatives of the Royal Family were in
> attendance. The couple will live together at Kensington Palace. For the
> time being, the Princess will be styled 'HRH The Princess Margaret,
> Mrs Pablo Picasso'. There will be no honeymoon.

The marriage was, by all accounts, a disaster. From the start, Picasso resisted all attempts to incorporate him in royal duties. Whenever he bothered to attend an official function, he seemed to make a point of dressing improperly. There was a national outcry, for instance, when he attended Ascot in 1968 wearing a grubby blue smock rather than the regulation tailcoat. Prince Philip is said to have walked out of a private dinner party in Buckingham Palace, slamming the door, when Picasso turned up bare-chested in shorts and a floral sunhat.

Convinced that he could be brought to heel, the Queen Mother persuaded the Queen and Prince Charles that Picasso's artistic leanings would make him the perfect choice to design the setting for the investiture of Prince Charles as Prince of Wales at Caernarvon Castle in 1969. Grudgingly attempting to save his marriage, Picasso accepted the commission, but his designs were deemed inappropriate, and were subject to widespread condemnation.

'The sight of a clearly nervous Prince of Wales wearing a cow-horn helmet making his formal entry on a bull made from papier-mâché was for most people the last straw,' read a strongly-worded editorial in the *Daily Telegraph* the following day. Even the more go-ahead *Guardian* felt the entire ceremony 'grotesque': 'There was simply no need for the sixty-one-year-old Garter King of Arms to be forced to dress as Pan in a bright green leotard, nor for the Queen Mother to be borne aloft on a bamboo platform by twelve minotaurs, each bearing a suggestive horn.'

Friends say that Princess Margaret was at first mesmerised by the forceful painter. If so, she soon came to regret her impulsiveness. 'Women are machines for suffering,' Picasso had told one of his mistresses in 1943, and he did not spare his British wife. The British public, who had extended such sympathy to the Princess during her Townsend years, and had rejoiced at her first wedding, now began to turn against her, condemning her as unfit for public office. Picasso's reputation took a beating too, particularly from the avant-garde. Those who had once heralded him as a great revolutionary artist now chided him as an Establishment lickspittle. Consequently the prices commanded by his works began to plummet, and his dealers grew restless.

By the end of the decade, the Picassos decided that it would be in their mutual interests to part. Their divorce was finalised in February 1970. Two months later, at the unveiling of Picasso's *Naked Woman Smoking Cigarette* at the Metropolitan Museum of Art in New York, sharp-eyed critics noticed what they took to be the Poltimore Tiara perched on the head of the weeping subject.

20

The serious-minded novelist John Fowles, four years older than Princess Margaret, shared the obsession of Pablo Picasso. In real life, as it were, he might well have cold-shouldered the Princess, as he had long considered himself an intellectual with no truck for social snobbery. But he cherished her as a fantasy object, particularly when comparing her with his more down-to-earth current girlfriend, whom he referred to in his diary only as 'G'.

'Physically I criticize her,' he writes of poor Miss G on 13 March 1951. 'That way I cannot blind myself. She is warm, nubile; but not beautiful. And I see her growing old quickly, fat, with the Jewish, Mediterranean strain coming out in her. I see her in all sorts of conditions – whenever they entail "chic", she disappoints me. She has all the DH Lawrence qualities, heart and soul and heat, humanity, intelligence, and simplicity when it is needed, the qualities of peasant stock, but no aristocratic traits. And aesthetically I need a little more aristocracy, a little carriage, fine-bred beauty.'

Later in the same entry, he declares that 'I think it would do me good to marry G just for this one reason. That I should then limit myself, and achieve a certain humility which is lacking at the moment. Shed some of my aristocratic dream-projections. For example, I have day-dreamed of seducing Princess Margaret. I suppose many men must have done that. For unattached men she must be an obvious evasion out of solitary reality.'

A year later, Fowles completed his first novel, *The Collector*, which he went on to sell for a record sum. It is the tale of a creepy man who kidnaps a beautiful young art student and keeps her imprisoned in his basement. In a letter to his publisher, Fowles explained that 'the whole woman-in-the-dungeon idea has interested me since I saw Bartok's *Bluebeard's Castle*'. He had also been intrigued, he said, by a news story concerning 'a man who had kidnapped a girl and imprisoned her for several weeks in an air-raid shelter at the bottom of his garden'.

In all his public utterances, Fowles took pains to express a more high-minded blueprint for his artistic purpose. In an essay on *The Collector*, he stated that by making his victim die in captivity,

> I did not mean by this that I view the future with a black pessimism: nor that a precious *elite* is threatened by the barbarian hordes. I mean simply that unless we face up to this unnecessarily brutal conflict (based largely on an unnecessary envy on the one hand and an unnecessary contempt on the other) between the biological Few and the biological Many … then we shall never arrive at a more just and happier world.

But to his diary, he confided that the novel had also been inspired by

> My lifelong fantasy of imprisoning a girl underground. I think this must go back to early in my teens. I remember it used often to be famous people. Princess Margaret, various film stars. Of course, there was a main sexual motive, the love-through-knowledge motive, or motif, has been constant. The imprisoning, in other words, has always been a forcing of my personality as well as my penis on the girl concerned.

21

In Italy with his wife in September 1962, Fowles was still mulling over Princess Margaret, though by now his lust had curdled into irritation. Never blessed with the sunniest of dispositions, particularly when thinking of England, he complained to his diary of 'The grey shock of England and the English ... I haven't had the extent of my exile from land and people so clear for a long time. They are foreign to me, and so the land seems foreign.'

He went on to chastise England for 'a colossal lack of style, an almost total inability to design life', and noted sulkily that 'The British sit like a fat pasty-faced bespectacled girl at the European party.'

For a man so desperate to put his own country behind him, his choice of holiday reading that September was perverse, and harked back to his trusty old obsession:

An extraordinary book we read in Rome – the banned-in-England *My Life with Princess Margaret* by a former footman. Written, or ghosted, in a nauseatingly cloying, inverted style: the man sounds like a voyeur and a fetishist. He constantly uses turns of phrase (and the sort of euphemism, in particular) that I gave the monster in *The Collector*. Again and again he praises, or smirks at, behaviour by the filthy little prig-princess that any decent person would despise; and the horror is not that he does this, but that one knows millions of silly men and women in America and here will agree with him. A whole society wrote this miserable book, not one man.

22

The book in question had been banned in Britain after the Queen Mother gained an injunction against it. The judge agreed that Princess Margaret's former footman, David John Payne, had signed an agreement preventing him from writing about his time in the royal household. But no such restriction existed in the US, where Payne's work was serialised in *Good Housekeeping* magazine, and had now been published in book form.

In 1959, while in service to Lord Rothermere, Payne heard of a vacancy for a footman at Clarence House.

He passed the interview. 'You are tall, smart, and seem to have the bearing required to carry out your duties,' said the comptroller, Lord Gordon, hiring Payne at a basic wage of five pounds ten shillings a week. Gordon then introduced him to Jack Kemp, steward to the household, who in turn presented him to HRH the Princess Margaret. Payne's first impression was of 'a tiny figure, beautiful in a pink and white cotton dress, her dark hair brushed into a bouffant style and a shining double row of pearls round her throat … She extended her small white hand – I had time to see the smoothness of the skin and the care which had gone into the manicure of her nails – and we shook hands … Margaret at twenty-nine was a beautiful woman. Her face, not too heavily powdered, had been made up by an expert – herself, as it later turned out. Her eyebrows had been pencilled in and her lipstick smoothly formed in a delightful cupid's bow. But her most striking, almost mesmeric features were her enormous deep blue eyes.'

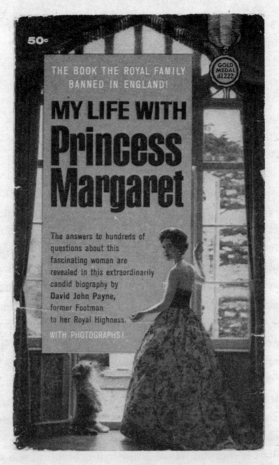

From the start there is, as Fowles suggests, something voyeuristic, even fetishistic, about Payne's memories of the Princess. And creepy, too: *My Life with Princess Margaret* is a strange, unsettling mixture of idolatry and loathing, suggesting they are two sides of the same coin. Payne is a forerunner of the Kathy Bates character in the film *Misery*, hero-worship turning, without warning, into almost passionate resentment, then back again, and all in the flicker of an eyelid.

A few months later, now part of the furniture, Payne entered the Princess's sitting room while she was lying full-length on the settee, her head pillowed on two pink brocade cushions and her dark hair spread out around her face. Her eyes were closed and she was concentrating on the music … She looked her very loveliest lying there in a midnight blue sequined cocktail dress with a tight bodice and flared skirt. She was lightly made up, her powder and lipstick applied with the delicate touch of an expert. Her shoulders above the low-cut neckline shone silkily in the soft lights. On the table by her side stood a half-glass of whisky and water and in the ashtray there were two or three inch-long stubs. She lay perfectly still, lost in the atmosphere of the romantic music, her eyes closed, her face serene. I stood there for a few seconds, inwardly moved by the sight of the lovely sleeping beauty.

Small wonder if Princess Margaret felt unnerved by these creamily intrusive reminiscences: Payne slips into a room as stealthily as a cat-burglar, prowling around, gathering everything up for future use, always the observer, never the observed.

'I was one of the very few servants who ever saw the Princess's bedroom,' he boasted. 'She would often send me up to get a jewel case or some item she particularly wanted to take with her on a trip … Once the Princess and myself were used to each other, she had no second thoughts about sending me up on such errands to her inner-most sanctuary.'

Throughout his time in her service, Payne seems to have been sizing up his mistress, her family and friends with the watchfulness of a boa constrictor. As Fowles suggested, the reader grows complicit with this particular Collector, perching voyeuristically on his shoulder as he slithers around the Princess's private domain.

Imagine, now, that you are with me as we walk up the main staircase and into the bedroom. It is deserted now, of course, but has been prepared for the Princess to retire. We tread the thick carpet of the corridor silently, with only the occasional creak of a floorboard to tell we are there … The 5-foot tall Princess has chosen a 6-foot, 4 inch bed topped by a foam-rubber mattress, firm but yielding gently to the touch … And just to complete the picture, Mrs Gordon has already laid out one of the Princess's flimsy, full-length nylon nighties.

And why stop there?

Let us take a closer look. We can see a collection of nail files, jars of face cream, tubes of lipstick, and a brush set comprising two green bone-backed brushes edged in gold, and a hand mirror in the same material. Next to them Margaret has thrown an ordinary comb. Also lying there is a half-filled packet of tissues which she uses for removing her make-up at night. In the morning there will be half a dozen of them smeared with lipstick and powder tossed on the dressing table.

Our tour continues into her bathroom, with its fitted carpet in oyster pink, its loo in the far left-hand corner, its white porcelain bath with two chromium-plated taps. Resting across the bath is a tray with compartments containing coloured scented soaps and a long-handled loofah. 'There is no shower as such, but in one of the lockers of the bathroom there is a rubber tubing hand shower which can be plugged into the taps.' Hitchcock's film *Psycho* was released while Payne was still in service at Clarence House, Fowles's book *The Collector* soon after he left.

Back in the bedroom, Payne leers long and hard at the Princess's bedside table, with its light-brown pigskin photograph case. 'It is on the table near the lamp. Look closer and you will see that the case contains three small head-and-shoulders portraits of a man. You may recognize him. And you will not be surprised when I say that to me, they constitute one of the most significant things I encountered during my service with Princess Margaret. But more of that later …'

Those three bedside photographs are all, it emerges, of Group Captain Peter Townsend.

23

Ah! The Group Captain! The rest of us are allowed to forget a youthful passion, but the world defined Princess Margaret by hers, bringing it up at the slightest opportunity. The two of them – the Group Captain and the Princess – had called it a day four years before, when she was twenty-five years old, but when you are royal, nothing is allowed to be forgotten. That is the price to pay for being part of history.

Those who think of Princess Margaret's life as a tragedy see the Group Captain as its unfortunate hero. He was the dashing air ace, she the fairy-tale Princess, the two of them torn apart by the cold-hearted Establishment. For these people, their broken romance was the source of all her later discontent. But how true is the myth?

Peter Townsend entered the scene in February 1944, when he took up his three-month appointment as the King's Extra Equerry. At this time he was twenty-nine years old, with a wife and a small son. Princess Margaret was thirteen, and a keen Girl Guide.

The King took to him immediately; some say he came to regard him as a son. Three months turned into three years, at which point Townsend was made a Commander of the Royal Victorian Order; after a further three years he was promoted to Deputy Master of the Household. Following the death of the King in 1952 he moved to Clarence House, as comptroller to the newly widowed Queen Mother.

When, precisely, did Townsend start taking a shine to the young Princess? For all the fuss surrounding him, it is a question rarely asked.

In his autobiography *Time and Chance*, published in 1978, when he was sixty-four, he fails to set a date on it, insisting that when he first set eyes on the two Princesses, he thought of them purely as 'two rather adorable and quite unsophisticated girls'.

But by the time of Margaret's fifteenth birthday in August 1945, he was already thinking of her in more affectionate terms. Describing a typical dinner party at Balmoral shortly after the end of the war, he writes that the gentlemen would join the ladies for 'crazy games, or canasta, or, most enchanting of all, Princess Margaret singing and playing at the piano'. By now, he was clearly quite smitten:

> Her repertoire was varied; she was brilliant as she swung, in her rich, supple voice, into American musical hits, like 'Buttons and Bows', 'I'm as corny as Kansas in August …' droll when, in a very false falsetto, she bounced between the stool and the keyboard in 'I'm looking over a four-leaf clover, which I'd overlooked before …', and lovable when she lisped some lilting old ballad: 'I gave my love a cherry, it had no stone.'

He accompanied the Royal Family on their 1947 tour of South Africa; by now the Princess was sixteen, and Townsend exactly twice her age. 'Throughout the daily round of civic ceremonies,' he recalls, 'that pretty and highly personable young princess held her own.' Margaret herself was more open, telling a friend, in later life, 'We rode together every morning in that wonderful country, in marvellous weather. That's when I really fell in love with him.'

The tour ended in April 1947. In his autobiography, Townsend insists that he returned home 'eager to see my wife and family'. But, as it happened, 'within moments' he sensed that 'something had come between Rosemary and me'. He now takes a break in his narrative to detail the difficulties within his marriage.

Townsend had married Rosemary Pawle in 1941. He paints it as a marriage made in the most tremendous haste. 'I had stepped out of my cockpit, succumbed to the charms of the first pretty girl I met and, within a few weeks married her.'

At this point, Townsend launches into one of the most curious parts of the book, a rambling homily against the perils of sexual attraction. 'I cannot help feeling that the sex urge is a rather unfair device employed by God,' it begins. 'He needs children and counts on us to beget them. But while He has incorporated in our make-up an insatiable capacity for the pleasures which flow from love, He seems to have forgotten to build a monitoring device, to warn us of the unseen snags which may be lurking further on.

'Sex,' he continues, 'is an enemy of the head, an ally of the heart. Boys and girls, madly in love, generally do not act intelligently. The sex-trap is baited and set and the boys and girls go rushing headlong into it. They live on love and kisses, until there are no more left. Then they look desperately for a way of escape.'

One of the anomalies of this passage is that, when Townsend rushed into this particular sex-trap, he was rather more than a boy. In fact, he was a distinguished Battle of Britain fighter pilot of twenty-six, the recipient of the DSO and the DFC and bar.

His marriage, he says, 'began to founder' on his return from South Africa. The couple's problems were 'intrinsic and personal', principal among them his yearning to go back to South Africa and 'Rosemary's fierce opposition to my ravings about South Africa and my longing for horizons beyond the narrow life at home'. He argues that while 'Rosemary preferred to remain ensconced in her world of the "system" and its social ramifications', he was a rebel who reacted instinctively against 'the conventional existence, the "system", the Establishment, with its taboos, its shibboleths and its obsession with class status'. At this time the Group Captain was the equerry to the King, and had applied (unsuccessfully) to be a Conservative parliamentary candidate, neither the hallmark of a rebel.

Halfway through 1948, the Princess shed the 'Rose' in Margaret Rose. It seems to have been her way of declaring that she was no longer a little girl but a young woman, a transition greeted with a certain lasciviousness by some of her biographers.

'Never before had there been a Princess like her. Though she had a sophistication and charisma far in advance of her years, she was young, sensual and stunningly beautiful,' observes Christopher Warwick. 'With her vivid blue eyes ... and lips that were described as both "generous" and "sensitive", she was acknowledged to be one of the greatest beauties of her generation. In addition, she was curvaceous, extremely proud of her eighteen-inch waist ... unpredictable, irrepressible and coquettish.'

Phwoarr! Tim Heald is equally smitten: 'At eighteen, she was beautiful, sexy ... the drop-dead gorgeous personification of everything a princess was supposed to be.' Furthermore, she was 'a pocket Venus ... an almost impossibly glamorous figure'.

Her emergence into adulthood had its drawbacks. She was burdened with a succession of royal duties, most of them bottom-drawer and dreary. 'The opening of the pumping station went very well in spite of the gale that was blowing,' she wrote in a letter that year to her demanding grandmother, Queen Mary. 'I am afraid that one photographer rather overdid things by taking a picture of me with my eyes shut.' A little later, she oversaw the official opening of the Sandringham Company Girl Guides' hut. The speech she delivered reflects the nature of the occasion:

Looking around me, I can imagine how hard Miss Musselwhite and the company must have worked ... I do congratulate you on the charming appearance of your new meeting place. I have been in the movement ten years as a Brownie, a Guide and a Sea Ranger ... I have now great pleasure in declaring this hut open.

At the same time, her elder sister was opening bridges, launching ships, taking parades and welcoming foreign dignitaries.

From now on, would Margaret have to measure her life in scout huts and pumping stations? Was that all there was? As her day job as her sister's stand-in grew ever more mundane, who could blame her if she looked for excitement elsewhere?

24

'Without realising it,' Peter Townsend writes of autumn 1948, when he was chosen to accompany the Princess to Amsterdam for the inauguration of Queen Juliana, 'I was being carried a little further from home, a little nearer to the Princess.'

In August 1950, Townsend's ongoing rebellion against the British Establishment continued along its mysterious path with his appointment as assistant master of the royal household, a promotion that elevated him to a smart carpeted office on the south side of Buckingham Palace, 'a little paradise compared with the gloomy equerry's room'. At home, though, 'conjugal life, practically, emotionally and sentimentally, had come to a standstill'.

Not so his enchantment with the Princess, who was now within an inch of her twentieth birthday. Townsend was entranced. 'If her extravagant vivacity sometimes outraged the elder members of the household and of London society, it was contagious to those who still felt young,' he writes, adding, a touch dolefully, 'whether they were or not.'

Written when he was in his sixties, his memories of the young Princess retain their sense of wonder. 'She was a girl of unusual, intense beauty, confined as it was in her short, slender figure and centred about large purple-blue eyes, generous lips and a complexion as smooth as a peach. She was capable, in her face and in her whole being, of an astonishing power of expression. It could change in an instant from saintly, almost melancholic, composure to hilarious, uncontrollable joy. She was, by nature, generous, volatile … She was coquettish, sophisticated. But what ultimately made Princess Margaret so attractive and lovable was that behind the dazzling facade, the apparent self-assurance, you could find, if you looked for it, a rare softness and sincerity. She could make you bend double with laughing; she could also touch you deeply.' No one else, before or since, has written about the Princess in quite such adoring terms.

By this time, a group of bright young blades surrounded the Princess. Townsend looked on with a sense of yearning, perhaps even entitlement. 'I dare say that there was not one among them more touched by the Princess's *joie de vivre* than I, for, in my present marital predicament, it gave me what I most lacked – joy. More, it created a sympathy between us and I began to sense that, in her life too, there was something lacking.'

While Princess Margaret admitted to having fallen in love with the Group Captain in the spring of 1947, when she was sixteen years old, Townsend claims to have noticed the first spark in their romance over four years later, in August 1951, following a picnic lunch in the middle of a day's shooting. He was dozing in the heather when he became aware that someone was covering him with a coat. 'I opened one eye – to see Princess Margaret's lovely face, very close, looking into mine. Then I opened the other eye, and saw, behind her, the King.' At this point, Townsend whispered to the Princess, 'You know your father is watching us?' In response she laughed, straightened up, and went over to her father's side. 'Then she took his arm and walked away,' adds Townsend, 'leaving me to my dreams.'

King George VI died early the following year. The Princess had been devoted to him, and he to her. 'Lilibet is my pride. Margaret is my joy,' he once said, adding on another occasion, 'She is able to charm the pearl out of an oyster.' Lilibet was dutiful and serious; Margaret wilful and fun. 'She it was who could always make her father laugh, even when he was angry with her,' wrote John Wheeler-Bennett, the official biographer of George VI. On one occasion she interrupted a telling-off by saying, 'Papa, do you sing, "God Save My Gracious Me"?' The King had burst out laughing, and all was forgiven.

His death hit her hard. 'It was a terrible blow for Princess Margaret,' a friend remembered. 'She worshipped him and it was also the first time that anything really ghastly had happened to her.' Margaret confirmed this to Ben Pimlott, the biographer of her sister: 'After the King's death there was an awful sense of being in a black hole. I remember feeling tunnel-visioned and didn't really notice things.' In her grief, did she seek refuge in love?

After the King's death, everyone moved up or down a notch: Queen Elizabeth became Queen Elizabeth the Queen Mother, Princess Elizabeth became Queen Elizabeth II, and Townsend was appointed comptroller of the Queen Mother's household. Only Margaret stayed the same, but now she had to live alone with her mother in Clarence House, eclipsed and to some extent marginalised by her sister, the new Queen, and with no clear role of her own.

The following December, after eleven years of marriage, nine of them in the service of the Royal Family, Peter Townsend divorced Rosemary, who was named as the guilty party. Two months later she married John de Lázsló, son of the fashionable society painter Philip de Lázsló.

That winter, according to Townsend, he and the Princess found themselves alone in the Red Drawing Room of Windsor Castle. They spoke for hours on end. 'It was then,' he writes, 'that we made the mutual discovery of how much we meant to one another. She listened, without uttering a word, as I told her, very quietly, of my feelings. Then she simply said: "That is exactly how I feel, too."'

Or that's how his story goes. But had this impetuous young woman really managed to hide her feelings for a full five and a half years? And had the Group Captain somehow exercised a similar restraint?*

---

* Possibly not. Princess Margaret's chauffeur, John Larkin, recalled a conversation with his employer when she replaced her Rolls-Royce Phantom IV with a Silver Shadow. Larkin asked

According to Townsend, they pursued their romance in the open air, walking or riding, always 'a discreet but adequate distance' from the rest of the party. 'We talked. Her understanding, far beyond her years, touched me and helped me; with her wit she, more than anyone else, knew how to make me laugh – and laughter, between boy and girl, often lands them in each other's arms.' Once again, he describes himself as a boy; but by now he was thirty-eight years old, and middle-aged. 'Our love, for such it was, took no heed of wealth and rank and all the other worldly, conventional barriers which separated us,' he continues. He doesn't mention less romantic barriers such as age, children (by now he had a second son) and his recent divorce. 'We really hardly noticed them; all we saw was one another, man and woman, and what we saw pleased us.'

The news of their pleasure, 'delivered very quietly', went down like a lead balloon with the senior courtier Sir Alan 'Tommy' Lascelles, at that time private secretary to the new Queen. 'You must be either mad or bad,' he informed Townsend. The Princess was to credit Lascelles with ruining her life. 'Run the brute down!' she instructed her chauffeur, decades later, when she spotted Lascelles, by now an old man, through her car window.

Margaret had already confessed her love to Lilibet, who invited her and the Group Captain to dinner *à quatre* with herself and Prince Philip, an evening that passed off, in Townsend's view, 'most agreeably', though 'the thought occurred to me that the Queen, behind all her warm goodwill, must have harboured not a little anxiety'.

Margaret also told the Queen Mother. Townsend insists that she 'listened with characteristic understanding', though he attaches a

---

her if she wanted her old numberplate – PM 6450 – transferred to the new car. 'No,' she replied. 'It refers to an incident in my past best forgotten. I want something that doesn't mean anything.' Larkin worked out that 'PM' stood for Princess Margaret, and '6450' stood for 6 April 1950. What had happened on that day? What was that incident in her past which was 'best forgotten'? Was it, as some have calculated, the day on which the nineteen-year-old Princess lost her virginity to the Group Captain?

disclaimer to this: 'I imagine that Queen Elizabeth's immediate – and natural – reaction was "this simply cannot be".'

But one of the hallmarks of the Queen Mother was resilience, maintained by a steadfast refusal to acknowledge anything untoward. Whenever she caught a glimpse of something she did not like, she simply looked the other way, and pretended it was not there. Margaret, on the other hand, liked to let things simmer, sometimes for decades.

25

The romance became public at the Queen's coronation on 2 June 1953, when Princess Margaret was spotted picking fluff off the Group Captain's lapel. It was hardly *Last Tango in Paris*, but in those days interpersonal fluff-picking was a suggestive business. The next morning it was mentioned in the New York papers, but the British press remained silent for another eleven days. The *People* then printed the headline 'They Must Deny it NOW', above photographs of the two of them. 'It is high time,' read the front-page editorial, 'for the British public to be made aware of the fact that scandalous rumours about Princess Margaret are racing around the world.' The writer then added, perversely, 'The story is, of course, utterly untrue. It is quite unthinkable that a royal princess, third in line of succession to the throne, should even contemplate a marriage to a man who has been through the divorce courts.'

Within days, the prime minister, the cabinet, the Archbishop of Canterbury, the newspapers and the entire British public had got themselves into a flurry of alarm, delight, concern, horror, approval, dismay, condemnation, joy and despair. Everyone, high and low, had an opinion, for or against. Lascelles himself drove down to Chartwell to inform Winston Churchill of the developing crisis. 'A pretty kettle of fish' was the verdict of Churchill's private secretary, Jock Colville – the very same phrase, incidentally, that Queen Mary had employed seventeen years before, on hearing that her elder son was intent on

marrying a double-divorcee from Baltimore. Readers of the *Sunday Express* turned out to be three-to-one against the union. Mrs M. Rossiter of Whixley, York, declared that 'I am not one of those who consider a married man with two children suitable for any girl of about 20.' On the other hand, when the *Daily Mirror* conducted a readers' poll, complete with a voting form, of the 700,000 readers who bothered to vote, a full 97 per cent thought that the couple should be allowed to marry.

Nella Last, who kept a diary for the Mass-Observation archive, noted that 'My husband was in a dim mood – & Mrs Salisbury [their cleaner] was in one of her most trying. Her *disgust* & indignation about Princess Margaret being "such a silly little fool" held her up at times … "It's *not nice* Mrs Last. I'd belt our Phyllis for acting like that. And a lot of silly girls who copy Princess Margaret's clothes will think they can just do *owt*! … And fancy her being a *stepmother* … And I bet she would miss all the fuss she gets …"'

Churchill agreed to Lascelles's curiously old-fashioned suggestion that Townsend be posted abroad, out of harm's way, and so too did Lilibet. And so, on 15 July 1953, Townsend found himself shunted off into exile, to the almost transparently farcical post of air attaché to the British embassy in Brussels. The idea was that in two years' time Margaret would be twenty-five, and would no longer require the official consent of the monarch, who would thus avoid being compromised. Those with harder hearts argued that absence makes the heart grow weaker, and that two years would be more than enough time for the fairy-tale romance to wither and die.

Townsend was unable to say goodbye, as he had been whisked abroad before the Princess and her mother had returned from their official tour of Rhodesia. For his part, Lascelles was glad to see the back of him: in a letter to a friend he described him as 'a devilish bad equerry', sniffily adding that 'one could not depend on him to order the motor-car at the right time of day, but we always made allowances for his having been three times shot down into the drink in our defence'.

Life has its consolations, even in Belgium. A few months into his involuntary exile, Townsend went 'by pure chance' to a horse show in Brussels. There he watched 'spell-bound, like everyone else, a young girl, Marie-Luce Jamagne, as she flew over the jumps with astonishing grace and dash'. As if in a fairy tale – or rather, a competing fairy tale – the horse fell, and the dashing young girl lay senseless 'practically at my feet'. Townsend rushed over to her, and was reassured to learn from one of the judges that she would make a full recovery.

At the time she landed at his feet, Marie-Luce was fourteen, a year older than Princess Margaret had been when he first set eyes on her, some eight years before. A friendship grew. Marie-Luce's parents invited Townsend to their home in Antwerp. It became a safe haven. 'It was always open to me and in time I became one of the family. That is what I still am today. Marie-Luce, the girl who fell at my feet, has been my wife for the last eighteen years.'

Quite how close had he grown to Marie-Luce by the time he returned to England, a year after his enforced departure? Did he mention her to Princess Margaret when they were briefly reunited in 1954? 'Our joy at being together again was indescribable,' he recalls in his autobiography. 'The long year of waiting, of penance and solitude, seemed to have passed in a twinkling … our feelings for one another had not changed.' We must take his word for it. By now they had only one more year to go until the Princess's twenty-fifth birthday, when she would be free to marry without her sister's consent.

The next year, Townsend returned from his unofficial exile, prompting fresh speculation that marriage bells would soon be ringing. 'COME ON MARGARET!' ran the *Daily Mirror* headline, imploring her to 'please make up your mind!'

Once again, everybody, high and low, had an opinion on the matter. Harold Macmillan noted, 'It will be a thousand pities if she does go on with this marriage to a divorced man and not a very suitable match in any case. It cannot aid and may injure the prestige of the Royal Family.' Mass-Observation's Nella Last entertained similar misgivings, while her husband was resolutely against the match. 'Mrs Atkinson came in. She had got me some yeast,' Mrs Last recorded in her diary. 'She said idly, "Looks as if you're going to be right, that Princess Margaret *will* marry Townsend – seen the paper yet?" We discussed it. We both felt "regret" she couldn't have married a younger man. Mrs Atkinson too has "principles" about divorce that I lack. We just idly chatted, saying any little thing that came into our minds, for or against the match. I wasn't prepared for my husband's wild *condemnation* or his outburst about my far too easy-going way of looking at things! I poached him an egg for tea.' By now, the nation as a whole seemed to have swung behind the idea of the marriage. A Gallup poll discovered that 59 per cent approved of it, and 17 per cent disapproved, with the remainder claiming indifference.

On 1 October the new prime minister, Sir Anthony Eden (himself on his second marriage), informed the Princess that it was the view of the cabinet that if she decided to go ahead with the marriage, she would have to renounce her royal rights, and forgo her income.

Townsend and Margaret were reunited once more on the evening of 13 October. 'Time had not staled our accustomed, sweet familiarity,' Townsend recalled, fancily. But after a fortnight of press attention, things no longer seemed quite so straightforward. 'We felt mute and numbed at the centre of this maelstrom.'

Ten days later, the Princess went to lunch at Windsor Castle with her sister, her mother and the Duke of Edinburgh. According to the Queen's well-connected biographer Sarah Bradford, the Queen Mother grew tremendously steamed up, declaring that Margaret 'hadn't even thought where they were going to live'. Prince Philip, 'with heavy sarcasm', replied that it was 'still possible, even nowadays, to buy a house'. At this, the Queen Mother 'left the room, angrily slamming the door'.

Towards the end of his life, Lord Charteris* voiced misgivings about the Queen Mother's behaviour throughout the Townsend affair. 'She was not a mother to her child. When the Princess attempted to broach the subject her mother grew upset, and refused to discuss it.'

After this fraught lunch, the imperilled couple spoke on the phone. The Princess was, according to Townsend, 'in great distress. She did not say what had passed between herself and her sister and brother-in-law. But, doubtless, the stern truth was dawning on her.'

The following day, *The Times* ran an editorial arguing against the marriage, on the grounds that the Royal Family was a symbol and reflection of its subjects' better selves; vast numbers of these people could never be persuaded that marriage to a divorced man was any different from living in sin. Townsend himself regarded this argument

---

* 1913–99. Assistant private secretary to HM Queen Elizabeth II, later private secretary, and later still Provost of Eton. Aged eighty-one, and imagining he was speaking off the record, he gave an interview to the *Spectator* in which he called the Queen Mother 'a bit of an ostrich', the Prince of Wales 'such a charming man when he isn't being whiny', and, most memorably, the Duchess of York 'a vulgarian, vulgar, vulgar, vulgar'.

as 'specious', and would never have allowed it to sway him. But, he claimed, 'my mind was made up before I read it'.

That afternoon, he 'grabbed a piece of paper and a pencil', and 'with clarity and fluency' began to write a statement for the Princess. 'I have decided not to marry Group Captain Townsend,' it began. With that, he went round to Clarence House and showed her the rough piece of paper. 'That's exactly how I feel,' she said.

'Our love story had started with those words,' he recalled in old age. 'Now, with the same sweet phrase, we wrote *finis* to it … We both had a feeling of unimaginable relief. We were liberated at last from this monstrous problem.'

26

How does a fairy-tale romance turn into a monstrous problem? 'I had offended the Establishment by falling in love with the Queen's sister,' was the Group Captain's simple explanation. But was it sufficient?

In *Time and Chance*, Townsend declares that 'It was practically certain that the British and Dominions parliaments would agree – but on condition that Princess Margaret was stripped of her royal rights and prerogatives, which included accession to the throne, her royal functions and a £15,000 government stipend due on marriage – conditions which, frankly, would have ruined her. There would be nothing left – except me, and I hardly possessed the weight to compensate for the loss of her privy purse and prestige. It was too much to ask of her, too much for her to give. We should be left with nothing but our devotion to face the world.'

When *Time and Chance* was published in 1978, it enjoyed a largely respectful reception, most critics commending the tact with which its author covered his relationship with Princess Margaret. 'Balanced and charitable', read a typical review.

But one critic broke ranks. Alastair Forbes was a cousin of President Roosevelt, the uncle of the future US secretary of state John Kerry, and a friend of the well-connected, among them Cyril Connolly, Randolph Churchill, the Grand Duke Vladimir of Russia, the Duke and Duchess of Kent, and Prince and Princess Paul of Yugoslavia. He was, however, seen as trouble by some of the more prominent royal households:

Princess Margaret used to refer to him as 'that awful Ali Forbes', while Queen Elizabeth II was once heard to yell, 'Will you please put me DOWN!' as he lifted her up during a Highland reel.

Like many of the most energetic stately-home guests, he traded in gossip, usually about those with whom he had just been staying. His fruity tales were peppered with nicknames, often based around puns. For instance, he retitled Temple de la Gloire, Oswald and Diana Mosley's home outside Paris, 'The Concentration of Camp'; Essex House, the home of James and Alvilde Lees-Milne, became 'Bisex House'.

Forbes was long rumoured to be some sort of non-specific spy, either for the CIA or MI6, or possibly both at the same time. His whole life was to some extent swathed in mystery, much of it of his own making. Sustained by a private income, he dabbled in politics and journalism and, in his sixties, took to reviewing books for the *Times Literary Supplement* and the *Spectator*. His prose had a Firbankian quality, its long, elegantly rambling sentences choc-a-bloc with foreign phrases, ribald asides, Byzantine names, incautious allegations and forensic examinations of abstruse questions such as 'Did the Duke of Windsor have pubic hair?'

He had a morbid side to his character. At funerals, some detected an air of triumph emanating from him as friends, enemies and chance acquaintances were lowered into the soil. He was also something of an early bird at deathbeds, pen at the ready to transcribe any last words. It was death that brought his competitive streak to the surface: he had, for instance, made it his mission to be the last man to see Diana Cooper alive.*

---

* The only time I met Forbes was also the only time I met Diana Cooper. It was at the launch party for my friend Hugh Massingberd's book about the Ritz in 1980. Hugh introduced me to Forbes, and the conversation turned to the subject of Lady Diana Cooper. 'Everyone used to go on and ON about Diana's beauty, but to my mind she was nothing LIKE as beautiful as Charlotte Bonham-Carter', said Forbes. At this point, who should appear but Lady Diana herself, wearing an extremely wide-rimmed black hat. 'DIANA!' exclaimed Forbes, with a great beam. 'We were just TALKING about you!'

Forbes was an egalitarian, in that he was as rude to the highest-born as to the lowest. Perhaps more so: he once dismissed Jesus Christ's Sermon on the Mount as being on a par with the mottoes contained in Christmas crackers. His review of Peter Townsend's autobiography, published under the heading 'The Princess and the Peabrain', followed this cock-snooking impulse. Throughout the piece he portrayed Townsend as an upstart – 'What might be pardonable as the dream of an assistant housemaid was entirely unsuitable for an assistant Master of the Household' – and his memoir as yet another attempt to cover the tracks of his social climbing. Rejecting the Townsend version of himself as a victim of love and circumstance, Forbes poured scorn over his every excuse and explanation:

'How to consummate this mutual pleasure was the problem,' writes the author in his best Monsieur Jordain style. You don't say! His imagination, he adds, never at a loss for a cliché, 'boggled at the prospect of my becoming a member of the Royal Family'. Boggled perhaps, but no more than it had been Mittyishly boggling away on the back burner for years. 'All we could hope was that with time and patience, some solution might evolve.' Meanwhile, he neither felt the slightest conscientious compulsion to resign from a position whose trust he had so weakly betrayed, his perverted taste for risk overcoming his sense of duty and gratitude to his Royal employers of eight years, nor did he feel able to say, after the fashion of those pretty inscribed Battersea enamel boxes: 'I love too well to kiss and tell.'

… Townsend, to judge him from this book and its predecessors, still makes a living solely from exploiting his life as the courtier who went too far a-courting. One must hope that he will find alternative ways of bringing up his nice-looking family in their nice-looking house in the Paris green belt and that this will be his last shameful pot-boiler about the unhappy Princess whose coronet he failed to chalk up on his fuselage in his second Battle of Britain, a pranging fall like Lucifer's from the first.

For Forbes, their final decision – to marry or not? – all came down to money. 'What would they have to live on and how would it compare to the quite unusually sybaritic *train de vie* of Clarence House? … In short, if the money was right the marriage was on; if not, it was off.'

Would Princess Margaret really have faced personal and financial 'ruin' if she had accepted Townsend's hand in marriage? Forbes doubted it, but observed that no one in the Royal Family had been 'eager to put the hat around for her. In marked contrast to her sister, whose kindness and courtesy behind a natural reserve are legendary, the Princess had already in her brief years of public life displayed a disagreeable lack of good manners and consideration to all and sundry, on right as on left, and such popularity as she possessed was to be found amongst those who had been neither in her employ nor in her circle of acquaintance, many of the latter having suffered sufficiently from her spoiled rankpulling and snubs to see her indefinitely marooned on Mustique or some more convenient island with her *cavalier servente*. Politicians had long prayed with added fervour for God to save Queen Elizabeth II, long to reign over them, lest they one day wake to find themselves living the nightmare of Tuesday audiences with her ill-educated, ill-informed and sullen sister.'

Forbes's view that their parting was more pragmatic than tragic has gained traction since he first expressed it. Old friends say the marriage would never have worked, largely because of the age gap. And HRH the Princess Margaret baulked at the prospect of losing her title. 'Who wouldn't?' says one friend. 'Much more fun than being Mrs Townsend!'

There was also the money to think about. 'Had she married Townsend, she would have been obliged to forfeit her Civil List income and all her royal privilege, to live quietly in the country on a very small income as the second wife of a middle-aged divorcé,' wrote Selina Hastings in a long profile of the Princess in 1986. And had Peter Townsend really been quite such a dish? 'The prospect of marriage was no longer quite so attractive: no money, and Peter Townsend with his thin mouth and crinkly hair: so reliable, so *wet*.'

Hugo Vickers is sure that the Establishment ruse had done the trick: over the course of those two years, their love had waned. 'Princess Margaret thought that the British public deserved some sort of statement, but it was over by then, and they both knew it.'

27

On Monday, 31 October 1955, the BBC announcer John Snagge interrupted regular broadcasting to read a brief statement from HRH the Princess Margaret:

> I have been aware that, subject to my renouncing my rights of succession, it might have been possible for me to contract a civil marriage.
>
> But, mindful of the Church's teaching that Christian marriage is indissoluble, and conscious of my duty to the Commonwealth, I have resolved to put these considerations before any others.
>
> I have reached this decision entirely alone, and in doing so I have been strengthened by the unfailing support and devotion of Group Captain Townsend.

When the statement emerged from his wireless, Philip Larkin was in the middle of writing another downbeat letter to his girlfriend, Monica Jones. 'Very cold here – large frosty moon, spilling chill light over the lifeless leaves. Mrs S. very poorly again – she appears to have been retching all day & is quite broken down by it – she is still coherent but very feeble. I tried to sit with her tonight, but she dismissed me in order to retch better. She gave me her right hand to shake. I do not like the look of her at all.'

He had, he added, turned on the wireless 'to drown the sound of retching from below, which is really upsetting, groaning & noises similar to those utilised by persons in the article of death'. 'As I write this I'm listening to one of the best Just Fancy programmes I've ever heard … Now it's over, & I'll have to switch off. Can I write any – Whoops! Just heard Princess M. *isn't* going to marry Group Captain Fiddlesticks – well, what a frost! And at 6.15pm tonight I was saying that any announcement wd be bound to be of an engagement, since you couldn't announce *nothing*. Well, apparently you can. How curious & strange. Well, well. What a romantic incident. Christian marriage. Well, well …'

On Alderney, the irascible author T.H. White was writing an awkward letter to his old friend David Garnett, who had posted him an advance copy of his new novel, *Aspects of Love*. Unfortunately, White had not liked the book, and was determined to let Garnett know:

Dearest Bunny, this is a hateful and stupid letter but I must face it and write it, otherwise I shall never be able to look you in the face again.

First of all, the letter you sent me with Aspects of Love filled me with such pride and pleasure that I could hardly sleep all night, I was so happy. But second, as you predicted, I DON'T like Aspects of Love. I kept fidgeting about and putting it down and starting again, it was only at the bottom of page 144 that light suddenly dawned on me like an atomic flash. You like cats and I loathe them. This is not a rational criticism, and God knows I don't claim to be right in loathing cats or that you are wrong in loving them …

… I hate Rose, like a cat, for going to bed with Alexis first, then tossing him over for Sir George, and then taking him and other lovers. Surely women are dependable people as well as men? My adored grandfather on my mother's side was a judge, but not a hanging judge. He would have simply … have answered your various dilemmas in two ways. He would have said … if a woman cannot behave herself

103

according to the laws I have given all my career to, as an Indian Civil Servant – the laws of honour – then take down her crenellated, lace, Victorian pants, and give her one resounding blow with the flat of the hand on the buttocks. In short, I think your Rose is a selfish, short sighted, self-admirer and a bore. Obviously you don't think so, and neither of us is right. It is the dog and the cat.

Perhaps to sweeten the pill of this forthright letter, White added this short paragraph:

Before I end this letter – which is bound to wound you – I must make one other confession. I was truly delighted a week or two ago to learn that Princess Margaret had decided not to marry Group Captain Townsend.

In London, Lady Violet Bonham Carter was far from delighted. She had spent the evening of the announcement with her brother, the film director Anthony Asquith, at a Royal Command Performance screening in Leicester Square of Alfred Hitchcock's 'very bad and slow' movie *To Catch a Thief*, followed by dinner at the Savoy Hotel. As they left the Savoy in the early hours, Asquith 'overheard someone saying something about Princess Margaret which sounded like "off"'. He immediately went back and bought early editions of two different newspapers. 'They had banner headlines, "Princess Margaret decides not to marry Group Captain Townsend". Underneath was a most poignant statement, perfectly expressed. It is a heroic decision and rends one's heart. She is so vital, human, warm and gay – made for happiness. And what she must be suffering doesn't bear thinking of.'

'Thank goodness that's over!' was the verdict of Nella Last's husband in Barrow-in-Furness. Mass-Observation charted the reactions of its predominantly middle-class panel of ordinary men and women. There was a sharp division of opinion between the sexes: the men largely indifferent or unsympathetic, the women more emotionally engaged. 'It is a pity she did not marry Townsend and thereby leave the country,' said a thirty-six-year-old man, a married bank cashier. 'I am no lover of Princess Margaret and the National Press does not help by its continuous publicity of this so called glamour girl. Princess Alexandra beats her hands down.' A twenty-five-year-old bachelor told Mass-Observation, 'My interest in this matter has not been raised above the "luke warm" stage and I have no opinions on this very personal subject.'

A forty-seven-year-old commercial traveller was among those men who came down hard on Townsend. 'Had Group Captain Townsend been a Gentleman he would not have put the Princess to the necessity of making such a decision. He would have gone off to Darkest Africa to shoot elephants or something.'

'Now perhaps we'll hear a little less of that over-publicised little lady,' observed Anthony Heap, a forty-six-year-old local government officer from St Pancras.

The women panellists of Mass-Observation were, on the whole, more sympathetic. A retired teacher aged sixty-five said, 'I am *very sorry* for Princess Margaret – as I feel their decision has been a *hard one*. At the same time, she realises that Great Privileges imply Great Responsibilities, which the Duke of Windsor was *too selfish* to do!'

A thirty-four-year-old secretary, a spinster, was less equivocal: 'I really do think that a man of his age & experience need not have allowed the equivalent of a schoolgirl crush to develop into a grand passion. The man's a Cad.'

A librarian aged fifty was profoundly upset: 'I'm deeply distressed by her decision. It came as almost a physical shock. It was as if we had suddenly started to move back towards the darkness of some primitive jungle – as if a beautiful young girl had been sacrificed to its gods.'

On hearing the news, the author and politician Harold Nicolson felt nothing but admiration for the Princess. 'This is a great act of self-sac-rifice, and the country will admire and love her for it. I feel rather moved,' he wrote in his diary. But, like so many other people, he was soon focusing on how the news might affect his own social arrangements: 'It will be awkward meeting the Duke of Windsor at dinner after this.'

On Wednesday, 2 November 1955, the *Daily Mirror* ran the headline across half its front page: 'THIS MUST NOT WRECK TWO LIVES', trumpeting an opinion piece by Keith Waterhouse, soon to become famous as the author of *Billy Liar*.

Today, as the self-satisfied chorus dies down, I would like to say something about the future of these two people who reached for happiness and found only a stone ... Without doubt the magnifying glasses are out in Whitehall today as the bureaucrats search for unlikely places at the end of the earth where Peter Townsend could be banished.

This must not happen.

The stiff-collar classes are already crowing in their clubs that Peter Townsend has been shown the door.

THESE ARE THE PEOPLE who would have bowed the lowest if he had married Princess Margaret.

THESE ARE THE PEOPLE who will want Peter Townsend plucked up and removed by jet plane whenever there is the slightest chance that Princess Margaret may come within a hundred miles of him.

THESE ARE THE PEOPLE who, from now on, will watch Princess Margaret like hawks crossed with vultures ...

That these two lives have not been wrecked already is due to the courage and immense strength of character of them both ...

LET THEM LIVE IN PEACE AND, IF THEY CAN FIND IT APART, HAPPINESS.*

---

* Waterhouse's valiant deed was never reciprocated. At a reception thirty years later, he noticed Princess Margaret's ash growing longer and longer, so he reached across her to grab an ashtray. 'She simply flicked her ash into my open palm as it passed,' he recalled. 'Thank God she hadn't decided to stub it out.'

Two days later, on Friday, 4 November, the *Daily Express* printed a 'We, the Undersigned' letter about the recent announcement from a mixed bag of figures from the arts world, including Lindsay Anderson, Humphrey Lyttelton, Wolf Mankowitz, Ronald Searle and Kenneth Tynan:

> First, it has revived the old issue of class distinctions in public life.
>
> Second, it has shown us 'The Establishment' in full cry, that pious group of potentates who so loudly applauded the Princess's decision.
>
> Third, it has exposed the true extent of our national hypocrisy.
>
> But above all the Townsend affair brings up the general question of 'national dignity', and its encroachments on personal freedom.

The final name on the list of the undersigned was that of Sandy Wilson, the writer and composer of the 1953 hit musical *The Boy Friend*. Princess Margaret had attended its original production. Among the show's catchiest numbers was 'I Could Be Happy With You':

> I could be happy with you
> If you could be happy with me.
> I'd be contented to live anywhere
> What would I care –
> As long as you were there?

These anti-Establishment types got on the nerves of the Princess's life-long though not wholly uncritical supporter, Noël Coward. A week before the announcement, he had affected boredom with the whole affair: 'I have noticed in the Press certain references to Princess Margaret wishing to marry someone or other,' he wrote in his diary on 24 October. 'I really must try to control this yawning.' But within a fortnight his interest had revived: 'Poor Princess Margaret has made a sorrowful, touching statement that she will not marry Peter Townsend. This is a fine slap in the chops for the bloody Press which has been persecuting her for so long. I am really glad that she has at last made the decision but I do wish there hadn't been such a hideous hullabaloo about it.'

Coward complained that 'It has all been a silly, mismanaged lash-up and I cannot imagine how the Queen and the Queen Mother and Prince Philip allowed it to get into such a tangle. At least she hasn't betrayed her position and her responsibilities, but that is arid comfort for her with half the world religiously exulting and the other half pouring out a spate of treacly sentimentality.' He looked to the future, though with trepidation: 'I hope she will not take to religion in a big way and become a frustrated maiden princess. I also hope that they had the sense to hop into bed a couple of times at least, but this I doubt.'

Despite it all, he felt the Princess had come to the right decision. 'Apart from church and royal considerations, it would have been an unsuitable marriage anyway. She cannot know, poor girl, being young and in love, that love dies soon and that a future with two strapping stepsons and a man eighteen years older than herself would not really be very rosy.'

Jessica Mitford was staying with her sister Nancy in Paris. 'On the Margaret thing,' she wrote to her husband Bob Treuhaft, who was back in America, 'the general consensus seemed to be that she is now one-up on the Windsors.* The Fr. papers were full of the incroyable attitude of the Anglais towards l'amour.' In the same letter she told her husband that, just before Princess Margaret's statement, she had heard that 'the Windsors have a new dog named Peter Townsend, my dear quel mauvais gout'.†

---

* i.e. The Duke and Duchess of Windsor.

† 'What bad taste.'

Three years later, the Duchess of Windsor was talking to James Pope-Hennessy, who was busy researching his authorised biography of her late mother-in-law, Queen Mary. While they chatted, the Duchess's three pugs gambolled about. Their names, she said, were Disraeli, Trooper and Davey Crockett. 'We did have a fourth called Peter Townsend,' she added with what Pope-Hennessy describes as 'her least nice grin', 'but we gave the Group Captain away.'

28

Mrs Peter Townsend, the former HRH the Princess Margaret (b.21 August 1930), died yesterday at her modest farmhouse outside Paris.

The younger sister of HM Queen Elizabeth II, she renounced her right of succession to the throne on 31 October 1955, issuing her famous statement: 'I would like it to be known that I have decided to marry Group Captain Peter Townsend. I am aware that, by seeking to contract a civil marriage, I must first renounce my rights to the succession, and this I have done. I continue to pledge allegiance to my sister, The Queen, who has been a great comfort to me during this difficult time. From this point on, I shall be participating no more in public affairs, but I shall continue to offer my support to Her Majesty in every way that I can.'

The Princess became Mrs Peter Townsend on 4 January 1956 in a private ceremony at Marylebone Register Office. Following a small luncheon party hosted by Noël Coward, the couple flew to their new home in France.

In addition to Townsend's two sons from a previous marriage, the couple had two children of their own, David, born in 1961, and Sarah, born in 1964.

In their self-imposed exile, the Townsends became regular visitors to the home of the Duke and Duchess of Windsor within the Bois de Boulogne. 'They had much in common,' observed a close friend. 'Margaret used to love gossiping with her uncle about the family they had both left behind, and the Duchess was always eager to join in, clapping her hands in delight at Margaret's waspish remarks. "Oh, but Margot, darling – you really shouldn't!" But poor old Peter would find their habitual sniping at those he still regarded with loyalty and affection a little awkward, and so would occasionally take himself off for a discreet walk.'

The Townsends' marriage ended in divorce in September 1972. Friends said they had been growing apart for some time. Margaret had never been wholly reconciled to her loss of status, and would entertain only those who were content to curtsey and address her as 'Ma'am'. While she was drawn to the artistic community, her husband, who worked in the wine trade, was said to prefer the company of those from military or business backgrounds. Sometimes, when her husband was talking, Margaret could be spotted yawning theatrically. Inevitably, Paris society buzzed with rumours of her romances with, among others, Yves Montand, Jacques Brel and Charles Aznavour. The latter's chart-topping 1974 hit 'She' was often said to be about her:

> She may be the beauty or the beast,
> May be the famine or the feast,
> May turn each day into a
> Heaven or a hell.

In November 1972, Peter Townsend married Marie-Luce Jamagne, the former wife of high-society party photographer Antony Armstrong-Jones. Margaret Townsend never remarried. Towards the end of her life she returned to England, where she lived in a small apartment in Kensington Palace, along with two pugs, Betty and Pip, inherited from the Duke and Duchess of Windsor.

29

Two and a half years after the Princess's brief statement announcing her decision not to marry Group Captain Peter Townsend, her silky young footman, David John Payne, was summoned to her sitting room. 'John, I am expecting a very special guest to take tea with me this afternoon. Lay three places in here because Her Majesty Queen Elizabeth will be taking tea with us.'

Payne set out the white china tea service with pale-blue edging on a card table in the centre of the room. At 4.25 p.m., he was stationed by the main door as a chauffeur-driven green saloon car drove up. 'To my utter astonishment, I recognized the suntanned figure of the passenger as that of Peter Townsend.' As he was leading Townsend down the corridor to Princess Margaret's sitting room, Payne received his next surprise. 'In complete abandonment of the usual Royal rules', the Princess and her mother were walking towards them, 'their faces smiling with anticipation'.

The Princess and the Group Captain had not seen each other since their parting. According to the fanciful Payne, Margaret ran to meet Townsend, put her hands on his shoulders and kissed him 'firmly, full on the lips. They lingered over this kiss, neither wanting to draw back … At last they parted and Margaret leaned back, taking his hands but keeping them still on her waist. Only then, for the first time that afternoon, did she speak. "Oh Peter …" was all she said. And I was close enough to hear the sigh in her voice and see the liquid sparkle in her eyes. Then: "It's wonderful to see you again."'

The couple were, at this most private moment, being keenly observed. First, by Payne ('I never saw two people lost in the magic of a moment like that. It lasted less than a minute, I suppose, though it seemed like a golden age to me at the time'). Second, by the Queen Mother, who was herself being observed by Payne. 'Only when they parted did it occur to me that throughout, the Queen Mother had been standing watching three paces away, having walked quietly after her daughter ... As Margaret and Townsend parted, she smiled fondly.'

The Queen Mother greeted Townsend. 'Good afternoon, Peter. It's been a very long time. It's so very lovely to have you here again.' Around this time, it began to dawn on the three participants in the drama – the Queen Mother, Townsend, and Princess Margaret – that there was someone else present: the ubiquitous Payne.

> Up until this moment, I had been an unnoticed observer, and the three had been oblivious of me. It was the Queen Mother who broke the magic spell for me. She released Townsend's hand and looked at me, half in surprise. With a warm smile, she said simply: 'I'm sure tea is quite ready now.'

Payne led them through to the sitting room, where their afternoon tea of cakes and sandwiches was waiting for them. He then retired to the pantry, and smoked a couple of cigarettes, 'musing on the scenes I had been privileged to witness'. He worked out – or later claimed to have worked out – that 'the real significance of this visit' was that it was 'Margaret's opportunity to say her final goodbye to Townsend before any other romance, this time of a permanent nature, prevented her from so doing'.

Half an hour later, the bell in the pantry rang. 'Our guest is ready to leave,' announced the Queen Mother. Payne watched as Margaret and Townsend walked 'slowly, almost reluctantly' out of the room, hand in hand. 'As they passed I smelled the exquisite perfume that Margaret had used ... something extra special, perhaps, I speculated.'

Outside, Townsend's car was waiting for him. 'With an audible sigh', Townsend turned away from Margaret towards her mother, and kissed her on both cheeks. 'Your Majesty, I … I am so happy to have seen you again, yet so sorry to be leaving you.'

The Queen Mother did not reply, but stepped back. All the time, Payne had been looking on. 'I watched, and I admit I felt the sting of tears in my eyes … I am not ashamed to say that I have rarely been so moved, so afflicted by the sadness of others on that day, that hot day at the unromantic hour of teatime.'

Townsend took Margaret by the hand and kissed her on both cheeks. 'He seemed overcome … As Peter Townsend kissed Margaret, I caught sight of the Queen Mother. She was watching them, a gentle look in her eyes. Then, at the moment of their kiss, she turned away. It was a truly majestic move, signifying that she approved and wished the star-crossed couple to embrace without the restraint of her stare.' Payne followed suit. 'I, too, lowered my eyes and stood impassively as I knew a Royal servant must. Yet I shall always remember Margaret best as I saw her in that moment.'

But Payne's eyes were evidently not quite so lowered as they might have been, as he managed to snatch a good peek at their embrace. 'Her chin, held high and proudly, trembled ever so slightly. I knew she was near to tears and I could almost feel the fight she was putting up to prevent them from filling her eyes.'

He opened the car door for Townsend. 'As I bent to shut the door, his eyes met mine and I read a chapter of despair in his look.' Glancing upwards, Payne noticed the windows of Clarence House dotted with the faces of his fellow servants, 'straining for a glimpse of the famous visitor'. At this point in his narrative, Payne grows self-righteous at the memory of others barging in on his grandstand view. 'And so the magic of the moment of farewell was lost. I felt I wanted to get the whole thing over, to urge Townsend to go, to shut the doors of Clarence House on the rest of the world and to allow my Princess to be alone with her thoughts.' Or at least alone with her thoughts and those of her footman.

With Townsend gone, the Princess and her mother disappeared into the sitting room and shut the door. 'To hell with the teacups, I thought. To intrude at such a moment would be ghastly.' Instead, he went up to his room and threw himself on his bed. 'It was ridiculous, I reasoned with myself, to feel so miserable at something which really had nothing to do with me. But had it nothing to do with me? For the first time, I examined my thoughts and feelings about the relationship between Margaret and her personal footman.' He had, he claimed, become 'emotionally bound up with my Princess. That day there was no escape from my enforced sharing of her sadness.'

Half an hour later, the bell rang. As he entered, Margaret was sitting at her desk, writing. 'When I drew near her, I saw that three-quarters of a page of her personal diary was filled with neat handwriting.'

Margaret barely looked up. 'I shall be dining with Her Majesty tonight,' she said quietly.

Dinner took place in complete silence. 'When I scraped a spoon over a silver salver, it sounded like thunder. That meal remains quite the strangest I ever saw. It was almost eerie.'

Margaret sat by herself, playing classical music on the gramophone, before going to bed. Payne took the opportunity to go into her sitting room, 'the air ... heavy with cigarette smoke'. On her desk was a glass of whisky and an ashtray containing half a dozen cigarette stubs, as well as her diary. 'What had she written against that day, I wondered?' He stared at it for two or three minutes. 'I knew temptation then, for it would have been simple to have opened that diary and read it.' But he resisted the temptation: 'It would be sacrilege.' Instead, he poured himself a glass of the Princess's whisky, drank it down with one gulp, and raised his eyes 'to where, through the bricks and mortar, Margaret would be sleeping'.

* * *

Life at Clarence House continued, its stately path paved with routines both big and small. In the first few moments of any given day, Payne would gauge the Princess's mood. 'The first words she spoke were the barometer of her temper ... My heart would sink if she stepped briskly out of the elevator, her head held high, glancing at me with a slight lift of an eyebrow but not a word before marching along to the sitting room. Then, I knew, things might be a little difficult. On really black days, she hurried into her room and gave the door a resounding slam.'

He would wait for the bell to sound. 'It was a fair guess that she would want a drink – vodka and orange juice it would be ... Just a short nip of this lethal drink, liberally laced with orange juice, would suffice her and she rapidly returned to her normal, pleasant self.' Executing one of his Misery-ish about-turns, he adds, 'Princess Margaret is really one of the sweetest people I have ever met and I can honestly say that it was always – or very nearly always – a joy for me to work for her.'

Payne seeks to paint a portrait of himself as the Princess's loyal knight in a hostile world. The most effective way to do this is first to repeat the world's most hostile gossip, and then to be gravely offended by it. 'I felt my blood boil to hear people make cheap and nasty remarks about Margaret. Only too easily they believed she was a spoiled, pampered and petulant girl who had no knowledge of the Royal Palace. Often I wanted to defend my Princess against these ill-mannered remarks.' This passage comes in the middle of his own hour-by-hour description of her slovenly daily routine:

9.00 A.M.: She has breakfast in bed, followed by two hours in bed
listening to the radio, reading the newspapers ('which she
invariably left scattered over the floor') and chain-smoking.

11.00 A.M.: She gets into a bath run for her by her lady's maid.

NOON: An hour in the bath is followed by hair and make-up at her
dressing table, then she puts on clean clothes – 'as one would

imagine of a Princess, she never wore any of her clothes more than once without having them cleaned'.

12.30 P.M.: She appears downstairs for a vodka pick-me-up.

1.00 P.M.: She joins the Queen Mother for a four-course lunch 'served in an informal manner from silver dishes', with half a bottle of wine per person plus 'fruit and half a dozen different varieties of native and Continental cheeses'.

And so on. In the afternoon, she catches up with her diary or brings her photo album up to date. If there is an appointment planned for the following day, she practises her speech.

More often than not, these royal duties proved tiresome beyond words, and the Princess returned in a sulk.

'Many of them were pleasant-enough chores but obviously the thrill of visiting schools, addressing umpteen societies, visiting factories and laying foundation stones would quickly pall ... I'm afraid that sometimes on her return to Clarence House after one of these outings Margaret would not be able to disguise her expression of gloom or outright relief.'

Every now and then, the Queen Mother would be there at the front door to greet her returning daughter. 'I well remember one rather revealing incident, which amused me very much indeed. It was a sullen rainy day. The Princess had been driven back from some tedious function and was greeted by the Queen Mother who waited with me just inside the half-open main door of Clarence House.'

The Queen Mother offered Princess Margaret a cheery greeting. 'Hello, darling. Did you enjoy yourself?'

At this, 'Margaret scowled and sighed: "Honestly Mother, I was bored stiff."

'The Queen Mother raised her eyebrows in surprise, threw me a glance and said confidentially to the Princess: "Never mind, darling. You must always remember to look interested even if you are not."

'But Margaret was not impressed. She huffed her shoulders and stomped off down the corridor leaving the Queen Mother looking after her with the glimmer of a smile round her mouth.' With that, the Princess shut herself in her sitting room, and played an LP by Frank Sinatra.

At 4.30 p.m. on a normal day, it would be time for afternoon tea. This consisted of scented China tea, a plate of sandwiches and two or three fancy cakes, served in her sitting room on a tray covered with a fresh white cloth. More often than not, the Princess wouldn't eat anything. At the same time, her mother would be served exactly the same spread, but in her own apartment upstairs.

At 5.30 p.m. it would be time to prepare for the evening ahead. 'With the help and advice of the faithful Mrs Gordon, the Princess selected a dress – either a simple cocktail affair for the more casual social occasion, or, for a big evening, one of the flamboyant, billowing evening gowns which she was able to wear to such a wonderful advantage. With a choice of shoes and her matching assessories [sic] laid out for her, Margaret would sit once more before her own reflection in her dressing table mirror and make herself up and carefully comb her hair into position.'

For Payne, 'evening at Clarence House began with the descent of Princess Margaret from her bedroom, changed, made-up and invigorated by the prospect of an evening out with her friends'. Meanwhile, he would have cleared away the tea things and arranged the evening drinks tray, 'ready for Margaret and her visitors'.

Invariably, these visitors were the Woosterian group of young aristocrats known by the press at the time as 'the Margaret Set'. After drinks they would go to a West End theatre ('their tickets obtained discreetly through a booking agency'), and from there back to Clarence House, 'tumbling out of their cars laughing and calling out to each other', ready for more drinks.

'They might even decide to have a little late dinner,' records an aggrieved Payne, adding that 'these decisions were always a thorn in my side, for they never thought about it until 11 o'clock or so, which meant I had to wait up all evening, and then stay up to serve dinner at midnight'.

After dinner there would be smoking, and the gang would stroll back into the sitting room. 'Within minutes, the record-player went on. Brandy and cigars were ordered in quantity and the Margaret Set let their hair down, kicking off their shoes to dance on the carpets, helping themselves to drinks and sorting through the Princess's vast collection of records, from pop singers to Dixieland to real cool jazz.' Payne notes, sniffily, that despite her 'very fine' collection of classical music, 'my Princess's taste was definitely low-brow, and for the most part, the symphonies, concertos and arias remained solidly in their covers'.

His work was not done until the last guest had left, and the Princess had finally gone to bed. 'I would be expected to remain up until Margaret turned in, maybe at two, three or four in the morning.'

So one day would end, and the next begin. 'These late nights were inevitably followed by the "morning after" which meant that Margaret would not be seen until the early afternoon. No such luck for me, of course. I was still expected to respond to the urgent calls of the Royal dogs and take them out for their early-morning exercise.'

For all her devil-may-care attitude to late nights and fun, Margaret was always a stickler for order, her timetable as rigid as can be. Every evening, the drinks tray was her first port of call. She would stand and check it to see that everything was in place. 'Chief object of her scrutiny was the special bottle of sealed Malvern water … which the Princess insisted on taking with her Scotch whisky,' Payne recalled.

In even the most ruthlessly calibrated hierarchy, it is these niggly little demands that can so often cause a rupture. Payne says he first realised the intensity of the Princess's love of Malvern water and hatred of all other brands when he accompanied her for a weekend in the country.

'I remember it was on one of these weekends away – it was actually at the Devonshire house of Margaret's cousin, Mrs Ann Rhodes* and her husband – that I realized how strong was my Princess's insistence on Malvern water with her drink. This ridiculous habit of always taking Malvern water had often caused me trouble and embarrassment, not to mention an occasional tongue-lashing, throughout my service with her. Now I was to see someone else put on the spot by my Princess's petty refusal to drink plain tap water.'

It was the evening of their arrival in Devon. Princess Margaret, 'a little weary after our long journey', had changed for dinner. Drinks were about to be served. 'Of course, none of the other guests could be served until Margaret had made her choice ... I knew that at this moment she would be looking forward to her usual whisky and water.'

Denys Rhodes said, 'What will you have to drink, Ma'am?'

'Whisky and water,' came the reply.

'Certainly.' First, Denys Rhodes filled a glass with 'a generous helping' of whisky. Then he raised a crystal jug filled with tap water, which he was about to pour into the Princess's whisky.

'Instinctively, I pushed forward to warn him. But I was too late. Before I could speak, the Princess had spotted what he was doing and in a voice which stilled all other conversation in the room said: "No Denys. Not that. I want WATER in my whisky."'

The room fell silent. No one could fathom what on earth she was on about. At the same time, Payne sensed that 'they seemed to be hoping – by the look on their faces – that they were about to witness a royal tantrum.

'Mr Rhodes was apparently quite puzzled too. He looked at Margaret as if she might have been joking and with a slight smile playing about his lips said: "But this is water, Ma'am."

---

* More accurately known as Margaret Rhodes, née Elphinstone (1925–2016). Her autobiography, *The Final Curtsey* (2011), was an unexpected bestseller.

'But Margaret wasn't having any of that, as I could have told him. She looked him up and down and completely ignoring the rest of the company said in her most Royal tones: "That is not water. It is only tap water."'

Princess Margaret beckoned Payne over. 'John knows exactly what I mean. Fetch my special water here immediately, will you?'

Payne went to the kitchen and picked a bottle of Malvern water from the crate he had brought with him. When he went back into the room, he found that the other guests were still not talking, while Mrs Rhodes, 'in a slightly vexed voice', was saying, 'But Margaret, water is water wherever it comes from. You've got to admit that.'

But no: she dug in her heels. Water is NOT water. Payne went over to the Princess and showed her the bottle of Malvern water. 'It was still sealed; Margaret always insisted on this.' The Princess nodded her head, and turned to her cousin.

'This, Ann, is water. Now do you see what I mean?'

With a bow, Payne presented the fresh glass to Princess Margaret. All was well; conversation recommenced.

The ever-watchful Payne logged the Malvern incident as a prime example of the Princess's unsettling combination of obstinacy and ignorance. 'This type of demonstration of stubbornness by my Princess never failed to amuse me, especially if it concerned her love of Malvern water. But I soon learned that Margaret could not recognise the taste of Malvern water from any other kind. It was only a Royal whim that made her an addict to this particular liquid.'

At this point in his memoir he reveals that on a number of their weekends away he ran out of Malvern water. 'And I knew that if a fresh bottle had not been produced when called for it there would be a stern reproach for me from the Princess. She had decided that without Malvern water she could not drink whisky and therefore I was depriving her of a decent drink. That is how Margaret's mind worked.'

To avoid a scolding, Payne would pick an empty bottle from the crate, then hunt around for a used Malvern seal. 'This could mean sorting through the rubbish in the waste bin or grubbing about on the kitchen floor.' Having ascertained that no other servant was looking, he would covertly fill the empty bottle with tap water before carefully fitting the seal in place. 'A little glue and some gentle re-arranging of the red and white paper seal and it would look as good as new.'

It was a trick that worked a treat. 'Of course, my Princess never spotted it. She would check the seal when I showed it to her, but, trusting me as she did, she never bothered to scrutinise the seal closely. I always felt a little guilty at fooling her but she drank her whisky and "water" as usual and never showed any ill effects. In fact sometimes I would swear she appeared to enjoy it more than the real thing.'

30

As she grew older, Princess Margaret turned pickiness into an art form, snubbing hosts who offered her items of food and drink that were not exactly what she wanted. Staying with friends on Corfu in the mid-1980s, she was invited to dinner by a neighbour who had never met her before. Prior to her arrival he went to an amazing amount of trouble, scouring the island for as many different types of whisky as he could find, so as not to be wrong-footed. When the evening came, he asked her what she would like to drink. 'Famous Grouse, please.' 'Ma'am, that is the only one I haven't been able to get.' 'Then I won't have anything, thank you.' And with that, she turned away to light a cigarette.

At times, it seemed as though she was taking a perverse pleasure in finding things not up to scratch. Hugo Vickers recalls the first time she came to dinner with him. 'She said, "You won't have a Robinson's barley water," and I said, "Of course I have," and she looked a little disappointed.'

Her hosts knew to serve her first. The more obsequious would withdraw any dishes she refused – potatoes, for instance – so that others could not have them either. Nor were her fellow guests permitted to carry on eating once she had finished. The Princess tended to wolf down what little food she ate, which meant that slowcoaches would have to down tools with half their food left uneaten.

Far more than her sister, she was given to pulling rank. She once reminded her children that she was royal and they were not, and their father was most certainly not. 'I am unique,' she would sometimes pipe up at dinner parties. 'I am the daughter of a King and the sister of a Queen.' It was no ice-breaker. Even in her youth, she would accept invitations only on the understanding that the names of her fellow guests were submitted to her lady-in-waiting beforehand, accompanied by a full CV. Throughout her life she delighted in exercising the power of veto. One hostess remembers an Indian friend being black-balled, on the grounds that the Princess didn't like Indians.

When exactly did she first show signs of being the world's most difficult guest? By the age of twenty-eight she had already developed a reputation: when Cynthia Gladwyn, the wife of the British ambassador to France, heard that the Princess would be accompanying the Queen Mother on a visit to Paris in April 1959, she felt very put out. 'This put a different complexion on the scheme,' she recalled in her diary some time later. '... Her reputation, when staying in embassies and government houses, was not an encouraging one.'

Lady Gladwyn could not have been aware of an unfortunate incident a few days before. On the morning of a lunch in Rome held in the Princess's honour, the ten-year-old daughter of a senior British diplomat had been taught to say grace. But when the big moment came, she grew tongue-tied. While the Princess and everyone waited expectantly, the little girl whispered to her mother that she had forgotten what to say.

'You remember, darling,' replied her mother encouragingly. 'Just repeat what Daddy and I said before lunch.'

'Oh God, why do we have to have this difficult woman to lunch,' piped up the little girl.

The Gladwyns met the Queen Mother and Princess Margaret off their plane at Orly airport. They had flown direct from Rome after a meeting with the Pope. Her diaries suggest that Lady Gladwyn was ill-disposed towards Princess Margaret from the start: while she describes the Queen Mother as 'radiant as always',* the Princess is, she notes, 'looking far from radiant' in a 'distinctly ordinary coat and skirt'.

Along with radiance, she emitted delight. Her authorised biographer, William Shawcross, chronicles this trail of delight. Wherever she goes, she delights everyone, and they are in turn delighted by her delight, whereupon she is delighted that they are delighted that she is delighted that ... and so forth. If you shut his book too abruptly, you'll notice delight oozing out of its sides. Returning from Australia, the young Elizabeth hears that the King is 'delighted with the enthusiastic reception'. For her birthday, the King and Queen give her a Chinese screen. 'She was delighted,' reports Shawcross. Off on another trip, she leaves the children with Queen Mary. 'The Queen was, as always delighted,' writes Shawcross. In time, George and Elizabeth are elevated to King and Queen. Her husband bestows the Order of the Garter upon her. 'She was delighted.' She meets President Roosevelt, whom 'she thought delightful'. She also found train drivers 'delightful', and 'delighted' in mimicry. After the coronation she visits Balmoral. 'It was delightful,' she says.

It clearly takes a certain steeliness to be quite so radiant, quite so delighted twenty-four hours a day. The famously effete Stephen Tennant, the brother of one of the Queen Mother's early suitors,

---

* Of all the adjectives used to describe the Queen Mother, 'radiant' is surely the most frequent. During her lifetime it almost became part of her title, like Screamin' Jay Hawkins or Shakin' Stevens. Radiant this, radiant that: she might have popped out of the womb radiant, and continued radiating morning, noon and night. As time went on, it became hard to imagine her ever unradiant, but then again, she never had to put out the bins, or book a ticket online, or trudge around a supermarket with a twelve-pack of toilet paper. She seems to have achieved her perpetual radiance by ring-fencing herself from anything unpleasant or – a favourite word, this – 'unhelpful'. She was singular in her pursuit of happiness, banishing anything upsetting from her walled garden of delight. She rarely attended funerals or memorial services, even of old friends, and was a stranger to deathbeds. Hugo Vickers cites a particularly chilling example of her ruthless contentment. When Sir Martin Gilliat, her loyal private secretary for thirty-seven years, was dying, she never once visited him. 'Before he died, perhaps because of the pain of his terminal illness, or perhaps because, due to Queen Elizabeth's ingrained dislike of dying friends, she had not gone to see him, Gilliat railed against his employer, declaring that he had wasted the best years of his life in her service.'

CRAIG BROWN

described her as 'hard as nails'. The Duke of Windsor agreed, calling both his mother and his sister-in-law 'ice-veined bitches'.

Queen Elizabeth II is also sometimes described as 'radiant', though less frequently so, perhaps because her efforts at radiance appear rather more dutiful. But from the age of twenty-five, Princess Margaret was rarely described as 'radiant', other than on her wedding day, traditionally an occasion on which the adjective is obligatory, to be withheld only if the bride is actually hauled sobbing to the altar.

On that April morning in Paris, Lady Gladwyn ascribed the young Princess's determined non-radiance at Orly airport to her late nights 'dashing around in Rome in a smart set'. She had mixed with aristocrats, artists and film stars, returning to the Rome embassy in the early hours of the morning. But this was, she felt, no excuse for her general off-handedness. 'Princess Margaret seems to fall between two stools. She wishes to convey that she is very much the Princess, but at the same time she is not prepared to stick to the rules if they bore or annoy her, such as being polite to people.' This was soon to become the accepted view of the Princess among those who bumped into her socially.

Her purpose in coming to Paris was twofold: to have her hair styled by the famous Parisian hairdresser Alexandre, and to be fitted for a dress by Dior. Any additional obligations she regarded as a bit of a chore. At a small cocktail party in the embassy, she proved to Cynthia Gladwyn that she was 'quick, bright in repartee', but also 'wanting to be amused, all the more so if it is at somebody else's expense'. This, she felt, was 'the most disagreeable side to her character'.

After the cocktail party, they all went upstairs to dress for the forthcoming dinner for sixty in the State Dining Room. On the way, Margaret asked her hostess, 'Will it be short or long?' Lady Gladwyn sensed a trap. 'I knew that this trivial detail had often been a stumbling block; that if it was decreed that we would all wear short dresses, she would embarrass everybody by making an entry in the most sweeping of ball dresses, and vice versa.' Even at this early stage, she had taken against the young Princess. Did she merit such instant disapproval, or was it a perverse reaction to her fame?

Cunningly, Lady Gladwyn pre-empted any mischief by informing her guests that either long or short would be fine. It took some time before they discovered which way the Princess would swing. 'Dinner was at 8.30 and at 8.30 Princess Margaret's hairdresser arrived, so we waited for hours while he concocted a ghastly coiffure,' complained Nancy Mitford, who was also present. When she finally emerged, she looked, according to Mitford, 'like a huge ball of fur on two well-developed legs'.* As for her dress, she had managed to find a loophole. Lady Gladwyn recorded that it was not just short, but too short. According to her, 'one Frenchman commented, "It began too late and ended too soon."' Nancy Mitford was also to repeat this witticism, adding, 'In fact the whole appearance was excessively common.'

The Princess was placed next to Jean Cocteau, who recalled, perhaps fancifully, that she had told him, 'Disobedience is my joy.' After dinner, the other guests trooped into the ballroom for a performance by the vocal quartet Les Frères Jacques. The Gladwyns and the royal party entered last, by which time the others were all sitting down. At a similar event in Britain, everyone would have greeted the royal party by rising to their feet; but not in France. 'Being French and republican and democratic and independent, and with nobody giving them the lead to rise, they remained as they were.'

The Queen Mother, 'with perfect manners and comprehension of the situation', didn't look in the slightest bit put out, but just 'smiled amiably and moved towards her chair'. Not so Princess Margaret. 'She exclaimed imperiously, "Look! they've sat down!" and showed that she was displeased.'

---

* Four years later, in a letter to Violet Hammersley written on 28 April 1963, Nancy Mitford varied the imagery slightly. 'Pss M unspeakable, like a hedgehog all in primroses,' she observed after seeing her at a wedding in County Waterford.

Lady Gladwyn had already worked out who should sit on either side of the Princess for the performance, but the Princess was having none of it, plonking herself beside Cocteau, who had already been next to her at dinner. 'She took such a fancy to him that she would hardly talk to anybody else the whole evening.' At one point, the former French ambassador in London approached Lady Gladwyn. 'I really must have a word with the Princess. Can you arrange it?' She did her best, trying to edge him into the Princess's little circle, but the Princess refused to catch her eye. 'She was well aware of my tactics, and determined to ignore them. In the end I gave up.'

After church on Sunday – at which the Princess accepted a bouquet 'with noticeable ingratitude, holding it by the stalks, with the heads of the flowers almost touching the pavement' – Lady Gladwyn had planned a visit to two châteaux, on which several young people had been invited, to keep the Princess company. But shortly before they were due to set off, the Princess wriggled out of it. 'The Princess came towards me and told me she had a cold and therefore could not come with us. Simultaneously she began clearing her throat, cooked up a few coughs, and said that her voice was going. The Queen Mother turned to me rather sadly and sweetly asked whether it would matter very much.' Lady Gladwyn bit her lip. 'Naturally I said that although everybody would be dreadfully disappointed, health was so important that if she felt ill of course she must not attempt to come.' At this, the Princess disappeared upstairs to bed.

While Lady Gladwyn was hastily changing from her church clothes into her lunch clothes, her maid, Berthe, told her that the Princess had secretly arranged for Alexandre to come over in the afternoon to do her hair. 'Clearly Princess Margaret's cold was a fake,' she commented huffily in her diary. In the car on the way to the first château, she told the Queen Mother's lady-in-waiting, Lady Hambleden, about the Princess's clandestine hair appointment. She was not, replied Lady Hambleden, in the least surprised: they were better off without her, and if the Princess had been dragooned into coming, she would have behaved disagreeably and spoilt the day for everybody else. 'You will see that this tiresome incident will have no effect on Queen Elizabeth at all. She will enjoy the day as much as though it never happened. Nothing will disturb her happiness.'

And so it transpired: the day went swimmingly, the Queen Mother never more radiant. On their return to the embassy, Lady Gladwyn accompanied her upstairs to see how the Princess was. 'Her elaborate coiffure showed that something rich and strange had been done to her. Nevertheless the farce of the cold was still kept up.' The Princess was not sure whether or not she would feel well enough to come down before dinner.

Lying in her pre-dinner bath, Lady Gladwyn took a phone call from Lady Hambleden. A little apologetically, she explained that Her Royal Highness wished to know the names of anyone of importance who would be coming. Lady Gladwyn replied, tersely, that there was a list in all the rooms, that she was at present in her bath, and that she really could not be expected to trot out the names of all thirty guests off the top of her head. However, she did know that the French prime minister, foreign minister and ex-president would all be there. Presently, word arrived that the Princess's voice had miraculously improved; she now felt well enough to come down to dinner.

'We must at least give her credit for being a good actress, for she played the role of somebody with a loss of voice effectively, even though her occasional cough, more difficult to simulate, was less effective.' Every now and then, forgetting she was meant to be ill, she began to speak perfectly normally. 'But what was really remarkable,' noted the undeceived Lady G., 'was her lack of desire to please.'

She was due to return to London on Monday morning, after an early fitting for her dress by Dior. Accordingly, Lady Gladwyn put in a request to say goodbye. Princess Margaret told her to come to her room at 10 a.m.

As she entered, she found the Princess wearing a beautiful sweeping negligée. How was she feeling? Much better, said the Princess. By this time, Lady Gladwyn considered that she had earned the right to the last word.

'As I curtseyed, I could not resist remarking, "I'm so glad, Ma'am, that having your hair shampooed did not make your cold worse."'

31

But might there be a different story? It has been said that history is written by the victors,* but, on the most basic level, this is not quite true: it is written by the writers. In her skirmish with Princess Margaret, this makes Cynthia Gladwyn the clear victor. But another story might as easily have been told, a story in which the beautiful young Princess is envied and resented in roughly equal measures by the catty middle-aged ambassadress. A less snooty, more easy-going hostess might have praised the Princess for her humility and common sense in wearing a 'distinctly ordinary coat and skirt' for her arrival in Paris. And, instead of condemning her for looking 'far from radiant', Lady Gladwyn might have complimented Princess Margaret on 'taking her responsibilities extremely seriously'.

Aged twenty-eight, did the Princess not show a refreshingly modern, independent outlook in refusing to bow to the dress regulations laid down by the dull old guard? Were Cynthia Gladwyn and Nancy Mitford the Ugly Sisters, seething with envy at this pert young Princess with her unabashed glamour and sex appeal? Given the choice, which of us would not rather sit next to Jean Cocteau than to a former French ambassador to London? And, when you are feeling below par, what could be worse than a middle-aged woman you've never previously

---

* Oddly enough, no one can agree on who wrote 'History is written by the victors.' Some say Churchill, others Hitler, Napoleon, Machiavelli, George Orwell or Walter Benjamin.

met tut-tutting and raising her eyebrows and implying, in bitchy asides, that you are simply putting it on?

When you are a Princess, every little step you take, no matter how small or insignificant, can be interpreted in any number of different ways, from comic to tragic, and all points in between.

32

'A story is told that Princess Margaret, having read Richard Holmes's biography of Coleridge, craved to see Nether Stowey. Accordingly she instructed her pilot on the way back from an official chore to circle several times around the Somerset cottage.'

TOBY BARNARD in the *TLS*, reviewing *The Oxford Guide to Literary Britain and Ireland*, third edition

Journalistic

Close friends are expressing 'deep concern' that in recent weeks Princess Margaret has become 'totally besotted' by an opium-addicted eighteenth-century poet who anxious friends described as a hellraiser.

The Queen is said to be suffering 'sleepless nights' over her sister's infatuation. Shocked onlookers who witnessed her appearance on an official visit said she looked 'dreadfully haunted', and that she could be seen 'performing endless "waving" gestures with her right hand'.

'This type of compulsive-obsessive behaviour is often a cry for help,' says a leading psychiatrist.

Fears increased yesterday after the Princess demanded a private plane, funded by the British taxpayer, to fly her high above the poet's West Country love-nest.

But as the plane arrived at the closely-guarded four-bedroom luxury hideaway, valued at over £1 million, the Princess was seen to be behaving erratically.

She refused to allow the plane to descend, instead peering longingly at the poet's bedroom window, say distressed onlookers.

Against all advice, the unhappy-in-love Princess then ordered the pilot – a married man – to fly around and around in terrifying circles. This led some traumatised villagers to describe the unexplained expedition as 'a nailbiting life-and-death journey to hell and back'.

There is no firm evidence that the Princess is addicted to hard drugs, but friends say she has found it hard to overcome rumours that she continues to struggle with cellulite.

'This was a wholly unsuitable expedition for anyone so close to the throne,' said one royal expert last night. 'Princess Margaret's behaviour continues to offer cause for concern.'

She seems to have it all. Wealth. Fame. Glamour. The most famous sister in the world.

But will she ever find true happiness?

Comic

Stop me if I've told you, but there was this Princess, see, and she'd just read this totally mind-boggling book about a poet, right, and so this Princess, she says, 'You know what I'm going to do, I'm going to get into this plane, and I'm going to say to the pilot, "Take me to the poet's cottage – and circle around and around until I say 'Whoah!'"' And that, my friends, is exactly what she did – only what the poor woman didn't realise was that the poet was dead and buried! Whoops!

Statistical

Princess Margaret (1930–2002) read *Coleridge: Early Visions* by Richard Holmes (1989), which was 409 pages long.

She was flying in a Cessna 172P Skyhawk, with a full, two-tube Lycomin O-320-D2J engine. They were cruising at about 201 mph at 3,000 feet.

It was a 73 per cent clear day. She looked down on the village of Nether Stowey (OS grid reference STI94308), with its population of 1,373. This was where the third most prolific Romantic poet, Samuel Taylor Coleridge, lived between 1797 and 1799.

The plane came in to land against a north-westerly wind at 16.36 hours precisely.

Discreet

Someone, who must remain nameless, was visiting the town or village of X in the West Country.* He or she had read somewhere that something had happened at a particular location,† and somehow managed to get another person to convey them by a certain means of transport to a location in some way related to it.‡ But for God's sake, this must remain strictly between ourselves.

Alliterative

The poems pondered and the pretty pointless parading partaken, the pert Princess primed the pertinacious pilot to pursue a path promptly to the pothead poet's pastoral pad to peruse the priceless panorama, perhaps pleading too pooped to pop out and participate in a painstaking potter.

Confrontational

'So you claim to have heard this story, is that correct?'

'Yes.'

'You read it?'

'Yes.'

'Ha! One moment you claim you heard it, and the next you claim you read it! I put it to you, sir, that you cannot have done both!'

---

* Private information.

† Private information.

‡ Private information.

'But I –'

'Very well. Let us now turn to the "story" itself. Did you or did you not suggest that it involved the late Princess Margaret, who is, I might add, in no position to defend herself?'

'Well, I –'

'And did you, furthermore, claim that a mysterious pilot was in some way involved?'

'Yes, but I –'

'Even though you don't know his name, and you haven't the foggiest idea what he looked like?'

'Well, I –'

'And yet you are seriously asking us to believe that the late Princess Margaret, a devoted mother of two, ordered this unknown pilot to fly over a wholly unremarkable cottage! And all because she had just read a book!'

'Well, if you put it like that …'

'Yes, I do indeed put it like that.'

'Well, I –'

'No further questions, m'lud!'

Gastronomic

1 Princess Margaret
1 Biography of Coleridge
1 Nether Stowey
1 Pilot
1 Plane

First, pour biography into Princess Margaret.

Mix well.

Place Princess Margaret in the plane with the pilot.

Wait until the mixture has risen.

Now, fly the plane over the village.

Add spice.

Serve with garnish, sauce, flavouring.

Chinese Whispers

'Princess Margaret flew in a plane over Coleridge's cottage.'

'Princes more regretfully play over coal ridge's cold itch.'

'Print cess replay overcoat rich cod id.'

'Priceless repair coat Trish curd.'

'Prepare catty skirt.'

Argumentative

I don't know who told this story and frankly I don't fucking care. Do you have an issue with that? Well, do you?

Just let me finish, for once. Whatever nutter told this load of bullshit said that Princess Margaret – God, I mean, who really gives a fuck about Princess Margaret, for Chrissake? – that Princess so-called Margaret once read Richard Holmes's unbelievably tedious biography of Coleridge, who honestly must be the most overrated so-called poet who ever lived. As the sister of the most boring and overpaid woman in the world, she then thought it perfectly reasonable to order her pig-ignorant pilot to destroy the ozone layer just that little bit more by circling around and around Nether Stowey, which, let's face it, is the single most boring place in the world, and if you don't agree with that then you're even more of a moron than you look. Do you have an issue with that? Well – do you? Typical!

Blurb

For the very first time, the extraordinary death-defying tale of Princess Margaret's secret flight to Nether Stowey can now be told.

The crazed poet who could never say no.

The pilot chasing his dreams.

The rebel Princess who had loved and lost.

And the legendary biographer who prompted her insatiable craving for the adventure of a lifetime.

Follow the tragic Princess on her amazing quest, and you will never be the same again. This landmark story of tragedy and triumph will change your life.

Forever.

Footnote

* Princess Margaret, HRH the (1930–2002). Sister of HM Queen Elizabeth II.

† *Coleridge: Early Visions* by Richard Holmes (Hodder & Stoughton, 1989).

‡ Nether Stowey, pop. 1,373.

§ The name of the pilot is unknown.

¥ Private information.

Haiku

Princess Margaret
Having read Coleridge flew
Over his cottage.

Oleaginous

This is one of the most marvellously touching of the many delightful stories that are told about that most beautiful of all Royal Princesses. Her Royal Highness was, of course, an inveterate book-lover, in fact one of the best-read women I have ever had the privilege of knowing, and she had simply adored lovely Dickie Holmes's quite wonderful life of Coleridge, as had we all. So lively was her curiosity, so quick her intelligence, that the divine Margaret managed to persuade her pilot (who, incidentally simply adored her) to fly his brilliantly nippy little plane over the delightful village of Nether Stowey. And thus, with characteristic wit, style and elegance did our most gracious of Princesses pay handsome tribute to the very greatest of poets.

Hypochondriacal

Her back hurt dreadfully and her ankles swelled to bursting as the frail plane spluttered and choked its exhausted way through the bruised skies.

Straining her neck to peer out of the window through her ill-fitting contact lenses, the Princess – who as a young girl had suffered not only mumps and chickenpox, but also German measles – would have known that if the elderly plane were to crash-land, her chances of survival would be minimal.

Hundreds of yards below, the inhabitants of Nether Stowey – a village stricken by a deadly plague three centuries before – coughed and sneezed, placed their heads in their hands, sighed, and prepared themselves for the end.

Non-sequitur

In order to finish an official function, Princess Margaret went round and round in circles. She flew over a cottage in Somerset because she had read a book. And that's why Richard Holmes wrote a biography of Coleridge.

Index

Coleridge, S.T. (*see* Nether Stowey)

Holmes, Richard (biographer; *see* Coleridge, S.T.)

Margaret, HRH Princess (*see* Holmes, Richard)

Nether Stowey (*see* Somerset)

Somerset (*see* Margaret, HRH Princess)

Optimistic

Margaret's heart soared as she stepped into the aeroplane. Her dream had finally come true: at last, she was to set eyes upon her beloved poet's cherished village from the air.

Her devoted pilot delighted in doing exactly what she wanted. Even the little birds bowed their heads as she swept by, chirruping their pretty songs in her honour. It was the smoothest flight imaginable, and she gasped with delight as the magical scene generously unfurled itself beneath her.

So this was where Samuel Taylor Coleridge had lived, so very long ago! How happy she was to see it! Oh, yes! she thought: life has nothing to show more fair!

Phonetic

Eh jest abite menaged to streggle through dyeeeah Richard's dreadfully lawng book on that tiresome little payit. After enduring a ghastly *événement* nearby, one prevailed upon one's pailot to flay one to the beck of beeyawned. Tairble waste of tame! Eh mean, realleh!

Suggestive

It's an open secret that the Princess had just been lapping up a biography of Coleridge, who was widely known to have been addicted to opium, and whose poems swell with sexual references. By the time she had gasped her way through it, she had become so overwhelmed with desire to visit his home that she climbed into her four-seater and commanded her pilot to pull hard on his joystick and dip and dive in smooth, luscious circles around the Somerset cottage that lay nestling in the cleavage of the Quantocks.

Limerick

There was an old Princess called Margaret
Who had downed rather more than a lager; it
Made her yearn to say 'Coo-ee!'
High above Nether Stoowey,
That contrary old Princess called Margaret.

Psychedelic

She's flying high, high, high in the sky, looking down, down, down on all those like crazy blades of grass and the red chimneypots open to the heavens like fishes' mouths when from out of nowhere the cat who once lived there, all those centuries before, appears like beside her in the cabin, telling her all the latest from Xanadu and Porlock and all that shit, and so together they soar into the evening sky on the outspread wings of this like great big bird, this albatross, and they circle around and around and around and she thinks, this is Nether Stowey, this is Stether Nowey, this is Weystone NeverNever Land, together forever, and everything is like far out and totally unreal, like totally unroyal.

Multiple Choice

1) Princess Margaret was in:
a) a plane
b) a car
c) a boat

2) She had just finished:
a) a fun-run
b) an official chore
c) her lunch

3) The book Princess Margaret had just read was:
a) *The Hobbit* by J.R.R. Tolkien
b) *The World is Full of Married Men* by Jackie Collins
c) *Coleridge: Early Visions* by Richard Holmes

4) The village over which she flew was:
a) Nether Stowey
b) Preston Candover
c) Bovey Tracey

Answers: 1 a; 2 b; 3 c; 4 a

Psychoanalytic

Because her dominant father had died as she entered into puberty, and her sibling had beaten her to become HMQ of GB, M. fell victim to the overwhelming urge to re-enter the womb that was her small private plane and to stare long and hard at the two sides of a particular village with which she had become obsessed: Nether (anus) and Stowey (vagina).

Nursery Rhyme

Her Royal Highness
Went up in a plane!
Her Royal Highness
Was never seen again!
Where did she come from?
What did she see?
Margaret flew over
The house
And
Never
Came
Back
For
Tea!

Queen's Speech

At this time of year, few sights evoke feelings of happiness and goodwill more readily than the lovely spire and rooftops of the peaceful West Country village of Nether Stowey.

And so, once more, our thoughts turn to the age-old story of my younger sister, journeying in her modest aeroplane high above a Somerset idyll in order to catch a glimpse of the home of one of that illustrious region's most distinguished poets, who is sadly no longer with us.

And as we remember this story, we take comfort from this heart-warming tale of valour in the air, and its eternal message of hope for all mankind.

Zippy
She read, ordered, flew, circled, peered, and went home.

Spoonerism
The tory is sold that Mincing Pargaret, Snowess of Countdown, had been laking a took at a tolarly schome about the Morantic poet Camel Sailor Toll Bridge.

Rather than shake in a toe or foot her peat up with a tug of me or bay on the pleach with a sucket of band, she cold the tapped-in cloud and lear on the bay wack from a dormal futy to wry in flings around the pate growit's Comerset sausage.

Tautological
The tale is told by a story-teller that a high-born Royal Princess read page after page of a non-fiction biography of the versifying poet Coleridge. Coming back on a return journey from an official function, she commandingly instructed the pilot in the cockpit to fly his plane up in the air over and above the rural country village where the book-ish man of letters had lived and breathed for a period of time before his tragic death.

Upwardly Inflected
Princess Margaret? read a book about Coleridge? and got the guy who was driving her plane? to fly her over his home village? so she could take a look?

Vague

I'm pretty sure I read somewhere that someone like Princess Margaret, or the other one, whatever she's called, or perhaps it was someone more like Prince, but basically someone incredibly famous, the name escapes me, apparently this man, or woman, had been reading a book about someone, I forget who, but someone pretty well known, and as they were near where he or she either used to live or still lived, and it was definitely somewhere in Britain, or possibly abroad, they asked their chauffeur – or was it their pilot? – yes, it must have been their pilot, because they were either in a plane or a helicopter – to fly over whatever the place was called, and I'm pretty sure that that's what they did, though I'm not sure I can remember every detail.

Tragic

Thousands of feet up in the air, the Princess had never felt so utterly, utterly alone. Did she consider, however momentarily, the possibility of throwing open the door of the aircraft and hurling herself out? And as she hurtled to her doom, who can say what her thoughts might have been? Would she have reflected on the futility of all human aspiration? Would she have felt that, in death, she would at last be the centre of attention? Or would she have let out one last, piercing yelp, a defiant outburst against the cruel whims of providence?

33

And there are also an infinite number of ways to interpret the young Antony Armstrong-Jones.

A clue to his character might be found in a list of items with which he decorated his ground-floor bachelor lodgings at 59 Rotherhithe Street, overlooking the Thames. It was carefully transcribed by his landlord, William Glenton, a shipping reporter, when Tony moved in:

A golden cage containing three stuffed lovebirds
A large ornate mirror
A miniature brass catafalque
Dusty wax flowers and a blue glass rolling-pin
A rocking-chair with a basketwork back
A papier-mâché chair inset with mother-of-pearl
A lifesize portrait of an eighteenth-century admiral on his flagship
A fishnet hammock
A stand carved in the shape of a Nubian page boy

Or in another list, like this, of his favourite clothes, circa 1958:

Hip-hugging slacks
Suede shoes
Rollneck jumpers
A fancy suede jacket

Tight jeans
Chukka boots

And there was, of course, always a camera around his neck: he would either walk around London with it, looking for suitable subjects, or stay indoors snapping his then girlfriend Jacqui Chan, a petite Chinese dancer from Trinidad. According to Glenton, the two of them looked 'like a pair of goblins' as they set about decorating the riverside *pied à terre*.

The young Tony was something of a tearaway, a sort of upper-class Mod. He used to enjoy riding pillion around London on his friend Andy Garnett's Triumph motorbike, performing cock-snooking japes on other drivers. Garnett's wife Polly Devlin recalls: 'Their motorbike would pull up at a red light alongside a glamorous open-topped car – preferably a two-seater XK120 Jaguar, usually driven by an odious young man in his dinner jacket showing off to his girlfriend who would be dressed to the nines; the car had its rear-view mirror fitted to the front wing, far forward from the cockpit. Andy would inch the motorbike alongside and Tony would lean over, turn the adjacent mirror around and then with his nose a couple of inches from it he would squeeze an imaginary spot and adjust the parting of his hair, occasionally jiggling the mirror to get a better view. Sometimes the driver would join in the fun, but more often he'd get into a rage, especially if his girl was laughing at him too – in any case, the motorbike was off before he had a chance to retaliate.'

It was when William Glenton noticed that his tenant had changed the flat's standard Bronco toilet paper* – hard, grey and almost aggressively non-absorbent, like tracing paper – for a brand that was not only softer and much more absorbent but also lilac-coloured, that he suspected something was up. And when his old friend Lady Elizabeth Cavendish, lady-in-waiting to Princess Margaret, cagily explained that

---

* Discontinued in October 1989, presumably owing to lack of demand.

she had just dropped by to 'tidy Tony's room', his suspicions multiplied. 'It did not need my reporting intuition to make me realise that there had to be some very special reason for a duke's daughter to act as a home help.'

A day or two later, Glenton was about to go upstairs when the door of the Armstrong-Jones flat opened. He recognised the silhouette in the candlelight as 'the unmistakeable figure' of Princess Margaret. Following an official visit to the Isle of Dogs, she had crossed the Thames by the Deptford ferry, disguised in a hat and a scarf, and then slipped into No. 59. This was to be the first of many visits. Before long, she was calling the flat 'the little white roomo'. Others described it as a 'love-nest'. 'She certainly didn't go short in that direction,' remarked one keen observer.

Tony was what might these days be called a 'metrosexual'. Like Princess Margaret, he had a strong taste for camp, perhaps fostered by his uncle, the stage designer Oliver Messel, whose photograph albums contained a few shots of his nephew in drag. Stuck in hospital with polio, the teenaged Tony had been visited by Noël Coward and Marlene Dietrich, who sang 'Boys in the Backroom' to him. The taste never left him. The author Philip Hoare recalls sitting behind the then Lord Snowdon at a first night of Coward's *Hay Fever*, and noticing that 'he greeted an actress's stage entrance with the exclamation, "Love the dress."' Decades later, Sir Cecil Beaton delighted in telling friends that he had once seen Tony and a male friend in New York performing wicked impersonations of his former wife. 'I didn't fall in love with boys,' Tony once said. 'But a few men have been in love with me.'

34

Princess Margaret felt most at home in the company of the camp, the cultured and the waspish. It was to be her misfortune that such a high proportion of them kept diaries, and moreover, diaries written with a view to publication. To a man, they were mesmerised less by her image than by the cracks to be found in it. They were drawn to her like iron filings to a magnet, or, perhaps more accurately, cats to a canary.

Some were blessed with peculiar prescience. As early as June 1949, when Margaret was only eighteen, Chips Channon spotted her at a ball at Windsor Castle. 'Already she is a public character. I wonder what will happen to her? There is already a Marie Antoinette aroma about her.'*

Seven years later, on 21 July 1956, the historian A.L. Rowse noticed the twenty-five-year-old Princess at a Buckingham Palace garden party. 'Interesting to watch her face, bored, *mécontente*, ready to burst out against it all: a Duke of Windsor among the women of the Royal Family.' She was also attracting opprobrium from other, less

---

* 'I wonder what he meant by that?' the Princess asked her authorised biographer, Christopher Warwick, when he mentioned this remark. There was something of the clairvoyant about Chips Channon. In 1991, when Tim Heald was interviewing Prince Philip for a biography, he was surprised by the way any mention of Channon's name met with a gruff response. 'So you've hit the Channon nerve,' said the Duke's old friend, Mike Parker. It emerged that fifty years earlier, in 1941, Channon happened to meet the young Philip in Athens. 'He is to be our Prince Consort and that is why he is serving in our navy,' he wrote in his diary. At that time, Princess Elizabeth was only fifteen years old.

well-connected diarists, among them Anthony Heap, the local government officer who was writing his diary for Mass-Observation. 'When is Princess Margaret going to be her age (which is 26) and behave like a member of the Royal Family instead of a half-baked jazz mad Teddy Girl?' he asked. 'For what should be reported in this morning's papers but that last night she went to see the latest trashy "rock 'n' roll" film [*The Girl Can't Help It*] at the Carlton – she never goes to an intelligent play or film – and, taking off her shoes, put her feet up on the rail round the front of the circle and waved them in time with the "hot rhythm".'

A few days after Channon's sighting of her at Windsor, the Princess merited her first mention in the diaries of the camp, waspish, etc. James Lees-Milne, after his friend, the camp, waspish, etc. James Pope-Hennessy, told him that the Princess was 'high-spirited to the verge of indiscretion. She mimics Lord Mayors welcoming her on platforms and crooners on the wireless, in fact anyone you care to mention.'

By the 1960s there were at least two more diarists biting at her heels: first Cecil Beaton, and then, towards the end of the decade, the up-and-coming young museum director Roy Strong. Beaton tended to zero in on her face and her clothes, on red alert for mishaps in both departments. On 4 May 1968, he went with his friend Dicky Buckle to watch the Danish Ballet at Covent Garden. He found the performance 'agony', but there was amusement provided by having 'a good gawk' at the Royal Box: 'Princess Margaret with an outrageous, enormous Roman matron head-do, much too important for such a squat little figure,'* and 'the common little Lord Snowdon, who was wearing his hair in a dyed quiff'.

---

* When her biographer Theo Aronson visited her some years later, in 1982, he nursed similar concerns about her appearance, which he expressed in diaries first published in 2000: 'Her hair is dyed a deep, glossy auburn; her lipstick is very bright. She is small, with a big bust that gives her a top-heavy look. She is badly dressed, in a black dress patterned in yellow and green squares and is wearing white, high-heeled, platform-soled sandals which, because her legs are so thin, give her a Minnie Mouse look.'

Ten days later, on 14 May, Princess Margaret spent the evening with yet another closet diarist, Lady Cynthia Gladwyn. We have already seen how Lady Gladwyn recorded with icy precision the Princess's wayward misbehaviour in Paris in the spring of 1959. Nine years on, at a party at St James's Palace, she noticed that Lord Snowdon's hair was 'tinted in a curious new colour. Sachy Sitwell afterwards described it as peach, but I would say apricot.' Six months later, she was invited to see a pair of Italian plays, *Naples by Day* and *Naples by Night*. Though she found them 'a little slow in places', her interest was again quickened by the recently refurbished hair of Lord Snowdon, who was sitting immediately in front of her. Against his fashionable white polo-necked jersey, it now seemed 'auburn coloured ... dressed in two handsome waves, the perfection of which seemed to preoccupy him very much'.

After the theatre, the group went on to the Italian embassy for dinner. Sadly, they found themselves trapped there, unable to leave before Princess Margaret, who clearly had another late night in mind. 'She kept on approaching the door, and just as we were encouraged to think she was really about to take her departure, she suddenly went back into the centre of the room and became engaged in animated conversation – all just to tease and annoy.'

Inevitably, the Princess's performance set tongues a-wagging. Diana Cooper told Lady Gladwyn of the time she had stayed at Hatfield. After dinner, there had been calls for the Princess to play the piano or to sing, but she had refused right up until everyone wanted to go to bed, at which point she had beetled over to the piano and played it until four in the morning. Needless to say, even the sleepiest guests had bowed to royal protocol, listening until the bitter end.

Roy Strong first encountered Princess Margaret on 27 November 1969, at a dinner thrown by the soon-to-be Lady Harlech to celebrate the opening of his exhibition 'The Elizabethan Image' at the Tate Gallery. In his diary, the thirty-four-year-old Strong noted that the Princess, 'wearing a cream sheath dress with a bolero in pink', refused to sit

down for three quarters of an hour, 'thus obliging the pregnant Ingrid Channon to remain standing for all that time'.

Placed next to Strong, the Princess made her dissatisfaction obvious, ignoring him until the pudding course. 'Then she wiped her plate slowly with her napkin, at which point Beatrix* leaned over and said, "The food here's great but let's face it the washing-up's rotten."' After escorting the Princess around the exhibition, Strong concluded that 'Princess Margaret is a strange lady, pretty, tough, disillusioned and spoilt. To cope with her I decided one had to slap back which I did and survived.'

* * *

---

* Beatrix Miller (1923–2014), editor of *Vogue* 1964–85.

Earlier that year, Cecil Beaton had been unimpressed by the television documentary *The Royal Family*, finding Princess Margaret 'mature and vulgar', and her husband, his professional rival Lord Snowdon, 'common beyond belief'.* He encountered the royal couple in the flesh at a party held at Windsor Castle in April 1972 for bigwigs in the arts, including Flora Robson, 'in a terrible wig', and Lord and Lady Olivier, who were 'cheap and second rate'. Beaton was, however, rather more forgiving towards Princess Margaret, who at least 'managed to create a solid, clean, well-sculpted simplicity of line and colour', though this pleasing effect was offset by the way in which 'she wore harsh white and hair scraped back like a wealthy seaside landlady'. But at least she fared better beneath his unforgiving gaze than Queen Juliana of the Netherlands, who, said Beaton, 'looked nice and cosy and sympathetic in spite of her ugly little face with unseeing small eyes and pig snout …'†

On Wednesday, 28 June 1972, James Lees-Milne and his wife Alvilde 'motored' to London for a private screening of John Betjeman's television documentary about Australia. They didn't know who else was going to be there, but Lord Snowdon arrived, 'full of vitality and cheer', and started talking to them about Bath, where they lived. Next came Princess Margaret, followed by the Prince of Wales. 'I was taken aback,' wrote Lees-Milne in his diary, 'not having expected such.'

---

* Princess Margaret was always in two minds about Beaton. She used to tell friends that as he was such a nightmare in company she felt obliged to have him to dinner *à deux*. He, in turn, would always be thrilled by such exclusive access, imagining he must occupy a special place in her heart.

† Beaton's pen-portraits are particularly spiteful towards women. At different times in his diaries he calls the Queen Mother 'fatter than ever, but yet wrinkled'; Joan Plowright 'like a deficient house-parlour-maid'; Katharine Hepburn successively 'a complete egomaniac', 'a goddamned bore' and 'a rotten ingrained viper'; and Elizabeth Taylor 'this monster'. He then goes on to single out for particular displeasure Taylor's 'breasts, hanging and huge, like those of a peasant woman suckling her young in Peru. They were seen in their full shape, blotched and mauve, plum … on her fat, coarse hands more of the biggest diamonds and emeralds.'

After the screening, they all went for dinner in a private room at Rules restaurant. The party consisted of Patrick Garland (director of the documentary), James Lees-Milne, John Drummond (producer of the documentary), Princess Margaret, John Betjeman, Alvilde Lees-Milne, Lord Snowdon, Elizabeth Cavendish (Betjeman's girlfriend), the Prince of Wales, Jenny Agutter (actress girlfriend of Patrick Garland), and Mary, Duchess of Devonshire.

By his own account, Lees-Milne 'hardly spoke a word to the royals but watched them closely'. He found Prince Charles 'very charming and polite', but considered Princess Margaret 'far from charming ... cross, exacting, too sophisticated, and sharp'. On the other hand, she was 'physically attractive in a bun-like way, with trussed up bosom, and hair like two cottage loaves, one balancing on the other'. In a letter to Betjeman he elaborated on this description, saying he found her 'very very very frightening but beautiful and succulent like Belgian buns'. He noticed that the Princess never spoke to Betjeman, but 'smoked continuously from a long holder'.

Prince Charles had to leave the dinner early in order to drive to Portsmouth. Elizabeth Cavendish had removed her shoes, so to see the Prince off she went downstairs and into the street without them, saying 'Mind you drive carefully' to the driver.

While she was out in the street, Princess Margaret leaned down to pick up the abandoned shoes, and placed them on her plate. This irritated Lord Snowdon. 'It's unlucky, I don't like it!' he snapped. In response, Princess Margaret removed the shoes from the plate, put them on her chair, and walked to the window in a sulk. Twice she said she wanted to leave; twice Snowdon insisted on waiting another five minutes. Eventually, Patrick Garland agreed to drive the Princess home in his Mini.

Snowdon then extracted promises from the rest of them to come back to Kensington Palace. Once he had left, they debated whether or not to join him, as he had asked. 'I did not want to go because I thought Princess M. would not be pleased,' reflected Lees-Milne. But in the end they decided to go; they were giving the Duchess of Devonshire a lift home, and were sure she would not want to linger.

On entering Kensington Palace, Lees-Milne found Princess Margaret 'more gracious to me ... but I did not find conversation very easy or agreeable'. As fate would have it, another writer was also there that night, jotting it all down, this time for an autobiography. From John Drummond we learn that they all remained at the palace until two in the morning, 'since the Princess never seemed to tire'.

Once home, Lees-Milne mentioned to his wife that after sitting down in a chair which Prince Charles had just vacated, he had drunk some water out of the Prince's glass, 'which I enjoyed doing', adding that 'I would not have drunk out of PM's.' Alvilde agreed with this judgement, and told him that she had gone into the loo with Princess Margaret and sat on the same seat after her, 'but would rather have sat on the one Prince Charles had just sat on'. Such are the more recondite pleasures of proximity to royalty.

The diarists hovered around her like hornets. In November 1972 Cecil Beaton took a good long look at her during the service of thanksgiving for the silver wedding of the Queen and the Duke of Edinburgh at Westminster Abbey, noting in his diary her 'set smile on a well-enamelled face', but condemning her 'fatal choice of putting on a black coal heaver's hat with a dark red dress'. But at least she did better than 'that awful John Colville,* his mouth now turning down like a croquet hoop'.

The following year, on Wednesday, 20 June 1973, James Lees-Milne attended ('honoured to be asked, but reluctant to go') a concert party at Windsor Castle. The ensuing dinner went on well past midnight. 'I avoided Tony Snowdon and Princess Margaret. In passing close to her

---

* Private secretary to HM the Queen when she was still Princess Elizabeth, and before that to Winston Churchill.

I overheard her saying to Angus Ogilvy, who happened to brush her arm in passing, "Must you do that?" in her snappish voice.'

The presence of royalty in a room acts as a magnet: some are attracted, others repelled. The diarists generally tended to experience both sensations at once, but on this particular evening Lees-Milne placed himself firmly in the camp of the repelled. 'I didn't want to get into conversation ... how obsequious most people look on talking to royalty, bowing and scraping ingratiatingly. How impossible to be natural. I am sure one must try to be. Yet when it came to saying good-bye to the Queen at the head of the staircase, all I could murmur was, "It has been the greatest treat, Ma'am." Really, how could I?'

Cecil Beaton came away similarly despondent from a ball at Buckingham Palace to celebrate the wedding of Princess Anne in November 1973. He had gone with 'high expectations' to the preceding dinner at Clarence House, but 'unfortunately I was disappointed ... It is a hideous house & the mixture of furniture makes for a rather sordid ensemble. Some of the pictures are so bad ... that it gives the appearance of a pretentious hotel.' Finding the women of the party 'unbelievably drab', he was also put off by the food: 'all too creamy'.

At the ball itself, he was surprised to find that Princess Anne had turned into 'an Aubrey Beardsley beauty. Never more was I astonished.' After all, when he had photographed her at the age of thirteen, 'she was a bossy, unattractive, galumphing girl', and 'the pictures were revolting'. Others at the ball included Begum Aga Khan, 'a common model, with too long fingernails'; Debo Devonshire with 'her ordinary farmwork hairdo'; Prince Charles, 'getting very red in the face and rather butch with huge butch feet and legs'; the Kent family, looking 'cretinous, ghoulish, a bit Addams cartoonish'; and the then prime minister, Edward Heath ('may I not be damned for saying tonight he exuded a certain sex appeal').

On his way out, Beaton spotted Princess Margaret, now aged forty-three. He did not like what he saw. 'Gosh the shock! She has become a little pocket monster – Queen Victoria. The flesh is solid and I don't think dieting can reduce a marble statue. The weighty body was encased in sequin fargets, of turquoise and shrimp, her hair scraped back and a high tiara-crown … placed on top. But the hairdresser had foolishly given her a vast teapot handle of hair jutting out at the back. This triple-compacted chignon was a target for all passers-by to hit first from one side, then another. The poor midgety brute was knocked like a top, sometimes almost into a complete circle.'

This diary entry goes on at almost manic length about the Princess's appearance, its malice all the more wounding for being coated with pity. 'As I talked, a waiter passed with a tray of champagne and once more a biff sent the diminutive princess flying. Poor brute, I do feel sorry for her. She was not very nice in the days when she was so pretty and attractive. She snubbed and ignored friends. But my God has she been paid out! Her appearance has gone to pot. Her eyes seem to have lost their vigour, her complexion is now a dirty negligee pink satin. The sort of thing one sees in a disbanded dyer's shop window.'

Nor does he miss the opportunity to take a poke at his real *bête noire*. 'The horrid husband was nowhere to be seen. It is said that the Queen would be willing to let Pss M get rid of him but Tony won't go.'

Beaton, Strong and Lees-Milne lapped up all the gossip about Margaret and Tony, particularly when it involved marital turmoil.* In his diary entry for Thursday, 11 July 1974, Lees-Milne noted that the Duchess of

---

* The diarists were no more loyal to each other than they were to the Princess. Both Lees-Milne and Strong turned on Beaton soon after his death on 18 January 1980. Hearing of 'appalling and brutal' caricatures Beaton had once drawn of Violet Trefusis and Vita Sackville-West, Lees-Milne wrote in his diary, 'Cecil was a bitch really.' On the day Beaton died, Strong wrote a glowing appreciation of him for *Vogue* ('I shall always recall him as he had no wish to be, a marvellous old man, gentle and warm …'), but seventeen years later he inserted an addendum into his diary: 'What one couldn't say then but can now is that I remember him too as a great hater … Snobbery, untold ambition, together with envy, were sad defects which marred this remarkable man.'

Devonshire had passed on a little gem she had originally heard from Snowdon's old friend Jeremy Fry, who had himself heard it from someone who had heard it directly from the Princess. 'P.M. told a friend the other day that she so hates her husband now she can hardly bear to be in the same room as him.'

At a dinner in celebration of the 'Scythian Gold' exhibition in Paris on Tuesday, 25 November 1975, Roy Strong observed the Princess 'in beaming mood, slimmer and wearing quite a weight of make-up, her thin hair heavily back-combed'. She looked, he thought, 'rather marvellous', though he felt that 'she addresses rather than speaks to you, but she revels in tough conversation and anecdotes. She is, as we all know, tiresome, spoilt, idle and irritating.'

Her escort for that particular evening, Colin Tennant, told Strong how the Princess had hated her recent trip to Australia. The traffic lights were not even cancelled any more to let her car through, nor was there a police escort, and no crowds cheering. Imagine the effect of their disappearance, said Tennant, on someone who had come to expect all those things. What did she have to fall back on? She had been brought up as the younger sister, not to offer competition, and was 'taught only to dance and sing and that was that'.

'She has no direction, no overriding interest,' concluded Strong in his diary entry for that evening. 'All she likes now is *la jeunesse doré* and Young Men.'

The following evening Strong bumped into her again, at a 'crashingly dull' dinner at which 'HRH slugged through the whisky and sodas'. But she cheered up when telling him all about her house on Mustique. Strong said he thought she had a cottage in West Sussex, but she told him it belonged to her husband. At this point, she started raving on and on against Snowdon: how he had upset both the nanny and the chauffeur when she was away in Australia, and how he 'went away for weekends she didn't know where and she didn't know his friends or anything'. Before Strong went to bed that night, he concluded that she was 'bitter and sad. She looked lonely and soured by it all.'

On 11 April 1976, James Lees-Milne was able to enjoy another 'good stare' at the Royal Family from his prime position in the middle of the nave in the church at Badminton, where they were all staying for a three-day event. He had a good view of the Prince of Wales, 'sporting a beastly beard', and the forty-five-year-old Princess Margaret, looking 'miserable, trussed up like a broody hen, pigeon-breasted and discontented'. Once again he reflected on his instinctive aversion to direct contact with royalty. 'I like the Royal Family to exist, but I don't want to know or be known by them.'

Six months later, on 25 October, Roy Strong had a correspondingly good view of the Queen, in 'floating apricot chiffon, quite hideous', as she arrived at the new National Theatre building for its official opening. While Her Majesty watched Goldoni's *Il Campiello* in the Olivier Theatre, Strong went with Princess Margaret to see Tom Stoppard's *Jumpers* ('a play of utter boredom') in the Lyttelton. The entire evening was, he complained, 'a washout in every sense of the word' – and this, he added, was the view of Princess Margaret too. She had, he said, 'been bored by the play but more by the fact that when she sat down the wall in front of her in the circle was so high that she couldn't see over it.'*

By the age of forty-two, Strong could claim to be on the inside of Princess Margaret's outer circle, and steadily inching closer to the centre. On Monday, 13 February 1978 he was invited to a dinner at Kensington Palace in honour of the Marchioness of Cholmondeley.

---

* Twenty-five years later, a heavyweight biography of Stoppard by an American academic called Ira Nadel paints an altogether sunnier picture of the Princess's reaction to *Jumpers*: 'Her presence and delight in the play prompted a long fascination with Stoppard's work, which grew into a friendship,' he writes optimistically.

The meal was lavish, 'starting with lobster and on through the usual game birds, the table heavy with silver and glass'. The Princess was less well covered: she was wearing a 'virtually topless' dress, 'apart from two thin shoulder-straps'. She had placed her young friend Roddy Llewellyn opposite her, 'in the role of host'. Strong considered Roddy 'a pretty young blond man but, unlike Tony, not bright. She seems to have thrown all discretion to the winds … It is all rather sad and pathetic and deeply embarrassing for the Queen, surely?'

On Tuesday, 4 April 1978, James Lees-Milne dropped in on Lord Snowdon's stepfather, the Earl of Rosse,* who was to die the following year. Rosse proved as keen to gossip about the royal couple as anybody. 'Talked of Princess Margaret and Tony, the latter having been to see Michael the evening before. Michael said the tragedy was that both of them only liked second-rate people. Their friends were awful.'

Two days later, the Strongs clocked up an overnight stay in Windsor Castle. Other guests included the prime minister, James Callaghan, the Turkish ambassador, the Australian high commissioner, and Kurt Waldheim, the secretary-general of the United Nations.† Never backward in coming forward, Strong thought Princess Margaret, suntanned in green, was 'obviously pleased to see us' amidst 'a bevy of people she probably regarded as "heavies"'.

The high point came when Strong found himself in a circle consisting of the prime minister, Princess Margaret and her son, the sixteen-year-old Lord Linley ('as tiny as his parents'). The avuncular Callaghan asked Linley what he wanted to be when he grew up. 'A carpenter,' replied the Princess on his behalf, adding, 'Christ was a carpenter.'

---

* Michael Parsons, 6th Earl of Rosse (1906–79). Irish peer, second husband of Anne Messel, whose first marriage, to Ronald Armstrong-Jones, had produced Tony Armstrong-Jones.

† And later discovered to have been a member of Hitler's SA.

At 8 o'clock the following morning, the Strongs took breakfast in their private sitting room at the Castle, 'with flunkeys in attendance'. Alas, all was not as it should have been: 'the three-minute egg arrived hard-boiled as no one had bothered to tap the top'.

35

After the Second World War, Ben Nicolson, son of Harold Nicolson and Vita Sackville-West, resumed his position as Deputy Surveyor of the King's Pictures, working under Anthony Blunt. In 1946 he was invited to Windsor Castle for ten days as a guest of the King and Queen. On four of those days, parlour games were played after dinner. He described them to the Labour politician Richard Crossman, who duly recorded them in his diary.

> The master of ceremonies took all the male guests outside and provided them with brass pokers, shovels, etc. After ten minutes' practice they were then made to parade as a squad, with the shovels and pokers on their shoulders, in slow goose step down the long drawing room past the King, the Queen and the Princesses, who found it exquisite fun seeing Stafford Cripps, Lord Ismay and Anthony Eden doing 'Eyes Right.'

Nicolson told Crossman that 'he hadn't seen anything like Stafford Cripps, who had been forced at two hours' notice to spend a weekend at Windsor and who humbly obeyed the Royal command but suffered the full humiliation which Royalty seemed determined to extract from its Commoner guests'.

Small wonder, then, if Princess Margaret grew up with an imperious streak, a presumption that the rest of the world had a duty to perform at the flick of a finger, and an unforgiving view of politicians. 'I hate them. They never listen to anything I say or answer my questions,' she complained to a friend. 'Even Sir Winston Churchill would just grunt.'

She relished making dismissive generalisations about those to whom she was obliged to engage in small talk during her Royal progress. 'All the town clerks are *exactly* the same,' she would say; and, of the university of which she was chancellor, 'All the students at Keele have just discovered Marx.' She was barely more approving of those in her own family, describing her grandmother, Queen Mary, as 'absolutely terrifying', and her grandfather, King George V, as 'a most objectionable old man' to a visiting biographer.

Though she affected a kind of monarchical indifference to party politics, her own opinions were deeply conservative. 'I don't mind who's in government so long as they're good at governing. What we must avoid at all costs is these windscreen wipers: left, right, left, right,' she opines in Edward St Aubyn's *roman à clef, Some Hope*. Giving money to the poor, she thought, somehow makes them less disciplined, and therefore less happy: 'What it really shows is the emptiness of the socialist dream. They thought that every problem could be solved by throwing money at it, but it simply isn't true. People may have been poor, but they were happy because they lived in real communities. My mother says that when she visited the East End during the Blitz she met more people there with real dignity than you could hope to find in the entire *corps diplomatique*.'

She offered a fuller view of her political outlook in a private letter to the then prime minister Margaret Thatcher, who had written to the Princess after she had been admitted to the London Clinic for an operation to remove a benign skin lesion. Mrs Thatcher's letter had touched on her recent visit to New York ('they are so easy to please and so delighted if you say what you really think') and the steel strike ('it is difficult to get across the message that more money has to be earned and not just demanded'). Princess Margaret's handwritten reply is dated 7 February 1980:

My dear Prime Minister

I write belatedly to thank you for your kind letter. I just had to have some things dug out of my face but luckily everything went well and we're not worrying.

I was so interested to hear about your visit to the United States. I expect you surprised them no end at answering their questions in a positive way, when they are used to waffling on for hours in figures of 8, not actually answering anything.

The steel strike is depressing. I well remember when Charles Villiers took it over. I congratulated him on his courage and he said, 'I am taking on a moribund, old fashioned, out of date, uneconomical, out of date industry' and I said 'Is there any hope of improving it?' and he said 'Very little'.

I suppose if one is an ordinary working man and one's union tells one not to vote for new machinery or technology because otherwise you will lose your job or your card – you just don't dare.

I went to Cambridge for a debate (rather dull, all about the church, lots of clerics) and found them all rabid conservatives – not a Trotskyite to argue with!

They were passionately against the Olympic Games in Moscow. I tried the 'isn't it hard on the athletes' bit but they were adamant. I suppose individuals must choose whether to go as it's up to the Olympic Committee.

If that silly boxer* doesn't make a hash of it he might get Africa to cock a snook at the Russians.

I find it quite impossible to find out what is happening in Afghanistan. Are they about to wheel into Iran and get all the oil? More power to your policy of nuclear power stations.

I wish they weren't called 'nuclear' as people always think of the bomb. I've been advocating this since I was 20!

---

* Muhammad Ali, who had been sent to Tanzania, Nigeria and Senegal by the US government to campaign for a boycott of the Games.

Many thanks for allocating £10,000 to the NSPCC. They are vital and I am President and support their free service.

With again many thanks for your letter.

Yours very sincerely,

Margaret

36

At the reopening of the Bath Assembly Rooms in 1979, James Lees-Milne cast his beady eye over Princess Margaret, who had recently fallen victim to severe criticism in the press.

Lees-Milne felt a twinge of pity for her. 'She looked extremely nervous,' he wrote in his diary. 'On the platform her hand was shaking. Making strange grimaces with her mouth. I suppose she is frightened of insults.' On a recent visit to Bristol, someone in the crowd had shouted, 'Whore!'

'I feel sorry for under-dogs,' he added, but by the next sentence his sympathy had dispersed. 'She is her own worst enemy of course, and if you are royal you must be immaculate, or expect the consequences. But she consorts with the raffish, and this the public does not like.'

The critic and connoisseur Brian Sewell was another exacting writer whose path crossed the Princess's around this time. In 1980 he had been invited to stay the weekend at the country house of an elderly friend, 'at the behest, she informed me, of Princess Margaret'. The Princess was to join them for dinner on the Saturday night.

It was not a success. 'Not even Stephen Sondheim foresaw the miseries possible in such a purgatorial occasion,' Sewell recalled. 'The Princess arrived an hour before midnight for a ruined dinner scheduled for eight; by then the servants from the village had gone home to bed and the rest of us, some half-dozen, absolutely plastered, had to buckle-to, and carry and carve the baked meats of sacrifice; she then kept us up until four in the morning, kippering us with her cigarettes. Long after the crack of dawn, with not a sniff of coffee nor sign of a servant in the kitchen to clear the mess from the night, I wandered into the village, called a friend and arranged a late morning death-and-doomsday telephone message requiring my immediate return home.'

Even in her own home, the Princess was never safe. On Thursday, 6 November 1980, Roy Strong expressed his disappointment at the state of her apartment at Kensington Palace. It was, he said, 'grubby and run-down'.

Before dinner, he had been obliged to guide twenty of her friends around his latest exhibition, 'Princely Magnificence', at the Victoria and Albert Museum. 'It's a curious set she attracts in some ways,' he reflected in his diary. Among his fellow guests were Derek Hart, Roddy Llewellyn, Colin Tennant ('looking very middle aged'), Luigi d'Orso, Ned Ryan ('Who is this man?'),* Jane Stevens and 'the usual top-up of members of the Household'. Strong and his wife Julia were given special leave to depart at 10.15 p.m., as they had to drive home to Hereford. 'It was awful to hear HRH droning on about how wonderful Anthony Blunt was but I've endured worse evenings with her.'

As the years rolled on, Princess Margaret became increasingly picky. Over dinner with Lady Harlech on 2 February 1982, she filled Strong in on all the latest shows she had failed to enjoy. 'No, she hadn't enjoyed the Gonzaga exhibition, the musical *The Mitford Girls* or the Evening Standard Drama Awards.'

On Wednesday, 7 December 1983, Strong had lunch with David Hicks in Mayfair. They took advantage of Princess Margaret's absence to exchange the latest gossip about her. 'Apparently no-one had told the British Consul in Miami that she was passing through, with the

---

* Ned Ryan (1933–2010), former bus conductor, dismissed after it was discovered he had never bothered to collect fares from the upper deck. He went on to achieve financial success in the property business, and social success as Princess Margaret's walker. A genial figure, he was sometimes dubbed 'The Sherpa' by those wary and/or envious of his skills as a social climber.

result that she was shunted through what we all endure. Bad temper resulted. Much funnier was when she had to walk through the arch which registers metal which she set off jangling like blazes. No one knew what to do because it had been set a-singing by the antiquated metal-supported corsetry she wore beneath!'

By the end of the 1980s, the Princess had grown too demanding even for diarists on the lookout for copy. In September 1988, Sir Edward Tomkins, the former ambassador to France, told the Strongs that Princess Margaret would be staying with him and his wife at the end of October. Would they come to lunch? 'I'm afraid we dodged it,' Strong confided to his diary. 'She had rung up and altered the date. Each time there is the ghastly listing off of people invited and the arrangements to HRH on the telephone and then waiting for her re-action: "Oh, I like them," "No, I don't think I want to do that" and "Can't stand them." Gill [Tomkins] then gets stuck with ringing up and somehow eliminating those not in favour.' By now her potential hosts, none of them getting any younger, were growing weary of the number of fresh amusements – new people, new places, new things – she expected to be laid on for her, and all the extra staff needed to cook and serve. 'Gill is a saint,' reflected Strong, 'but I really wondered whether it was all worth it.'

37

Servants tend to become proprietorial, but none more so than the ever-watchful David John Payne. He never felt that Tony was quite up to scratch. Margaret's new romance had taken him and the rest of the staff by surprise: up to then, they had written off the society photographer as just a passing acquaintance. After all, 'he was still a commoner, and no match, so we all thought, for the Princess'.

Payne first set eyes on Tony (as the staff called him behind his back) at a lunch thrown by the Queen Mother in honour of the high commissioner for Rhodesia and Nyasaland in July 1959. Tony was wearing a navy-blue suit with a white shirt and a plum-coloured tie. 'His fairish hair was groomed in his characteristic manner, which I thought rather ridiculous then. But I didn't know that one day it would set a new style for men's hair fashions.'

Payne had no idea who the young gentleman might be, but noticed his eyes darting around the room at the other guests, taking them all in, 'and he kept eyeing me and the other servants in our liveries with a sort of obvious wonder'.

Bending over to serve him, Payne glanced at his name card. 'It said simply … Mr Antony Armstrong-Jones.' An unspoken exchange then took place between guest and servant. 'He glanced up as I spooned vegetables on his plate and smiled. I was quite shocked. I had come to expect only a stony stare from top people when I served them. Now here was this young man smiling at me in an obvious attempt to be friendly. I wanted to smile back then because I knew he felt out of his depth in that company but I dared not. It was just not done.'

Payne was intrigued, and his interest quickened still further when he spotted Princess Alexandra chatting to the newcomer like an old friend. Who was this dapper young man?

After lunch, Payne kept a sharp eye on Mr Armstrong-Jones. 'I noticed something funny about Tony's walk. He was stepping along with a strange spring-heeled action … His slim figure was emphasized by the tightness of his trousers which tapered away to about sixteen-inch bottoms.'

As the time came for the guests to leave, Armstrong-Jones button-holed Payne near the front door. 'He smiled and said, "I don't think I've seen you before have I?"'

'"No sir," I replied. "I don't think you have."'

'This was hardly surprising as it was the first time to my knowledge that he had been invited up to the house.'

Armstrong-Jones asked Payne what his name was.

'"Oh, you are John, who is with her Royal Highness. She has mentioned your name to me. I must say I have always been impressed by the way in which she has spoken of you to me. She has often told me, 'John did this for me today' or 'John did that.' Now I know who she meant. I hope to be seeing a lot more of you in future, John."

'"I hope so too, sir."

'"I think you will John."'

Despite this chummy exchange, or perhaps because of it, Payne entertained misgivings. Like most of the servants, he was more of a Townsend man. 'I never really felt happy myself at the match. While Townsend seemed to project force and vigor, Tony was not that type of man. I felt my Princess was wasting herself on this friendly but unsuit-able man. Often I think back to that first day I saw him and how I watched him briskly stepping out along the pavement with his head in the air and a spring in his step and I wish that he had walked away and never returned to claim Margaret's hand in marriage.'

38

Yet, for all Tony's faults, she might have done worse. After all, many men, not all of them quite savoury, had once entertained the idea of walking her up the aisle.

Like many a schoolboy, Jeremy Thorpe enjoyed indulging in fantasies about his future. Aged sixteen, he entertained his fellow Etonians by delivering the balcony speech he would one day address to a tearful crowd upon standing down as prime minister. Another fantasy ran alongside it: one day in the not-too-distant future, he planned to marry Princess Margaret. A year older than the Princess, handsome, well-connected and amusing, he felt himself well placed to achieve this ambition.

Fifteen years later, Thorpe was the up-and-coming young Liberal MP for North Devon. One of his schoolboy fantasies was in with a fighting chance of becoming a reality. Small wonder, then, that he was taken aback by the announcement, in March 1960, that the Princess had just become engaged to his old chum Antony Armstrong-Jones.

Two friends recalled the strength of his reaction. One described him as 'completely furious'. The other, a business associate, remembered seeing him on the day of the official announcement:

In March 1960, Thorpe dined with me one evening at the Dorchester. He arrived late and appeared to be upset. It was the evening of the announcement of the news of Princess Margaret's engagement. I asked what was the matter and he utterly dumbfounded me by saying he was furious at 'Maggie pulling the wool over his eyes and getting engaged'. He went on to say he had been after her for a long time and considered himself in with a top chance. I thought he was joking but very soon saw he was in earnest.

Around the same time, Thorpe posted a characteristically indiscreet House of Commons postcard to his friend Norman van der Vater* about the royal coupling. By now his anger had subsided into regret. 'What a pity about HRH,' the card read. 'I rather hoped to marry the one and seduce the other.'

Following Jeremy Fry's withdrawal from the role of best man at the forthcoming wedding 'owing to a recurrence of jaundice',† Armstrong-Jones put forward the name of Jeremy Thorpe. A discreet investigation on behalf of MI5, the Chief Constable of Devon, Colonel Ranulph 'Streaky' Bacon, revealed that while the friendship of Armstrong-Jones and Thorpe was 'nothing more than two Old Etonians catching up with each other', it was 'fairly common knowledge in Devon' that Thorpe was homosexual. It was felt that this was enough to disbar him

---

* Born Norman Vivian Vater, later to rejig his name to Brecht Van de Vater, before achieving a compromise with Norman van de Vater. The number of characters employing bogus names in the Thorpe saga is spectacular. Norman Scott was born Norman Josiffe, later upgrading to the Hon. Norman Lianche-Josiffe. Staying with Thorpe's mother, he signed his name 'Peter Johnson' in her guest book. When staying in Los Angeles, Thorpe's one-time partner in crime and fellow Liberal MP Peter Bessell called himself Dr Paul Hoffman 'for security reasons', while the mustachioed hitman Andrew 'Gino' Newton introduced himself to Scott as Peter Keene. By the 1990s, Newton had changed his name to Hann Redwin, which on close investigation turns out to be an anagram – inappropriate, given his circumstances – of Winner Hand.

† Fry had stepped down, in the words of the *New Yorker*'s Mollie Panter-Downes, 'for the highly unusual reason, as reported in the press, that he expected to be ill between now and May'. In fact he had been fined £2 for homosexual importuning eight years previously, and the press had got wind of it.

from being best man, though not apparently from being an MP, or, a little later, leader of the Liberal Party.

Nineteen years after the royal wedding, Jeremy Thorpe was on trial for conspiracy to murder his former lover, Norman Scott. Scott had worked for Norman van der Vater as a stable-boy. On leaving his employ, he had purloined a number of cards and letters of an intimate nature from Thorpe to van der Vater. This is how the 'marry the one and seduce the other' postcard came to be in the possession of the police. It would almost certainly have been produced at the trial had the judge not been determined to stop the Royal Family being dragged into the proceedings.

39

Lord Thorpe of Barnstaple and HRH The Princess Margaret, Lady
Thorpe, Welcome Us Into Their Beautiful Home
From *Hello* magazine, 1999

Theirs was the fairy-tale wedding that captured the heart of a nation. As the beautiful Princess and the handsome young politician walked back down the aisle of Westminster Abbey on that beautiful summer's day in 1962, the dreams of a nation seemed to have been fulfilled.

'I remember it as the most splendid possible occasion!' says Lord Thorpe. 'Don't you, darling? I'm sure you do!'

HRH Princess Margaret raises her glass. She is a woman of few words, but her restrained smile says it all.

Many other suitors had been mentioned in the press – Group Captain Townsend, of course, but also man-about-town Colin Tennant and fashionable photographer Antony Armstrong-Jones, now better known as Tony Jones.

'I was tickled pink when Princess Margaret was good enough to accept my proposal,' laughs Jeremy. 'To be frank – I never thought I stood a chance!'

We are sitting in the private drawing room in the royal couple's beautifully furnished apartment in Kensington Palace. Souvenirs of their glamorous life together are scattered hither and thither. On the grand piano by the window there are photographs of some of the key moments in Jeremy's political career: his first day as home secretary in Edward Heath's government, his elevation to the House of Lords in 1977, and, in his judicial robes, as lord chancellor. There are, inevitably, those who suggest that marrying the Queen's sister might have smoothed his upward trajectory. 'There will always be the failures and malcontents, sniping from the sidelines, bless 'em!' he laughs.

It seems to have been a glorious career, but have there been any hiccups along the way?

'Well, some wonderfully kind souls have suggested that one might have risen to the highest office in the land had not one's role as consort obliged one to speak at all times with such impeccable restraint,' he smiles. 'Obviously, one's wings have been clipped. But, all things being equal, one hasn't done too badly, I suppose!'

And has Her Royal Highness ever felt that the hurly-burly of her husband's political life meant that he wasn't around when she needed him?

'Not really. No. In fact I would have preferred to have seen rather less of him, to be perfectly frank,' she jokes, producing gales of laughter from her husband. Famous for her deadpan sense of humour, the Princess herself somehow manages to stop herself breaking into a smile.

At this point their butler, Norman, enters the room. Norman – or 'Bunny', as they know him – has been with Lord Thorpe and Princess Margaret ever since their wedding, and seems very much part of the furniture. I ask him how he first came to work in the royal household all those years ago.

'Bunny,' interrupts Lord Thorpe, 'has been a complete godsend, don't you agree darling?'

The Princess seems about to reply.

'Very kind of you to say so, Your Lordship.' Once again, her ever-dutiful butler has beaten her to it!

And how did they first come to employ the trusty Norman?

'Oh, dear me, all that's very much lost in the mists of time!' laughs Lord Thorpe. 'Now, Norman, you mustn't let us keep you from your duties, must you? You'd better run along!'

'Yes,' agrees the Princess. 'Some of us are positively PINING for a drink!'

Lord Thorpe and Princess Margaret have a reputation for remaining fiercely loyal to old friends. Lord Thorpe's former fellow Liberal MP, Peter Bessell, is now the Princess's private secretary, and his associate David Holmes is the Comptroller of the Household. 'If Her Royal Highness ever attempts to lift a finger,' jokes Lord Thorpe, charmingly, 'Peter and David come down on her like a ton of bricks!!'

40

After their initial meeting, Payne kept tags on Tony's progress. He noticed the tell-tale letters 'T.A.J.' appearing with increasing frequency on the top right-hand corner of the envelopes he collected every morning from the on-duty policeman. They were delivered by hand, and often topped brown paper packages containing photographs. 'But at this time and throughout their courtship I never once saw a photograph of Tony in Princess Margaret's possession or even in Clarence House. One thing did strike me though. Even up to the time of her engagement those three tiny portraits of Peter Townsend never left the Princess's bedside table.'

After Tony's first weekend at Royal Lodge, Payne noticed that the young man 'had made a hit' with the Queen Mother. 'But I have often wondered whether the Queen Mother would have approved so much of their friendship then if she had known what it was going to lead to later on.'

Why did Payne entertain such strong misgivings about Tony? In his memoir, he lists a number of what he calls his 'bad habits'. For a start, he always stayed too long in bed. On that first morning, Tony arrived downstairs 'well past eleven', by which time 'Princess Margaret had already finished her early morning vodka and orange juice'. After reading the newspapers for three quarters of an hour, 'he got up slowly and stretched a few times' before going back upstairs, 'rubbing his eyes sleepily', to fetch a camera. 'I then watched him lazily idle down the steps and out into the garden.'

And so Payne became a snooper. 'I stood out of sight at the window to the lounge and studied him as he pottered from spot to spot in the garden in an aimless sort of way … He looked like such an energetic young man in the evening. But now I was seeing him at his most listless.'

Without warning, the Queen Mother burst into the room, having returned from exercising her dogs. 'She must have realized that I was watching someone out of the window because she came across and glanced out on to the garden.' She asked Payne whether any of the guests were still in the house.

'"I believe Mr. Armstrong-Jones is in the garden, Your Majesty," I replied. But I knew that she had already seen him from the window.

'"I will go out and join him, then," she said, and after giving me a searching look walked out of the lounge.'

Payne's curiosity was excited. Going about his household chores, he kept an eye on the Queen Mother and Armstrong-Jones from different vantage points in the Lodge. Presently, they were joined by Princess Margaret; the three of them enjoyed the sunshine, apparently unaware that the eyes of Payne were upon them.

Lunch was followed by a break to 'change into lighter clothes' before the party went out on the terrace. Payne still had his eyes glued to Tony. 'Every few minutes he would glance up from the magazine which lay open on his lap and look at the Princess. Their eyes would meet and a meaningful smile would pass between them.'

Payne studied 'my Princess', in her light wide-necked summer dress, her face, arms and shoulders 'a soft honey brown'. Her hair, 'rippled by the gentle breeze, had never looked more lovely'. Looking back on that moment in the months to come, he decided that 'it must have been then that Tony lost his heart completely to my beautiful Princess'.

A couple of weeks later, Payne's vigilance paid off once more. It was a Friday evening. Returning to Royal Lodge for the weekend, the Princess was 'playing with a lighted cigarette between her fingers. She seemed to be nervous.' Glancing at her watch, she told Payne that Mr

Armstrong-Jones 'should be here at any moment. Please go and look for him.'

The Royal Lodge steward, Mr Havers, informed Payne that a car driven by Mr Armstrong-Jones had just passed through the gates of the park.

The car pulled up 'with a crunching skid on the gravel driveway'. Tony leapt out, wearing a pair of cavalry twill slacks, a striped shirt, a red tie 'with a blue flowered motif' and a brown sports jacket. 'His hair was disarranged and looked very boyish as he sprang lightly from the driving seat and slammed the front door.' Payne was 'astonished' to find that his luggage consisted of just one 'rather soiled' brown zippered holdall.

He led Tony to the Octagonal Room, where the Princess was waiting. 'Margaret was so relieved to see Tony that all thought of royal procedure must have been swept from her mind. As she reached him Tony's arms went up and he caught her fingers in his. Then with their hands held in front of them they leaned towards each other and kissed. It was a tender moment and one which I will never forget. Obviously it was not their first kiss, but it was their first in someone else's presence.'

Payne was mesmerised. 'I watched as Tony's arms slowly crept down and around Princess Margaret's tiny waist and pulled her closer to him. Her fingers, freed from his, caught at the back of his coat and she clung to him.'

This, he observed, 'was by no means a Royal escort's kiss – those I had seen many times'. Rather, 'it was a full-blooded lovers' embrace. Their lips were tight to each other. Indeed, it was the same sort of heartfelt embrace which I had seen the Princess offer to only one man before – and that man was Peter Townsend.

'After what seemed an age to me as I stood by the door, slightly embarrassed,' their embrace came to an end.

'Tony. How wonderful it is to have you here,' said the Princess. All ears, Payne judged her words 'adequate yet inadequate to the situation'.

On the other hand, 'Margaret had at that time no real experience of dealing with the one she loved.'

But 'if Margaret's remark was simple, Tony's was ridiculous: "Ma'am, it's delightful to see you again."'

Payne found Tony's formality theatrical and overdone: 'I almost felt like laughing.'

Only now did the Princess appear to notice Payne's presence by the door. 'With a smile and a nod she dismissed me.' Payne seized the opportunity to carry Tony's grubby little bag upstairs. Inside the bedroom, 'anxious to get my chores done quickly', he unzipped it, only to be gravely upset by what he found within. 'The sight which met my eyes made me step back a pace and I stared aghast at the contents.'

What had he found? A sawn-off shotgun? A blow-up sex doll? A copy of *Socialist Worker*? Payne had in fact been catapulted into this peculiar state of horror by the sight of unpressed clothes: a screwed-up dinner jacket, an unlaundered evening shirt, a pair of crumpled pyjamas wrapped in inky newspaper. 'Everything seemed to have been rolled up in a ball. With a feeling of great consternation I remembered that Tony would have to dress for dinner with my Princess within the hour.'

Down the side of the holdall, Payne discovered a dark-grey suit 'carelessly tossed in', a black bow tie, and an ordinary red tie. His indignation was unfettered. 'The whole jumbled mess would have been a disgrace to the average man – but to a man who was to dine with his country's favorite Princess it was worse. It was a sin. Especially as the clothes were well cut and of good material. But it was typical of Mr Armstrong-Jones' attitude, which was slap-dash and lazy at this time. I wondered what his flat and studio could be like if they were anything like the state of that bag.'

Finally, Payne fished out a leather washbag and busily rootled around in it, finding after-shave lotion, talcum powder, deodorant, hair cream and an electric razor. One particular item had the effect of making him feel more tenderly towards the young gentleman: 'I noticed that Mr Armstrong-Jones favoured the same talc and toilet water as myself and later I was to see Princess Margaret give an appreciative sniff whenever I passed by.'*

With less than an hour to go, 'I made up my mind I could not allow Tony to appear downstairs to dine with my Princess in such shabby gear.' So he nipped down to the kitchen with the clothes under his arm, pressed the trousers and 'did what I could' with the jacket. He then set about sponging the worst stains off the shirt and ironing it dry, before returning the freshly laundered clothes to the bedroom. Having drawn the curtains and run a bath for Tony, he went downstairs. The Princess told him that they had decided to have dinner watching television, and asked him to lay out two tables.

'"Yes of course, Your Royal Highness," I replied and with a meaningful glance at Mr. Armstrong-Jones I said: "I have laid your things out ready for you, sir. They are all in order now."'

The Princess 'looked puzzled by this remark and looked at Tony'. In turn, Tony 'just stammered a thank you and I could see he knew what I meant'.

Dinner passed without a hitch. 'I remember the grateful look which Mr Armstrong-Jones cast me while I was clearing away the empty soup bowls … I knew he was trying to silently thank me for making his dinner jacket presentable. And indeed when on it looked as smart as any I had seen.'

Dinner over, Payne asked the Princess if she would be requiring him further that evening.

'I think so. Yes.'

He retired to the servants' sitting room and read a magazine. After two hours, she summoned him back. 'You will not be required again tonight.'

---

* In his memoir *Adventures of a Gentleman's Gentleman*, the former Palace footman Guy Hunting identifies Snowdon's trademark smell as a 'particularly stinky eau de Toilette called Zizzani with which he drenched himself'. He adds that 'finding Snowdon was always pretty easy'.

'Thank you, Your Royal Highness,' he replied, and bade them both a polite goodnight, though he was 'inwardly fuming' that he should have been 'kept from my bed for two hours after being told that I would be needed that night'.

The following weekend, Payne and Tony met again, this time at Balmoral. In Payne's opinion, Tony seldom appeared relaxed, despite putting considerable effort into it. The British upper classes rarely take kindly to those who try too hard, and nor do their servants. On the moors, Tony wore plus fours, a corduroy jacket and a sharp peaked cap, pulled down well over his eyes. 'I can only say that he invariably looked awkward and very much ill at ease whenever he wore this uniform ... In actual fact Tony looked out of place in just about every place they went except the drawing room.'

The lure of the lie-in was Tony's undoing: he was always the last to appear for breakfast, late for the sporting day ahead. This did not go down well with the Royal Family, and particularly not with Prince Philip. The Land Rovers would be waiting outside for fifteen or twenty minutes for Tony to join them. After half a dozen of these late starts, Prince Philip finally lost his temper.

'He sat patiently for about ten minutes and then he started to give long blasts on the horn every few seconds and appeared to be getting very agitated. At last he turned to one of the guests and snorted in a loud voice:

'"Where has that bloody man got to? Still in bed I suppose." And his companions grinned. For to them Tony's late rising was a standing joke. And the Prince's impatience a source of amusement.

'"I think he is coming now," one of them said to Philip.

'"And about time too," snapped the Prince with a withering look in Tony's direction.'

Payne suspected something deeper than irritation beneath Philip's attitude. 'I feel sure there was something else, something much stronger behind it. It is a well known fact that Prince Philip has always been particularly fond of Princess Margaret and never loses an opportunity to talk to her or help her in and out of a car or onto a horse.'

Tony's tardiness made him an unpopular figure with the household staff, too. Some weeks later, on a Friday night in Royal Lodge, the bell rang in the servants' sitting room. When Payne entered, the Princess's sitting room was in semi-darkness. 'Do switch off the television,' said Margaret, without looking up.

'Certainly, Your Royal Highness.'

She remained cuddling up to Tony on the sofa, as though Payne were not in the room. 'I was embarrassed,' he recalled.

'I want you to take up a breakfast tray to Mr Armstrong-Jones's bedroom at 10 o'clock in the morning John.'

'Yes, I will see to it Ma'am.'

'You can leave us now, John. We will not be needing you again tonight.'

As Payne shut the door behind him, he heard a tune from *Oklahoma* playing on the record player. A police guard later informed him that the couple had stayed up listening to records until 2 a.m.

At 10 o'clock the next morning, tray in hand, Payne entered Tony's pitch-dark bedroom. He switched on the light and drew back the curtains. 'Then, setting down the tray on a bedside table, I gave Mr. Armstrong-Jones a shake. Trying to wake Mr. Armstrong-Jones at any time before midday was always a struggle and I had to shove him violently before he showed signs of waking up.

"What do you want?" he asked, testily.

'I knew he had been late getting to bed and ignored his gruff comment.

"I've brought your breakfast as the Princess ordered last night sir."'

Tony denied ordering it. Payne repeated that it was the Princess who had ordered it. '"Did she?" grunted Tony, pulling the bedclothes over his head.'

Payne left the tray where it was, and went downstairs. At midday the bell rang again.

Payne returned. Tony was now lounging in his bed, 'the top half of his bare body – he never wore pyjamas if he could help it – uncovered'.

'I want breakfast immediately,' he snapped.

Exasperated, Payne snapped back, 'You have had one breakfast already today, and have let that one get cold.'

'Do as you are told and bring me another breakfast,' said Tony, 'glaring at me through his red sleep-filled eyes'.

'Yes, sir.'

Payne removed the untouched tray and took it down to the kitchen, where the cook was busy preparing lunch. Her mood, already poor, turned worse. 'You go and tell him I'm cooking lunch now and if he's too lazy to eat his first breakfast he can go without as far as I'm concerned. I'm not going to start preparing another breakfast at this time of day for anyone.'

'Do you really want me to go and tell him that?'

'Yes I do.'

Payne went back upstairs, and repeated what the cook had just said, word for word.

At this point, the narrative becomes a touch opaque.

'"Oh did she say that?" he asked in a vexed tone.

'"Yes. I'm afraid she did sir," I told him.

'"We'll see about that," he snapped and kicked the bedclothes off him. I heard him muttering about his breakfast and the cook.

'"That to the cook," he said.

'I was rather shocked. It was not gentlemanly at all.

'"Please, sir. Remember who you are … and why you are here," I told him.

'He looked a bit taken aback and then said: "Oh very well. But I do not think it is at all right that I should be treated this way."

'I watched him dress and he did not speak to me again that morning.'

What was the rather shocking, ungentlemanly act that Tony had performed? Did Payne's American editor judiciously censor a few words prior to publication?

Strangely, not a single one of Princess Margaret's numerous biographers ever mentions Payne by name, though they are all happy to plunder his material, ascribing it to 'a royal servant' or 'a Buckingham Palace insider'. Only one of them – Noel Botham, a boozy old Fleet Street hack, as far from a courtier as could be – goes into the nature of the ungentlemanly act.

Botham summarises it thus: 'After receiving the message from the kitchen, Tony had, so we're told, kicked off the bedclothes and, stark naked, made a rude gesture saying, "That to the cook."'

Botham then elaborates on the episode in his usual saloon-bar mixture of the lewd, the euphemistic and the grandiloquent: 'Nature had been very generous to Tony Armstrong-Jones in endowing him magnificently in his most private appendage. This he had grasped and pointed in a light-hearted and jokey way, so the story went, which was soon recounted throughout London.' Regardless of its rackety raconteur, this explanation seems the most plausible.

That same summer, Payne also saw more of the Princess than he considered quite appropriate, though perhaps rather less than he might have hoped for. Standing beside the swimming pool at Royal Lodge, he kept his beady eyes peeled as the couple frolicked in and out of the water. 'Standing in the sun, her tanned skin glistening with water, my Princess looked absolutely adorable ... Her supple figure was shown off to its best advantage in ... a brief yellow bikini two-piece affair with a halter strap around the neck.' He cast his mind back to the first time he saw her so scantily clad. He had just been sunning himself in the garden when the bell in the pantry rang: he was needed in the Octagonal Room. 'Hurriedly buttoning my tunic, I trotted up. On opening the door, I gaped.'

The Princess was standing there in a bikini, a towel loosely draped around her shoulders. 'Her body glistened and little droplets of water trickled down from her arms and legs ... I was too astonished to speak. I simply stood and looked, my eyes taking her in from head to toe.'

The Princess stood, hands on her hips 'and a pleased smile on her lips'. They exchanged glances. Payne felt himself blushing, 'but she smiled more broadly than ever' and asked him to bring them tea at the swimming pool at 5 o'clock.

'Certainly, Your Royal Highness.'

The Princess was 'apparently enjoying the situation. It was one of her playful moods.'

This fruity encounter inspired mixed feelings in Payne. 'I felt at the same time awkward and in some way flattered that I had reached a point of intimacy with this Royal Princess which made her capable of standing before me, covered only in the briefest clothing that the law permitted without any apparent embarrassment – on her part, anyway. I flatter myself that so complete was our relationship that only to me did she ever show such a complete abandonment of her royal pedestal. No other servant could have been given that accolade.'

Parallels with the topsy-turvy world of Dirk Bogarde in Joseph Losey's film *The Servant* also appear in what Payne describes as 'a disastrous gaffe' by Tony, which left 'my Princess' in 'a state of white-faced supercharged Regal fury which was terrible to see'.

Towards the end of the Indian summer of 1959, Payne was in the sitting room of Royal Lodge, kneeling on the floor next to the cross-legged Princess, helping her sort through her records. She was in what he described as a 'wonderfully happy frame of mind', picking up each long-player, looking at its cover, perhaps humming a snatch from one of its songs.

After they had sorted through one pile, the Princess asked Payne to take the records to the car. Suddenly, the door burst open and in came Tony, saying, 'John, I've been looking everywhere for you. Be a darling, will you, and ...'

Tony had clearly not seen Margaret, still tucked on the floor behind the sofa. 'I could do nothing to stop him from greeting me in this breezy way – as if she were miles away,' recalled Payne. 'But something of the alarm I felt must have shown on my face, for he stopped short, the smile fading from his lips.'

The Princess jumped to her feet and stared stony-faced at Tony.

'What on earth do you mean? Whom are you talking to?'

Tony was clearly discomfited. He had, he spluttered, no idea she was there. 'I didn't see you. I wanted John for something.'

"'And what do you mean by 'darling'?" asked Margaret fiercely, ignoring my presence.

"'It's an expression often used in the theatre world, Ma'am. I'm afraid I have picked it up …'"

The Princess stared at him coldly 'for what seemed like half an hour'. She then broke the silence.

"'You may go,' she said, looking at me frostily, her chin jutting out, her fists clenched at her sides.'

Closing the door behind him, Payne found himself 'soaked in perspiration. Sweat trickled down the fingers which had been holding the records and I felt its prickly sting down my back.'

Why was the normally unflappable Payne quite so flustered by a mistake that was, after all, entirely Tony's? He offers no explanation.*

---

* In her heavily disputed book *The Royals*, Kitty Kelley suggests that this passage contains an 'allegation of having been the object of a sexual overture from Antony Armstrong-Jones'. This, she claimed, was the principal reason the Queen Mother 'sued to prevent publication in England'.

41

On the morning of 21 April 1956, an up-and-coming young photographer arrived at Holkham Hall in Norfolk, charged with taking the photographs of the wedding of Lady Anne Coke to the Hon. Colin Tennant. Throughout the day, the bride's father, the Earl of Leicester, referred to the photographer as Tony Snapshot, though he knew full well that his real name was Antony Armstrong-Jones. For the rest of his life, the photographer would blanch at the memory of this snub. Furthermore, he had been treated as a tradesman, obliged to use the servants' entrance, even though he had overlapped with the groom at Eton. Nor had he been invited to join the wedding guests for champagne in the state rooms; instead, he had to make do with a cup of tea in the servants' hall.

At that time, the social status of a photographer was roughly on a par with that of a tailor – above a hairdresser, but below a governess. Over the course of the 1960s the poor old governess was to find herself overtaken by the other three. The rapid social ascent of Armstrong-Jones, whose persona had a hint of both the tailor and the hairdresser, served as a beacon for this social upheaval.

Yet neither time nor status could soften the rebuff Armstrong-Jones had suffered at the hands of Colin Tennant. Up to Tennant's death, and beyond, he felt unable to mention Tennant's name without appending the epithet 'that shit'. His loyal biographer Anne de Courcy records that, soon after his humiliation, Armstrong-Jones threatened Tennant, saying, 'I'll get even with you for that!' He then added, perversely but prophetically, 'I'll marry your best friend!'

De Courcy interviewed both men for her biography – Armstrong-Jones at great length – so the memory of that perverse threat must have come from one or the other, or both. Or had there been a scullery maid or a court dwarf hidden behind the curtain, who tearfully confessed what she had overheard on that fateful day, half a century before?

Tennant's equally loyal biographer, Nicholas Courtney, confirmed de Courcy's evidence. 'There was always bad blood between Colin and Tony, which Colin believed stemmed from that unintentional slight at his wedding ... Tony always referred to Colin as "that shit". When Courtney phoned him to request an interview, Tony exploded, 'I *loathed* the man. I want nothing to do with his biography!' And with that, he slammed down the receiver.

Was there a degree of sexual jealousy in the feud between Colin Tennant and Antony Armstrong-Jones? In the mid-1950s, Tennant had been widely tipped in the press as the front-runner for the Princess's hand in marriage. Some in her inner circle thought it a strong possibility too. 'I believe that Colin is serious and would enjoy being a Prince Consort,' wrote Ann Fleming to Patrick Leigh Fermor. Others were not so sure. 'The sudden arrival of Princess Margaret into our lives in the Fifties brought unfriendly reactions from some of the family,' wrote his sister Emma Tennant after his death in 2010. 'It was thought that we'd never find any privacy again, and, worst of all, if an engagement was announced between the Princess and Colin, then Colin was likely to become a pompous bore and all our fun and games would be over. That this didn't happen we might have guessed. Colin remained as irrepressibly funny and unimpressed by people who thought highly of themselves as he had ever been. Princess Margaret, as is well known, could be offensively sure of her superior status.'

Half a century on, Colin Tennant claimed that marriage had never been on the cards. Though he and the Princess had indulged in 'heavy petting', they had certainly never embarked upon what he called 'a serious affair'. Or so he told his biographer.

Like many euphemisms, 'heavy petting' is frustratingly opaque. Where does light end and heavy begin? *The Cambridge English Dictionary* defines heavy petting as 'an occasion [sic] when two people kiss, hold, and touch each other in a sexual way, but do not have sex'. *The Oxford English Dictionary* goes a little further: 'Erotic contact between two people involving stimulation of the genitals but falling short of intercourse.' But what do Oxbridge lexicographers know of heavy petting? Only the more worldly *Urban Dictionary* goes the whole hog: 'Foreplay ranging from breast massage to masturbating one's partner, yet no coital contact.'

Was it Tennant who decided that things could only go so far, but no further? Or was it Margaret? The evidence suggests it was Margaret who pulled up the drawbridge. Tennant always found the Princess 'ravishing, terribly funny, and such good company', but he confessed to Courtney that, for her part, the Princess had never found him all that attractive. 'I was not at all her type, unlike Peter Townsend, and then Tony and then Roddy. They were smaller, foxy, talkative men.'* He then added, sportingly, that, all in all, he was glad not to have fitted the bill: 'If I had actually been more of a lover and less of a companion, we would not have remained such friends.'

In other circles, a youthful stint of heavy petting, however circumscribed, might have licensed the use of Christian names; but not in this case. A private letter penned from Mustique two decades later by Tennant to Princess Margaret begins 'Madam', and ends with the

---

* In fact, Townsend was neither foxy nor talkative, and six foot two inches tall. A photograph of him standing immediately behind the Princess shows the top of her hair only just reaching the bottom of the knot on his tie, and her hair was always artificially puffed-up, lending it added height and volume. Incidentally, might her desire to be addressed as 'Highness' have been a form of wish-fulfilment, a subliminal reaction to her lack of inches?

complaint that though 'all is by no means gloom', things are 'rather flat without Your Royal Highness'.*

---

* Beyond her family, her old dresser, Ruby Gordon, was the only person allowed to call her 'Margaret'. Her insistence on being addressed as 'Ma'am', 'Madam' and 'Your Royal Highness', even by old friends and lovers, is a thread that runs through the life of the Princess. There was always an element of Hyacinth Bucket about her, a tendency to keep her high horse tethered for use at all times, even in the company of old friends. Clearly, the Princess felt that being called 'Margaret' involved crossing an invisible line which heavy petting did not. Or might she and her beaux have found a Chatterleyesque charge in the anomaly of maintaining social niceties while engaged in a steamy sexual encounter?

42

Staying at Balmoral in October 1959, Margaret received a letter from her old suitor Peter Townsend, telling her that he was engaged to be married to a Marie-Luce Jamagne, who was, he failed to mention, ten years her junior.

Her letter back was immediate, passionate and furious. She had been under the impression that, when they parted, they had both vowed never to marry anyone else; and now he had broken that vow.

'She believed I had betrayed her,' Townsend told his friend and co-author Anne Edwards, close to the end of his life. He had kept the letter, and let Edwards have a glimpse of it. 'It was an angry, bitter letter, written in M's hand on her personal stationery,' Edwards explained. 'She did indeed accuse him of betraying their great love and the vow they had both made when she made her decision to remain in England (for she would have had to leave, had they married) that neither would ever marry another. She also asked him to burn all of her love letters to him. He had saved a few and quite impassioned they were (in later years he told me he had destroyed these as well as that last letter from her).'

When Margaret received Townsend's letter, Tony Armstrong-Jones was staying at Balmoral for the first time. She told him about it, and added that, on this particular day, a proposal was out of the question.

Anne Edwards believed that Princess Margaret married Tony Armstrong-Jones 'out of pure spite towards Peter for marrying against their vow (which he had agreed to) … She was head over heels in love with Peter – the sad thing was she was also arrogant, loved being a princess with all its perks, and perhaps even harboured the idea that she could continue to have a secret affair with him and still be able to carry on otherwise as before.'

Shortly after Margaret received his letter, Townsend publicly announced his engagement to Marie-Luce Jamagne. David John Payne found himself having to deliver the evening newspaper to the Princess, its headline, 'Townsend to Marry', uppermost. For others, less bold, this might have posed a problem, but for Payne it was an opportunity. Normally he would have left the room after delivering the paper, but not today; he was eager to see her reaction. Of course Townsend had forewarned the Princess by letter, but Payne was not to know this, so he was on tenterhooks.

While he occupied his time emptying the ashtrays and 'putting the settee cushions to rights', the Princess continued to sit at her desk with her back towards him. 'I watched her, fascinated, as she put down her pen, picked up the paper and leaned back in her chair … I had a premonition that something violent was going to happen.'

Suddenly, Margaret 'flared into action'. She grabbed the paper with her left hand and hurled it across the room. Payne stood 'rooted to the spot', while Margaret returned to her desk and carried on writing, 'as if nothing had happened'.

The following day, Margaret went to stay at a house party in Kent. Word went round that she was not to be shown any of the daily newspapers, and no one was to mention the news. When most of the party embarked on a walk, Margaret stayed behind, singing melancholy hymns to a piano accompaniment. One of them was 'Nearer My God To Thee', the hymn that was played as the *Titanic* went down.

Tony and Margaret finally became engaged at Christmas. Tony seems to have been in two minds about it too. There was so much he would have to give up, not least his other girlfriends, one of whom confided to a friend that Tony had wept on her bare breasts at the prospect of getting married to royalty.

Just before travelling up to Scotland to stay at Balmoral that October, Tony had carried on his affair with his old friend Jeremy Fry's wife Camilla. Without him knowing it, Camilla was now pregnant with his child.

Polly Fry was born three weeks after the royal wedding, though it was not for forty-four years that she was to discover who her true father was. 'Those were different times, back then,' explains a member of their circle.

43

Never one to pass up an opportunity for an anecdote, Harold Macmillan claimed to have heard the news of the royal engagement from a distraught Duke of Gloucester. Apparently the Duke had greeted the prime minister on his arrival at Sandringham with the words, 'Thank heavens you've come, Prime Minister. The Queen's in a terrible state; there's a fellow called Jones in the billiard room who wants to marry her sister, and Prince Philip's in the library wanting to change the family name to Mountbatten.'

On 22 February 1960, Macmillan passed the news to his cabinet. Later that day, he recorded the occasion in his diary:

> I told ministers about Princess Margaret's engagement. No-one was in any doubt as to what advice – shd advice be necessary – ought to be given to the Queen. I think myself that the marriage will be very popular. All our people like a 'love match' – and the D Mirror etc will like a commoner ...

The engagement was officially announced four days later, on 26 February. In a television interview, Barbara Cartland, the prolific romantic novelist, expressed her joy. 'No bride, whatever her class, is immune from feeling that love is the most wonderful thing in the whole world, and that applies to a certain princess who wrote to a friend saying: "No two people have ever been so much in love."'

At the time she was criticised for this indiscretion, but in her memoir *I Search for Rainbows* she claims to have been quoting from an unnamed ancient Greek play. 'But how satisfactory it is to add, however indiscreet I was then, that seven years later no two people have ever looked more in love than they do today.'

Cecil Beaton reacted with mounting fury. How could his callow young rival have pulled off such a coup? 'Not even a good photographer!' he yelled. Subsequently, he suffered two or three sleepless nights, self-reproach criss-crossing with self-analysis and self-pity as he desperately tried to work out quite why the news was causing him such misery. He finally put his finger on it: envy that nothing so momentous would ever happen in his own life, and envy also 'that all my excitements and interests paled in comparison'.

Dozing in his study in Swansea, the novelist Kingsley Amis was nudged awake by his house guest Geoff Nicholson. 'It's just been announced that Princess Margaret is going to marry Tony Armstrong-Jones.'

'Look, sonny,' he replied testily, 'try and think of something a bit less obvious next time.'

'Come out and look. It's on now.'

The two men made their way to Amis's kitchen, where the BBC's court correspondent Godfrey Talbot was saying, '… and everybody is so delighted because this is so obviously a real love match.'

At this point, Nicholson chipped in, 'Weren't you telling me something about you telling him something about Princess Margaret being a bloody fool?'

'I expect I was,' replied Amis. 'Anyway, I did.'

It had occurred over a lunch at an advertising agency just a month before. Amis, then at the height of his fame as a comic novelist, was to be photographed, along with various other celebrities, enjoying, or at least pretending to enjoy, a glass of Long Life beer. He had been chatting away to the photographer when the subject of Princess Margaret had come up. Never one to beat around the bush, Amis had ranted on about her stupidity, based on something she had recently said.

'… the woman obviously has no mind at all – you remember that crap of hers about it not being any good our sending the products of our minds up into space while our souls remained stuck down below in the dives and the espresso bars – schoolgirl essay stuff.'

'I can assure you you're quite wrong,' the photographer had replied. 'She is in fact an extremely intelligent and well-informed woman.'

'Oh, you know her, do you?'

'I have met her on several occasions.'

Now it struck him that this photographer was the same man who was engaged to the Princess.

'Such a symbol of the age we live in,' Amis wrote to an American friend, 'when a royal princess, famed for her devotion to all that is most vapid and mindless in the world of entertainment, her habit of reminding people of her status whenever they venture to disagree with her in conversation and her appalling taste in clothes, is united with a dog-faced tight-jeaned fotog of fruitarian tastes such as can be found in dozens in any pseudo-arty drinking cellar in fashionable-unfashionable London. They're made for each other.'

On holiday in Athens, Evelyn Waugh was also taken aback by the news of the royal engagement, declaring it a 'fiasco'. On the day of the royal wedding he was invited by Ann Fleming to a celebratory party, but he firmly refused:

> Like all loyal subjects of the monarchy, I am appalled by the
> proposed mesalliance. The happiest solution would be for the press
> photographer (who I read is constant in his attendance at church) to
> be ordained a Protestant clergyman & made Archbishop of
> Canterbury. This would give him precedence immediately below the
> royal family. It confers no precedence on his wife, but she might be
> granted the style of a duke's daughter. They can then rock and roll

about Lambeth Palace. I understand Jones likes the smell of the lower Thames. There are several other surviving Anglicans – David Cecil, Betjeman, Lancaster, Piper, Elizabeth Cavendish and two (I think Lesbian) spinsters in Combe Florey who could compose their court.

In her garden in Barrow-in-Furness, the Mass-Observation diarist Nella Last was 'pegging out some tea towels on the line' when her friend Mrs Atkinson popped round. 'She was *shocked* at Princess Margaret's engagement to a common photographer – for once, not asking me what I thought before she began … She said, "Why, she will be Mrs Armstrong-*Jones*." I said, "Oh no, she is a princess & will keep her title – perhaps they will give her husband a title." She said "I hope they *do*."'

Mrs Last's counterpart in St Pancras, Anthony Heap, disapproved of the 'gush and ballyhoo' over the engagement announcement. On the other hand, he hoped that 'maybe marriage will help her to acquire a little more dignity and decorum'.

Most upset of all was Betty Kenward. At a party in 1959, the pseud-onymous author of *Queen* magazine's 'Jennifer's Diary' had brushed aside a photographer who was trying to introduce himself to her. 'Don't you dare address me!' she had snapped, as she turned on her heel. 'I don't talk to my photographers!'

A year later, the announcement came through that the shunned photographer was engaged to be married to HRH the Princess Margaret. Mrs Kenward took the news very badly indeed, occupying the rest of her afternoon with kicking and re-kicking her office waste-paper basket, saying over and over again, 'What a turn-up this is! What a turn-up this is!'

Shortly afterwards, she telephoned Tony Armstrong-Jones for a quote. He was afraid he couldn't help her, he replied, since he knew she never spoke to photographers.

It is said that she never quite got over the shock of that royal engagement. Nor could she find it in her heart to forgive the groom. For decades to come, whenever the royal couple appeared in Jennifer's Diary she would refer to them only as 'HRH the Princess Margaret and her husband'.

44

Princess Margaret's Wedding Book (1960) sits on my bookshelves alongside *Debrett's Book of the Royal Wedding* (1981) and *Debrett's Book of the Royal Engagement* (1986), all of them souvenirs of dashed hopes.

'There was no doubt about the nation's delight at the announcement of this engagement after weeks of speculation,' reads the introduction to *Debrett's Book of the Royal Engagement*, 'and the general consensus seemed to be that Prince Andrew was a fortunate man indeed in having chosen such an obviously warm-hearted and beautiful girl as Sarah Ferguson.'

The same note of optimism can be found in *Princess Margaret's Wedding Book*, though its expression is more tortured:

Now the future lies before the young couple. May there be many more pictures that they and all their well-wishers can turn to with pleasure, and may all the hopes the young bride holds for her married life be as richly fulfilled to her as the promises she made at the altar are certain to be nobly vindicated by her.

... When Princess Margaret walked up the nave of Westminster Abbey to the High Altar on the arm of the Duke of Edinburgh she was not only celebrating a uniquely happy personal event but setting a notable precedent for the British Royal Family. She was marrying a commoner ... It is fitting that it should have been left for Princess

Margaret to take this final step, since there has always been in her a modernity, a feeling for the constantly shifting patterns of twentieth century living that marked her as an innovator.

The newspapers of the time were every bit as jubilant, perhaps more so. The *Evening Standard*'s Anne Sharpley set great store by the groom's lack of blue blood:

> In splendour, sunshine and great sweetness, Princess Margaret married Mr Antony Armstrong Jones, the young man without title, without pretension, today in Westminster Abbey.
>
> It was something that could have happened only in the 20th century – a Sovereign's daughter marrying a photographer with all the force of the centuries of this ancient land bringing dignity, grace and deep approval.
>
> Princess Margaret – perhaps we have never known before how beautiful she is – kept a sweet gravity about her that we had never seen.
>
> The simplicity and lightness of her gown, her quiet air. She was a woman surrounded by all the white mystery of womanhood.

Sharpley's report was topped by two lines from a poem specially composed by the eighty-one-year-old poet laureate, John Masefield:

> All England here, whose symbol is the Rose,
> Prays that this Lady's Fortune may be fair.

Printed in full in the souvenir programme, the poem was called 'Prayer for this Glad Morning'. Like many royal verses, it favours simplicity over verve:

... Now, here, a nation prays, that a bright spring
May bless the day with sunlight and with flowers,
And through this ever-threatened life of ours,
May bless the lives with every welcome thing ...

Masefield left no notes or first drafts for this poem, and omitted it from his letters and diaries, so we can only guess at the manner of its creation. As he wrote the line 'Now, here, a nation prays, that a bright spring', was he hoping that the perfect rhyme would crop up, out of the blue, three lines further on? But what? 'Bling'? 'Fling'? 'Ring'? 'Sting'? Sometimes, the magic fails to materialise. 'May bless the lives with every welcome *thing*'. At this point, did he look at it, sigh, and think, like so many poets laureate before and after, 'It'll *do*'?

On the other hand, Noël Coward's delight flowed effortlessly. It had, he thought, been 'the big week, the glamorous week, the Hurrah for England week!' ('In spite,' he added, 'of a hacking cough.')

On the Wednesday, a court ball at Buckingham Palace had, in his opinion, seen 'everybody looking their tiptop best and the entire Royal Family charming'. He had enjoyed chats with Prince Philip, the Queen Mother, the Queen ('brief but amiable'), the 'dear' Duchess of Kent and 'the radiant engaged couple'. And he had been particularly entranced by the groom: 'He is a charmer and I took a great shine to him, easy and unflurried and a sweet smile.'

On the Friday came the wedding itself. 'God in his heaven really smiling like mad and *everything* in the garden being genuinely lovely ... The morning was brilliant and the crowds lining the streets looked like endless vivid herbaceous borders. The police were smiling, the Guards beaming and the air tingling with excitement and the magic of spring.'

The service was, he thought, 'moving and irreproachably organized. The Queen alone looked disagreeable; whether or not this was concealed sadness or bad temper because Tony Armstrong-Jones had refused an earldom,* nobody seems to know but she *did* scowl a good deal.' Princess Margaret herself 'looked like the ideal of what any fairy-tale princess *should* look like. Tony Armstrong-Jones pale, a bit tremulous and completely charming. Prince Philip jocular and really very sweet and reassuring as he led the bride to the altar. The music was divine and the fanfare immensely moving. Nowhere in the world but England could such pomp and circumstance and pageantry be handled with such exquisite dignity. There wasn't one note of vulgarity or anything approaching it in the whole thing … it was lusty, charming, romantic, splendid and without a false note. It is *still* a pretty exciting thing to be English.'

Once it was over, Coward went to 'a wild but beautifully organised lunch party' with a motley group drawn from the worlds of politics and the arts, among them James Pope-Hennessy, Lucian Freud, Bob Boothby and Hugh Gaitskell. Later, he sat down to watch the wedding on television, enjoying footage of the royal couple leaving for their honeymoon on the royal yacht *Britannia*. 'It was moving and romantic and the weather still held, and when the Tower Bridge opened and the yacht passed through with those two tiny figures waving from just below the bridge I discovered, unashamedly and without surprise, that my eyes were full of tears.'

Just short of his tenth birthday, Alan Johnson, who was to grow up to become Home Secretary and Chancellor of the Exchequer, watched the wedding on television with his mother and sister in their slum dwelling in Walmer Road, London W11. 'Up until then, I had never been able to figure out why a woman could not have babies before she was married. During the Royal Wedding service, after the couple were pronounced man and wife, the cameras had focused on the altar while the bride and groom went somewhere with the Archbishop of Canterbury, out of sight of the congregation and the cameras.

'It came to me in a flash that this must be the point at which a bride

---

* He did not become Lord Snowdon until the following year.

was injected to enable her to have babies. It all made sense. Princess Margaret had been injected and the following year she'd had a child.'

He held firm to this belief for a full two years before his older sister Linda, 'with a knowing smile', disabused him. 'I listened with mounting horror. How could a man do that to a woman? ... A simple injection seemed, to my twelve-year-old self, to be preferable in every respect.'

Sixteen years later, following the announcement of the royal couple's separation, Auberon Waugh was to look back on their wedding day with mixed emotions. As an undergraduate at Oxford, he had witnessed 'many scenes of dignified grief in the Christ Church Junior Common Room as she walked up the aisle with her Welsh dwarf of "artistic" leanings. But we may have felt that after her somewhat chequered past she was lucky to catch anyone, and certainly there was nothing like the shock of humiliation we all suffered when Princess Anne announced that she was going to marry her grinning speechless stable-lad.'

45

During their engagement, Tony and Margaret were invited to dinner by Colin and Anne Tennant. The conversation turned to their honeymoon: they would, they said, be sailing around the Caribbean.

'Why don't you stop off at Mustique?' asked Tennant. On a whim, he had bought an entire island for £45,000 three years before, despite it having no fresh water or electricity. 'It's very primitive but it has magical beaches. Anne and I will be there, living in our hut, and we won't bother you at all.'

Thus the newlyweds first set eyes on Mustique from the deck of the royal yacht. Not unusually for the Princess, she was disappointed. 'The island looked like Kenya,' she recalled. 'Burnt to a frazzle. We drove down a path, the only road, and sat in the brush whacking mosquitoes.'

The royal couple were greeted by the Tennants on the newly built jetty, Tony Snapshot moodily lurking three paces behind the bronzed, beaming Margaret. The Tennants had cobbled together a little bamboo hut to provide shade. Beneath a roof of coconut fronds, the four of them sipped glasses of lukewarm lemonade. Sensing that she was in a good mood, Colin turned to Margaret and reminded her that he still owed her a wedding present. 'Look, Ma'am, would you like something in a little box, or' – and here he swung an arm around – 'a piece of land?'

'A piece of land,' replied Margaret, without missing a beat. Tony managed a smile, but inwardly he was bristling with irritation. Why hadn't he been included in the offer? Why was Tennant always trying to do him down? Knowingly or unknowingly, Tennant had just delivered Tony yet another grievance ready for the nursing. 'Odd, don't you think?' Tony remarked to Princess Margaret's biographer, Tim Heald, nearly half a century later. In the same conversation he would refer to Tennant once again as 'that shit'.

46

'I'm delighted that our castaway this week is Her Royal Highness Princess Margaret, Countess of Snowdon,' announces Roy Plomley, the oleaginous presenter of *Desert Island Discs*.

'Ma'am, have you a big collection of records?'

'Ears, quate.'

'Have you kept your old 78s?'

'Oh ears, they're all velly carefully …' – she pauses, as if searching for the right word – '… preserved.'

'They're very heavy of course – you've got them down in the cellar?'

'Eh hev them up in the ettic, eckshleh.'

These abrupt replies set the tone for the interview. Princess Margaret says the bare minimum. Often she sounds slightly testy, as though grudgingly filling in a form. Or had she not been warned that an interview involves answering questions?

Their conversation turns to music, and her own piano-playing.

'Do you compose yourself?'

'Oh nyair – well Eh have composed one or two things, but er velly slight.'

'What – songs?'

'Ears.'

'Did you find it very difficult to choose just eight records that may have to last a long long time?'

'Oh ears, Eh found it velly difficult INDEED.'

She sometimes emphasises words, as if forcing unearned wit or irony upon them. Her first choice is, she says, 'King Cotton' by Souza.

'Who would you like to play it?'

'The Marine Bend, if possible, please.'

'Well here it is, conducted by Lieutenant Colonel Sir Vivian Dunn.'

'Well, thet'll be velly nice indeed, because he was my childhood hero.'

'Really?'

'Well, you see, whenever the Queen goes on the yacht, she still takes the Marine Bend and of course there's always a Director of Music and it's usually the senior one end he was the senior one for a gret number of years.'

They talk of her childhood.

'What's your earliest memory as a child?'

'In my prairm, Eh think, being told not to push my prairm up and down by moving about in it … after a little while Eh succeeded in tipping up the prairm and was rescued, screaming loudleh.'

Some vowels are elongated rather than clipped. 'Yes' emerges as 'ears', 'no' as 'nyair'.

Her second choice of record?

'"Scotland the Brave", please. Eh hape that it's recorded by the pipes and drums of my rairgiment, the Royal Highland Fusiliers.'

After 'Scotland the Brave', they talk of her schooling.

'Did your early education include some rather unusual subjects like protocol?'

'Nyair, I don't think it did rarely because one was brought up to be able to twalk to anybody … the Prime Minister or Archbishop or somebody like that were friends.'

'Did you study constitutional history?'

'Nyair, I didn't. My sister did.'

'Much of your life has been spent in historic buildings. Do you have a strong sense of the past?'

'Oh, ears. Tremendously.'

They talk about the family's sudden change of fortune in 1936.

'My first impression was of having to leave home. Bettling through these enORmous loving crowds.'

'Buckingham Palace itself must be a very daunting place from its sheer size.'

'Well, nyair, Buckingham Pellis is a vair cazy hice.'

They discuss the childhood pantomimes in which she took the lead role.

'I believe they were your idea, weren't they?'

'Nyair, they were my father's.'

'It's said that on VE-night you were outside Buckingham Palace in the crowds joining in the peace celebrations?'

Suddenly, her voice becomes animated. 'Ears, INDEED we WAIR.'

'Were you disguised in any way?'

'Nyair. It was MOST EXCITING. We went out with a party of friends, of course they were all in uniform then, including my sister, who was in the ATS. We went everywhere, we rushed down the street. We hed an uncle with us – my mother's brother – who was velly jolly and gay and encouraged us to behave bedly as usual.'

She first heard her third record in a 'treffic jem': 'Sixteen Tons', by Tennessee Ernie Ford. 'It chaired me up velly much.'

'When did you carry out your first solo public engagement? Do you remember what it was?'

'Well, I was twelve.'

'As early as that?'

'Ears. Eh went to present the school praizes at the Princess Margaret School in Windsor.'

'Were you very nervous?'

'Eh felt DREADFULLY sick, ears.'

'The first of so very many. I have a list of your presidencies and patronages of various welfare organisations and children's societies, a very long list, scores of them, and they must all be visited of course? … And of course you are now President of the Girl Guides?'

'Ears, eh took over from my aunt, the Princess Rahl.'

'– and you're Colonel-in-Chief of several regiments?'

'Ears, three.'

'Someone with a taste for figures has listed about 170 engagements you fulfil in a year. Does that seem reasonably right?'

'Well, Eh don't think Eh've ever counted! One seems to keep pretty busy.'

'It seems a lot of work. You have your own office staff, which arranges all the details?'

'Oh ears, Eh couldn't do without them.'

'You're usually accompanied by a lady-in-waiting. Are they appointed by yourself from among your personal friends?'

'Ears, not particularly PERSONAW friends, some are appointed because they are SYOOTABAW, and they are perhaps a friend of a friend who – you know – hez recommended them …'

'Right, we've got to number four.'

'May I hev please a small portion of Brahms' Symphony Number Two?'

'Why did you choose this one?'

'Eh think et's the maist beautiful tune in the weld (sighs impatiently). In fact et's beautiful all the way through, but Eh know we can only have a little bit of et.'

Her next record?

'Eh should like "Rule Britannia", pliz. Eh would like a recording, pliz, of the Last Night of the Proms, with the people joining in and sanding veh patriotic, which is veh important nardays.'

'Ma'am, you take a very active interest in arts organisations … Dancing has always delighted you.'

'Eh've always loved the bellay, and from a long time ago, Eh've had something to do with it.'

Plomley asks her whether she prefers classical to modern ballet. The classical, she replies. 'I suppose because of the music … If the music is baird or non-existent or ugly, I find thet it takes away from the dancing.'

'And you are a very regular theatregoer – all sorts of theatre?'

'Ears, wall sworts of theatre, but I really like the bellay best.'

'... You have a gift for mimicry, you're a good musician and you love dancing. In other circumstances, do you think you would have been a performer?'

'Nyair, I dain't think so. Eh wasn't any good at any of them. Eh mean, you're kind enough to say that Eh'm a good mimic but Eh can't ectually *mimic* people velly well. There are other members of my family who are better at that, end, erm, Em not a velly good musician. Eh can strum on the piano a little bit for other people to sing to. I never did any dancing other than ballroom dancing, so I dain't think I would have been accepted at an waudition.'

'Let's have another record. What's number six?'

'May I have a bit out of *Swan Lek*, pliz ... I think the conductor calls it number 13 waltz, second ect.'

After *Swan Lake*, they talk about her teenage children. David, she reveals, is 'velly good with his hends'.

At no point in the programme are her marriage or divorce mentioned, nor any of her romances, before or after the marriage. But now Plomley broaches the subject of her sometimes erratic press coverage.

'Few people have suffered more than you from wild and inaccurate and irresponsible press stories, especially in foreign papers. Can you laugh at them, or do you find them aggravating?'

'Eh find them EXTREMELY eggrevating. Of course, if they're ebsolutely invented, like sometimes they are, one can laugh at them with one's friends. But Eh think that since the age of seventeen Eh've been misreported and misrepresented.'

'A lot of it is beneath contempt,' Plomley loyally chips in, 'and of course you can't keep on issuing denials.'

'Well, they're not worth denying, relleh, because they're usually ineccurate.' Is this a Freudian slip? Would she only consider denying those that were accurate?

'Let's get back to music. What's record number seven?'

'Well, this is a record – quate an eld record Eh think – about 1948, when Eh was a young –' here she pauses, as though rootling around for the right word. '– thing and quite enjoying life' – her voice sounds momentarily melancholic – 'called "Rock Rock Rock" by Carl Ravazza end Sid Phillips and his Bend end long before what we know as rock.'

'Now, the practical problems of survival on the island. You've made many visits to the tropics, you've visited many islands. Any deserted ones?'

'Ears.'

'What sort of shelter would you build?'

'Eh think it would depend on what sort of stuff there'd be to build it with.'

'Well, you've got palm trees and undergrowth.'

'Well, then Eh think palm fronds and, erm, ears, that would do very well.'

'Would you plan to escape?'

'Oh ears, Eh like life too much to live on a desert island.'

Her favourite record? '"I Would Tek the Swan Lek".'

Her luxury? 'Eh think Eh'd take a piano.'

Book? 'Eh should like *War end Peace*.'

'A good long read.'

'A good long read, and rather needs reading several times, so that would keep me geng for a lawng time.'

'I should think it would! And thank you, Your Royal Highness, for letting us hear your Desert Island Discs.'

'Thenk you, too.'

'Goodbye, everyone.'

In his history of Radio 4, *Life on Air*, David Hendy reports considerable criticism of this episode within the BBC. Already upset by Plomley's 'reluctance to follow up interesting statements, or to raise topical issues, or even to change the relentlessly chronological running order of his questions', the powers-that-be felt that his handling of

Princess Margaret almost brought the programme to a grinding halt. It was not helped by the Princess's tendency towards the monosyllabic. Perhaps, thought the controller of Radio 4, Monica Sims, the Princess felt 'she had to weigh every word'. A current affairs producer argued that Plomley had simply been too obsequious, while a BBC governor judged that the final result had been, quite simply, 'terrible'.

Some years later, sitting next to the novelist A.N. Wilson at a dinner party, Princess Margaret said that she couldn't recall which luxury she had chosen on *Desert Island Discs*.

'I believe it was one of your regiments, Ma'am,' replied Wilson.

47

Back from honeymoon, their married life began swimmingly. Tony and 'M', as he called her, seemed set to become the golden couple of the Swinging Sixties, gaily swinging from royal to commoner, from grand to groovy, as and when the mood took them.

As though to usher in the new decade, 1A Kensington Palace had been submitted to a full refurbishment, closely supervised by Tony, who made sure the dining room was painted in apricot, and his dressing room had a dark-green carpet offset by tan cork walls and a gilded Napoleonic day-bed. A full staff had been assembled to look after the pair of them – butler, under-butler, footman, chef, housekeeper, kitchen maid, dresser, chauffeur. But at the drop of a hat the newly-weds were able to nip down to Tony's old digs by the Thames, Tony in his black leathers on his Norton, Margaret, anonymous in her crash helmet, riding pillion. Once in Rotherhithe they could play at being a groovy young couple, smoking (Gauloises for Tony, Chesterfields for M) and frying sausages and drinking and having a high old time. 'They were both very sweet and obviously very happy', Noël Coward observed in June 1961, having kicked off his evening at Kensington Palace and finished it in Rotherhithe, tossing empty Cointreau bottles into the Thames with gay abandon.

Glamour feeds off glamour. Margaret's new friend, the writer and journalist Angela Huth, asked them for dinner. 'Happily, it worked. George Melly sang, Edna O'Brien and Shirley MacLaine entered into

some profound, inextricable conversation; there were a couple of Rolling Stones, the barefoot Sandie Shaw and many others. She danced non-stop and stayed till dawn.' Thus, the Snowdons leapt head-first into the sixties, mixing with others of the jet set, sipping their Napoleon brandy, living in a fancy apartment, knowing the Aga Khan, na, na-na-na, na-na-na, na-na-na-na-na-na-na.

Her style changed, to keep up with the times: shorter skirts, hair-pieces, pale lipstick, heavy eye make-up. In 1962 the Earl of Snowdon (as he became in October 1961) took a black-and-white photograph of her in the bath, with diamonds and pearls in her hair, naked but for the Poltimore Tiara balanced on her beehive hairdo. The playful combin-ation of formality and informality, regality and nudity, pomp and sex, clearly suited her. Never again in a photograph was she to look so happy or at ease. Out of sight is the glass case containing the collection of exotic seashells which she polished whenever she found herself at a loose end. But in the corner of the photograph Snowdon can be spotted in the bathroom mirror, like an apparition, sitting bare-legged, the camera to his eye. At the beginning of the year he had been appointed artistic adviser to the bright new *Sunday Times* magazine, a contract that gave him £5,000 a year, with an extra £500 in expenses for each feature he organised; he earned a further £5,000 a year from his work for magazines like *Vogue*.

For that brief period, the two embodied the sixties dream: modern, go-ahead, and above all with-it. To complete the perfect picture, they were even in touch with the Beatles.

48

On 4 November 1963, the Beatles appeared in the Royal Variety Performance at the Prince of Wales theatre, watched by HM the Queen Mother and HRH Princess Margaret. A mixed bag of entertainers included Flanders and Swann, Steptoe and Son, Max Bygraves, Marlene Dietrich (singing 'Where Have All the Flowers Gone?' and 'Lili Marlene'), Charlie Drake and Pinky and Perky. Though the Beatles appeared seventh on the nineteen-act bill, they were the centre of attention.

They kicked off their set with 'From Me to You', and went on to play 'She Loves You' and 'Till There Was You'. At this point, John Lennon said, 'For our last number, I'd like to ask your help. The people in the cheaper seats clap your hands. And the rest of you, if you'd just rattle your jewellery. We'd like to sing a song called "Twist and Shout".'

Backstage, they met Marlene Dietrich, with whom Ringo Starr was particularly taken. 'I remember staring at her legs – which were great – as she slouched against a chair. I'm a leg-man: "Look at those pins!"'

Afterwards they were presented to the Queen Mother and Princess Margaret. 'Where are you playing tomorrow night?' asked the Queen Mother.

'Slough,' replied John.

'Oh, that's just near us.'

They were never to appear in another Royal Variety Show. John Lennon recalled: 'We were asked discreetly to do it every year after

that, but we always said, "Stuff it." So every year there was a story in the newspapers: "Why no Beatles for the Queen?" which was pretty funny, because they didn't know we'd refused. That show's a bad gig, anyway. Everybody's very nervous and uptight and nobody performs well. The time we did do it, I cracked a joke onstage. I was fantastically nervous, but I wanted to say something to rebel a bit, and that was the best I could do.'

The following year, the Beatles went on a world tour on a scale unprecedented in terms of both mileage and popularity. In America alone they played thirty concerts in twenty-four cities in the space of thirty-two days, covering 22,441 miles. In Holland, 100,000 people lined the streets to see their car whizzing past. In Adelaide, their journey from the airport to their hotel was witnessed by 300,000 people, far more than had ever been recorded for a royal tour.

On 6 July 1964 they returned to Britain for the Royal Premiere of their first film, *A Hard Day's Night*, at the London Pavilion, Leicester Square. The guests of honour were Princess Margaret and the Earl of

Snowdon, whom Lennon had renamed 'Priceless Margarine and Bony Armstrove' in his recent book of poems and sketches, *In His Own Write*.

Lennon's wife Cynthia was 'determined to look gorgeous', so spent days looking for the right clothes to wear. She finally found a full-length sleeveless dress in black and beige silk at Fenwick's, which was, she declared, 'one of London's classiest department stores'. She teamed it with a Mary Quant black chiffon coat, bordered with exotic black feathers. Fenwick's had agreed to shorten the dress, and to have it delivered in time for the premiere. But that morning it still hadn't arrived, and she had begun to panic. Her mother rushed out to collect it for her, returning with barely half an hour to spare.

Cynthia asked John if she should wear her hair up or down. 'Let's have a change – give us a bit of Brigitte and wear it up this time,' said John, who at that time measured all women against Brigitte Bardot. 'And don't wear your specs. You look great without them. Don't worry, I'll guide you.' With a black velvet bow in her hair, Cynthia set off for the premiere 'feeling like a princess'.

The Beatles brought traffic to a standstill in the centre of London, with 12,000 youngsters struggling to catch a glimpse of them. Passing through streets lined with cheering fans held back by rows of police, John looked out of the window of their chauffeur-driven car and wondered, in all innocence, what was going on. 'Hey, fellers, what's happening? Why are all these people around? What's on, a cup final or something?'

The band's manager Brian Epstein told him that they were actually waiting to see the Beatles. Cynthia noticed John's genuine surprise. 'Despite the screaming crowds he'd been confronted with over the past nine months, he still wasn't prepared for them.'

Stepping out onto the red carpet, with flashbulbs popping, Cynthia found herself smiling and laughing 'with unadulterated happiness'. Only a year ago, she reflected, she had been living at John's Aunt Mimi's house, hidden from the world, managing on a pittance.

After the screening, the Beatles were presented to Princess Margaret. Cynthia spotted John blushing. 'When it came to meeting royalty in the flesh, John was as much in awe as the rest of us. He was so pleased and proud that the Princess had come to see the film that his anti-establishment views flew out of the window and he stood red-faced as she spoke to him.'

Cynthia felt that though Princess Margaret was fascinated by the four Beatles, she showed a conspicuous lack of interest in their entourage, including Cynthia herself. In turn, Cynthia found the Princess's questions 'clipped and superficial', citing one as particularly dreary: 'How are you coping with all the adulation?' At one point, John attempted to draw Cynthia into their conversation: 'Ma'am, this is my wife, Cynthia.' But the Princess offered her only the most cursory glance. 'Oh, how nice,' she said, before returning her attention to John.

After the premiere, there was a party at the Dorchester Hotel. Princess Margaret and Lord Snowdon arrived with a few friends. They were clearly enjoying themselves, and seemed set for the long haul. The twenty-one-year-old George Harrison began to feel peckish, so he approached the film's producer, Walter Shenson, asking, 'When are we going to eat?'

Shenson explained the protocol: no one could eat until the Princess had departed. Harrison waited patiently, but after a further fifteen minutes he couldn't take it any more. He went up to the Princess and said the words that so many people, before and after, dreamed of saying: 'Your Highness, we really are hungry and we can't eat until you two go.'

'I see,' said the Princess obediently. 'Well, in that case, we'd better run.'

Six months later, the Beatles were interviewed by *Playboy* magazine in America. 'Is there any celebrity you would like to meet?' asked the interviewer.

'I wouldn't mind meeting Adolf Hitler,' replied Paul.

'Would you like to meet Princess Margaret?'

'We have.'

'How do you like her?'

'OK.'

The Beatles' second film, *Help!*, was premiered a year later, on 29 July 1965, once again at the London Pavilion. Once again it was attended by Princess Margaret and Lord Snowdon, who had delayed their summer holiday just to be there.

John Lennon invited his Aunt Mimi. No slave to the sixties, she failed to enjoy it. 'So you liked "*Help!*"? Well I didn't, although the Colour was very good,' she wrote to a young Beatles fan, Jane Wirgman. 'I went to the Premiere & it was like a mad house at the Show. I Sat immediately behind P. Margaret & when the Beatles came in I was panic Stricken, almost anyway. The girls in top balcony yelled & leaned over the edge & only for an attendant – one of them was nearly over.'

Aunt Mimi was struck by the number of stars of stage and screen in the audience, '& Some of the most outlandish dresses and hair dos – all there to be Seen, not to See the film. It was for Charity. So did good.'

Afterwards, both Princess Margaret and Aunt Mimi went to the after-party at the Dorchester. They made no further contact, but Aunt Mimi was not bothered. 'John was in great form & our table was in an uproar and Jane Asher* is really a delightful girl.'

On Tuesday, 4 March 1969, Margaret spent six hours at Twickenham Film Studios watching Ringo Starr and Peter Sellers shooting *The Magic Christian*. Described by its producers as 'an essentially genial indictment of capitalist society', the film was really just a hotchpotch of famous actors doing unexpected things: Richard Attenborough as a rowing coach; Raquel Welch whipping female galley slaves; Peter Sellers as Sir Guy Grand, the richest man in the world; John Cleese as

---

* Paul's actress girlfriend at the time.

the director of Sotheby's; Wilfrid Hyde-White as an alcoholic captain; Laurence Harvey performing a striptease while reciting Hamlet's 'To be or not to be'; and Yul Brynner in drag singing Noël Coward's 'Mad About the Boy' to Roman Polanski. Margaret spent a lot of time chatting with Paul McCartney, who happened to be visiting the set too.

Just over a week later, on the morning of Wednesday, 12 March,* Pattie Boyd, the wife of George Harrison, drove to London from their bungalow in Esher to pick up a dress from the showroom of Ozzie Clark. George and Pattie were due to attend a party on the theme of 'Pisces' thrown by the artist/singer Rory McEwen in Chelsea that evening. She was keen to look her best; after all, Princess Margaret and Lord Snowdon were due.

Coming out of the shop with her new dress, she noticed that, in her absence, someone had placed a packet of Rothmans cigarettes on the dashboard of her car. Inside the packet was a small lump of hashish, a phone number, a man's name and the message 'Phone Me'. Pattie placed the cigarette packet in her handbag and set off back to Esher. Once home, she had a bath, and was drying herself when the doorbell rang.

At the door was Detective Sergeant Norman Pilcher of the Drugs Squad, along with eight other policemen and a police dog called Yogi, specially trained to sniff for drugs. Another half-dozen policemen then arrived through the back door, and there were even more in the greenhouse.

'We're looking for dangerous drugs,' explained Det Sgt Pilcher.

'I'm terribly sorry but we don't have any,' replied Pattie, a former convent-school girl.

The police search uncovered the hashish in her handbag. Though she told Det Sgt Pilcher how it came to be there, he was unconvinced. She telephoned her husband at the Beatles' Apple office at 3 Savile Row. 'Guess what?' she said. 'It's a bust.'

---

* The same day, incidentally, on which Paul McCartney married Linda Eastman.

George was sceptical, so she handed the phone over to Det Sgt Pilcher, whose commanding tones quickly convinced George that she was not pulling his leg. He immediately set off for Esher, together with a lawyer and the Beatles' press officer, Derek Taylor.

As they waited for them to arrive, Pattie asked Det Sgt Pilcher what he hoped to achieve from the raid. 'To save you from the perils of heroin,' came the reply. Another policeman entered the room with a small brick of hashish, weighing 570 grams, which he claimed Yogi had just sniffed out in a bedroom cupboard, hidden in one of George's shoes.

'You're lying,' said Pattie. 'If we had that much hash we certainly wouldn't hide it in one of George's shoes. And if you're looking for grass, we keep it in the sitting room, on a table in a cigarette box.'

The atmosphere had grown a little tense, so they all had a cup of tea. One of the policemen asked if they could switch on the television. Pattie agreed. While some watched, others made a stab at conversation.

One of them asked, 'Have the Beatles been doing any new music lately?'

'Yes,' snapped Pattie. 'But you're not going to hear it.'

The mood remained sticky until the arrival of George. 'The police were obviously excited to meet him,' recalled Pattie. 'They stood to attention and were almost elbowing each other out of the way to get closer to him.' Looking at the assembled officers, George, the most spiritually-minded of the Beatles, calmly observed, 'Birds have nests and animals have holes, but the son of man hath nowhere to lay his head.'

'Oh, really, sir?' replied Det Sgt Pilcher. 'Sorry to tell you I am arresting you …'

Pattie and George were escorted to Esher police station, where they were questioned and fingerprinted, before being formally charged and released on bail. 'We got home feeling gloomy,' recalled Pattie. 'So George said, "Come on, let's go to the party."'

On their arrival in Chelsea, they found Princess Margaret and Lord Snowdon already there. The Harrisons joined their group. 'Hey, you can't believe what happened,' George said. 'We got busted.'

'What a shame!' said Princess Margaret.

'Can you help us?' said George. 'Can you use your influence?'

'Oh, I don't think so!' said Princess Margaret, with a look of horror.

At that moment, Pattie's younger sister Paula came over, removed a joint from her purse, and lit it. 'I couldn't believe it, it was the early evening of the same day that we'd just been busted and there was my sister trying to hand Princess Margaret a joint!'

Everyone looked daggers at Paula. Failing to read the signs, she dutifully passed the joint to Princess Margaret. 'Here, do you want this?'

Margaret immediately turned on her heel and left the party, taking Lord Snowdon with her. Between them, the Harrisons had thus been responsible for curtailing two of the Princess's appearances in the space of five years.

At the end of the year, on 11 December 1969, the Princess encountered the Beatles for one last time when she attended the premiere of *The Magic Christian* at the Odeon, Kensington. Unfortunately, her arrival was upstaged by John Lennon and Yoko Ono emerging from a white Rolls-Royce, bearing a banner saying 'Britain Murdered Hanratty'.

49

The most sixties of the Snowdon inner circle was Peter Sellers, the comic actor whose extraordinary talent for mimicry seemed to have invaded his body, depriving him of a fixed accent, or even a fixed character. This allowed him to be whoever he wished to be, but with no way home. Himself something of a chameleon, Snowdon was mesmerised by Sellers, and in turn Sellers was, in the words of the screenwriter Wolf Mankowitz, 'completely obsessed with royalty. He was always going on about Princess Margaret. His biggest thrill was to present people to her.'

In February 1964 Sellers brought his young fiancée, the blonde Swedish actress Britt Ekland, to meet Tony and Margaret. On their way to Kensington Palace he drilled her in the correct way to address the Queen's younger sister: 'Your Royal Highness' on first being presented, and 'Ma'am' thereafter. A preliminary curtsey was mandatory.

As things turned out, Her Royal Highness was as relaxed as could be. The four sat down to what Ekland described as a 'quite informal' lunch: consommé, roast beef, red wine. Over the brandy, Snowdon put it to Ekland that she might just possibly like to pose for what he described as 'glamour pictures'.

'What a good idea!' exclaimed Princess Margaret, at her most easy-going. 'He's actually quite good, Britt, if he remembers to put film in the camera!' Ekland took this remark as an affectionate tease. But did it also hint at Snowdon's lasciviousness?

If so, Margaret was happy to aid and abet him. 'The Princess showed me to her first-floor bedroom to change,' recalled Ekland. 'They each had their own separate bedrooms and bathrooms, and Tony came through and tossed me one of his shirts. I was in a tweed costume and once the royal couple had gone I slipped off my jacket and blouse and bra and exchanged it for the shirt.'

Meanwhile, Sellers and Snowdon were hunting out suitable places for their forthcoming shoot. They settled on the wide hallway, and opened the front door to let in a blaze of sunlight. This ensured that the silhouette of Ekland's breasts would be clearly visible through the shirt.

The session went like a dream, and from that point on, according to Ekland, 'we became close friends of the Royal couple'. Peter and Britt and Tony and Margaret: theirs was a very sixties friendship, a symbol of fame's sudden new supremacy in the British class system. Of her two new friends, Britt found Tony the easier; he was always 'well-meaning, friendly and considerate', whereas Margaret 'wasn't any less friendly but I think we were always conscious of her position and sometimes she was to impose that if anyone upset her'.

It wasn't long before Sellers was taken up as court jester to the wider royal court. Shortly after their marriage, he and Ekland were invited to Windsor Castle for a shooting party. On receiving the invitation, Sellers ordered himself a £1,200 shotgun from James Purdey & Sons, plus a shooting jacket, breeches and boots, with a deerstalker hat to complete the picture. The couple soon became regulars at Windsor: Prince Charles, in particular, was a starry-eyed fan of the Goons, and to this day is known to bring fixed smiles to the faces of weekend guests with his unstoppable medley of Goon impersonations.

'We were now very much part of the royal social whirl; hardly a week went by without contact somewhere,' Britt Ekland remembered years later. On one occasion, everyone played charades after tea at Windsor Castle. 'By now I was so beetroot that in portraying a "lobster" in the game Prince Philip had no difficulty in guessing my disguise, while Sellers warmed to the occasion throwing in Goon-like animations to confuse everyone.'

Weekending with mutual friends in Kent, Peter Sellers created a short film in which Princess Margaret impersonated Queen Victoria and Lord Snowdon a one-legged golfer. Sellers himself resurrected his 'Goodness Gracious Me' Indian doctor, and Ekland played an old-fashioned Hollywood vamp. At one point in the film, Sellers announces that he is about to perform his famous quick change impersonation of Princess Margaret. He then nips behind a screen, and hurls his shirt, jacket and trousers over the top of it; a split-second later, Princess Margaret emerges as if by magic, blowing theatrical kisses to camera. The film ends with the assembled company linking arms to sing 'We're Riding Along on the Crest of a Wave' from *The Gang Show*.

Sellers spent £6,000 – £80,000 or so in today's money – editing the film and adding a musical score. He then gave it to the Queen for her thirty-ninth birthday, after going with a group comprised of the Queen and Prince Philip, Prince Charles, Princess Anne, Sellers and Ekland to see Spike Milligan starring in *Son of Oblomov*.

The friendship between the two couples blossomed at roughly the same pace as their marriages deteriorated. In June 1966, Cecil Beaton was agog to hear all the latest gossip from his new butler, Ray Gurton, who had previously been employed by Sellers. 'He was paid £25 a week but never had a moment off as even when in one of his many cars Sellers would telephone to Ray: "Go up to nanny and tell her she's sacked. She's a cow." At three in the morning: "We're on our way home. We're passing through Berkeley Square now. See that hot soup is ready for us in seven minutes."

'He has become accustomed to the promiscuous sex, the violent rows, the hysteria and the bad manners, and he finds our household slightly dull in comparison. Nevertheless there are moments. But he tells Eileen of the Sellerses and the Snowdons, and he does not think much of either party. Once Sellers was having lighting for some sculpture installed in the garden and asked Tony's advice which he was giving when Margaret, sucking at a long cigarette holder, sidled up and asked, "Don't you think it would be better if –" to which Tony answered her by telling her to piss off.'

As her marriage fell apart, Britt Ekland grew nauseated by the vast sums her husband spent on sucking up to the Snowdons. Peter would supply Tony with any number of photographic lenses, cameras and flash-guns, and let him have his customised silver-blue open-topped Aston Martin for the knockdown price of £3,000. 'I would squirm with embarrassment at the demeaning lengths he would stoop to in order to ingratiate himself with the Royal Family. It was contemptible.'

Sellers welcomed the Princess onto the set of the zany James Bond spoof film *Casino Royale*, not least because it offered a chance to get even with his old enemy Orson Welles. 'The fact that Princess Margaret was stopping by every day at my house was unknown to Sellers,' said Welles. 'One day she came to the set to have lunch with Peter, or so he claimed. He couldn't wait to tell the cast and crew who he was dining with. Then she walked past him and said, "Hello, Orson, I haven't seen you for days!" That was the real end. That's when we couldn't speak lines to each other. "Orson, I haven't seen you for days!" absolutely killed him. He went white as a sheet, because *he* was going to present *me*!"'

By 1968 both marriages were in a state of collapse. Sellers' principal object of desire was no longer Britt, but Margaret. Around this time, his personal clairvoyant, Maurice Woodruff, expressed his concerns to the comic actor Harry H. Corbett, best known as the junior rag-and-bone merchant in *Steptoe and Son*. 'Peter is getting himself all in a twist over Princess Margaret,' said Woodruff. 'He keeps hinting that he's on the brink of a big affair with the Princess and wants me to give it my blessing … I know he wants me to be more positive but I'm damned if I'm going to encourage him. I can't see it and I'm not going to make something up just to keep him happy.'

Corbett gave the matter consideration. 'Well, you can't knock the bloke's taste. She's a gorgeous piece of stuff, you've got to admit.'

Sellers refused to take his clairvoyant's advice.* A few weeks later Woodruff reported: 'Peter has come right out in the open and admitted he is in love with the Princess. It is very worrying. He says he is splitting with Britt and has started an affair with Margaret. If so, then it can only end badly.'

Shortly after the divorce of Peter Sellers and Britt Ekland in December 1968,† Sellers was looking around for a suitable Christmas present for the Snowdon children. His eyes lit on Buttercup, a pony belonging to Victoria, his three-year-old daughter by Britt. Later the same day, Buttercup was delivered in a horsebox to Kensington Palace. Victoria never saw her again. She was heartbroken. 'She loved Buttercup beyond anything else,' recalled Britt.

By early 1969, Sellers couldn't stop boasting to friends that he was having an affair with Princess Margaret. She had greeted him at Kensington Palace in a very low-cut dress, and things had gone on from there – or so he claimed.

In the spring he escorted her to Ronnie Scott's club in Soho. Scott read a poem to the audience, specially written by Spike Milligan: 'Wherever you are, wherever you be, please take your hand off the Princess's knee.' The *Daily Mirror* cited this as proof of an affair, but Sellers issued a public denial. 'We are just good friends. You mustn't read anything else into it.' Some suspected that this was simply another way to draw attention to the rumour. He told friends and acquaintances that he was in love with her, and that he wanted all her love letters to be buried with him. These letters have never been discovered. Was it all another of his fantasies?

One night, Sellers employed his uncanny skills as a mimic to phone Princess Margaret in the guise of Lord Snowdon, telling her the ins and

* If he ever gave it: Woodruff had a reputation for telling his clients what they wanted to hear.

† 'He bit off more than he could screw,' was apparently Snowdon's comment. On a single night in April 1964, Sellers suffered eight heart attacks in three hours, having taken too much amyl nitrite before sex with Ekland. The response of the film director Billy Wilder was brusque and to the point: 'You have to have a heart before you can have a heart attack.'

outs of his affair with Lady Jackie Rufus-Isaacs. Halfway through, he sensed a *froideur* on the other end of the phone, and realised he had taken the joke too far. Typically of Sellers, what had started as a giggle had fast descended into torture. Not knowing how to undo the Princess's distress, he ended the conversation without revealing his true identity.*

Fuelled by marijuana, he told his friend Laurence Harvey of the ill-judged telephone conversation. He was worried that the Princess had by now twigged that it had been him all along. Would their relationship ever recover? He loved her, he said. 'The whole thing is, you see, she has the same size breasts as Sophia Loren. The same cup size exactly.'†

Harvey attempted to reassure him. 'In my experience, actresses and princesses have the most dreadful memories for trivia,' he said.

Princess Margaret finally dropped Sellers after teaming up with Roddy Llewellyn. By that time Sellers had already married and divorced a third wife, Miranda Quarry, and had become too volatile to remain an acceptable royal escort; in the middle of a row with Quarry over the correct way to pass the port, he had let off steam by releasing all her pet birds from their cages and hitting them around the room with a tennis racquet.

---

* Sellers was always more at home being someone else. Due to appear on the Michael Parkinson chat show in 1974, he withdrew at the last moment, saying, 'I can't walk on just as myself.' After a brief negotiation, it was agreed that he could assume a role. He eventually walked on dressed up as a member of the Gestapo.

† 34C, at least in the case of Sophia Loren; no official announcement was ever issued concerning Princess Margaret's cup size.

50

As we have seen, Princess Margaret was drawn to the world of well-heeled bohemia: writers and musicians and actors and other fast-living artistic types who could nevertheless be relied upon to show a fair measure of deference. She liked the louche hours they kept, their smoking and drinking, their refusal to take responsibility or to do the right thing. In this she differed from her sister, who, given the choice, would make a beeline for trusty fresh-air types, in their wellingtons and their Land Rovers; sensible, unflashy men and women who would never let one down or poke fun at one behind one's back, people in whose company one always knew where one stood.

From their point of view, the bohemians enjoyed the cachet – ironic, satirical, tongue-in-cheek, but cachet nonetheless – of having a royal on display, a real-life Princess to lend a bit of pageantry to things. It didn't really matter that she could be difficult. In a way, it was her party piece. If she happened to round off an evening with a display of her famous *hauteur*, then so much the better.

As for Margaret, she never quite understood the stuff and nonsense to which she found herself drawn – or perhaps she understood the stuff, but not the nonsense. 'What is a *bohemian*? What does it *mean*?' she once asked a lady-in-waiting, in all innocence. 'Well, Ma'am,' came the reply, 'with Tony it means he won't always turn up to lunch when he says he will.' Bohemians were, as she never quite appreciated, not entirely to be trusted: the moment you left the room they would start making their silly little remarks, and on returning home they were prone to penning catty little observations about you in their diaries.

Her introduction to *la vie bohème* coincided with the first reference to her in a literary diary as 'the Royal Dwarf'. The author was the *femme fatale* Barbara Skelton; the entry was for 2 December 1951, when Princess Margaret was twenty-one.

That evening, Skelton and her first husband, the eminent man of letters Cyril Connolly, had been invited to a Tennessee Williams play, followed by a large party thrown by Lord and Lady Rothermere, at which, they had been promised, Cyril would be placed next to Princess Margaret. Cyril was almost giddy with anticipation, but Barbara remained defiantly unimpressed. 'He had spent his day in preparation having nose-trims, haircuts and all his ear whiskers removed,' she confided sniffily to her diary.

On their arrival at the Rothermeres', the fractious couple were ushered into a drawing room, and then downstairs, where there was a parting of the ways, with some guests allowed into the dining room, and others cordoned off into a sort of holding area for the also-rans. Barbara made for the dining room, but 'on reaching the room where the supper tables were laid, I have the folding doors shut in my face by a swarm of butlers. Find myself in an adjoining room which has been turned into a bar where about four well-heeled couples have gathered and are quietly sipping champagne. They look at me, as much as to say, we got it too, but we're pretending to like it in here.'

A waiter offered her a bowl of soup. At that moment, Barbara spotted Cyril at the far end of the hall, 'trying not to catch my eye'. Never one to nod things through, she rushed up to him and screamed, 'It's no good turning your back on me.' But Cyril was already 'being hustled away to the Royal Dwarf's table by Diana Cooper'. With that, 'he disappears through the magic doors and from the throwouts' foyer I see him eating a hearty supper and beaming across at the Royal Dwarf'.

Skelton stood fuming in the corner. She had clearly had a bit to drink. The way she remembered it, everyone was doing their level best to avoid her. The up-and-coming painter Lucian Freud came in and followed suit, but she was determined, and 'pushing my way through the huddle of throwouts', attempted to engage him in conversation. Suddenly, Lady Rothermere, from her chair at the royal table, spotted his dilemma, and beckoned frantically. '"There's a place for another GENTLEMAN here," she shouted, and came over to drag him away.'

Stuck in her *salon des refusés* with no one to talk to, Skelton sat down with a glass and said out loud, to no one in particular, 'There's only one thing to do. Get drunk.' She then pinioned Renée Fedden, wife of the diplomat and author Robin Fedden, and talked at her for a solid hour, after which, 'with a look of desperation', Mrs Fedden seized the opportunity to ask a man for a taxi fare before beetling off. Skelton asked this benefactor what on earth was the matter with her. 'She doesn't like you, my dear,' he explained.

At last, the smart dinner in the other room came to an end, and 'Cyril reappears well-supped and beaming, followed by the rest of the privileged suppers. They all emerge with a healthy tan, the acclaimed heroes of a Shackleton expedition, and mingle with the throwouts.'

Skelton judged that this was the perfect time to tell Cyril exactly what she thought of him, 'but we are interrupted by Orson Welles, so I try to be offensive to him but he doesn't notice.'

Sensing trouble, Connolly told Skelton that he was going home, and left. Making no bones about her drunkenness, Skelton was beginning to draw comment even from those paid not to notice such things: as a waiter passed by, she overheard him mutter, 'Fill her up.' Undeterred, she dragged her friend Mark Culme-Seymour upstairs for a quick dance, but within seconds of launching themselves on the dance floor, they were interrupted by 'a fearful crash'. Looking over her shoulder, she noticed an enormous vase in pieces on the floor. Though her dance partner said he didn't think it was their fault, she nevertheless decided that now was a good time to leave for home, until it dawned on her that she had no money for a taxi.

What Connolly never seems to have confessed to Barbara Skelton is that his own encounter with the young Princess that evening left much to be desired. The truth was to emerge twenty-three years later, following Connolly's death. In an obituary of his old friend for the *TLS*, Stephen Spender recalled asking him what had happened on the night in question:

> He said (as I noted in my diary): 'When we were introduced I expected she would say: "What, THE Cyril Connolly!" Instead of which she didn't even look at me, but hurried by, followed by a Lady-in-Waiting saying: "Temper! Temper!"'

51

Social historians may point to Skelton's 1951 diary entry as the first reference to Princess Margaret as a Royal Dwarf, but it was certainly not to be the last. In future, her height was often invoked by those who wished to scorn her, but as the years rolled by, it was joined by other weapons in their armoury.

'Fat, ugly, dwarflike, lecherous and revoltingly tastelessly behaved Princess Margaret', the maverick Tory MP Alan Clark wrote in his diary on Thursday, 10 June 1982. In a letter to Maya Angelou on 30 April 1992, Jessica Mitford remarked on 'Princess Margaret, & smallness of her: Nancy used to call her the Royal Dwarf'. Writing to the actor Denis Goacher on 14 December 1975, the comic actor Kenneth Williams mentioned that 'I saw Gordon Jackson in the canteen. He said he had been lunching with the Queen the day before. When he congratulated Princess Margaret on Snowdon's documentary about midgets – "The Little People" – she replied "not my cup of tea at all. Bit too near home I'm afraid" and he said "I suddenly realised, they're all TINY! The Queen, and Margaret, and the mum …!"'

Chatting to Snowdon in June 1980, James Lees-Milne noted in his diary, 'How small he is, almost a dwarf …' To Auberon Waugh, the Snowdons were 'the two highest paid performing dwarves in Europe'.

Nor was her sister spared. After Ted Hughes received the Queen's Gold Medal for Poetry from the Queen, he mentioned his alarm at her height to his editor and fellow poet Craig Raine. '"You know she's small," he said, shaking his head, "but you don't know how small. She's this big." He measured an inch between his finger and thumb. "It's like meeting Alice in Wonderland.'"

52

In August 1967, Cyril Connolly was given a second chance to impress the Princess, having been invited to a house party on Sardinia by Ann Charteris, who in a previous incarnation had been Lady Rothermere, but after a divorce, a marriage and a death was now Ann Fleming, the wealthy widow of Ian Fleming, the creator of James Bond.

Ann Fleming described the comings and goings in a letter to the Duchess of Devonshire. Roy Jenkins had left a few days before, his departure followed by 'a temporary lull shattered by the arrival of M. Bowra and further shattered by C. Connolly'.

Connolly, it emerged, had been distracted by the presence in the sea below of 'a flotilla anchored below our windows, the Snowdons and the Aga',* a spectacle which was, observed Fleming, 'better than the Derby through the field glasses'. Knowing that Princess Margaret was so near, Connolly found himself unable to relax. 'Cyril made fearfully restless by vicinity of Snowdons, saying not to meet them was like being in Garden of Eden without seeing God!'

A man she described as a 'local tycoon', but failed to name, then phoned to invite Ann Fleming, and Ann Fleming alone, to dine with 'Margaret and Tony', as he breezily called them. When she told Cyril of her destination, he was 'distraught' at the idea of missing out, so

---

* Not the costly cast-iron cooker, but His Royal Highness the Aga Khan.

she kindly engineered an invitation for him, and for Maurice Bowra too.

This dinner proved a huge success. As she was leaving, Princess Margaret happened to mention that she and Tony had no plans for the next day. Ann Fleming noticed that this sent the tycoon into a state of apoplexy, as 'the poor brute was lunching with me', but she niftily solved the problem by inviting the Snowdons along too. 'Cyril beams,' she reported.

> Next morning Cyril rises at 11.30 and asks what I have ordered special for lunch, I say nothing since I can only communicate with Italians in deaf and dumb language.
>
> He scowls, and says did I notice what the Princess drank last night, I say no, he says it was white wine and martinis and may he go to hotel for the right stuff. I say yes, and have to pay enormous bill. Illustrious guests arrive, and since it is buffet I am the parlour maid; they stay till 3.30 and ask if they may return at 6.30 to record Maurice singing 1914 songs, I go to bed, they return at 5.30 from the sea and walk straight into my bedroom while I am struggling into skirt, then they have acrimonious discussion because she does not want to be alone while he water skis, finally he departs and we all talk daintily, then repair to her hotel swimming pool.

Princess Margaret was, she continued, 'marooned by the Aga who is gone to collect a new yacht'.

From the side of the pool, Bowra and Fleming watched Lord Snowdon water-skiing in the distance, and 'best of all princess and Cyril in pool, Cyril looking like a blissful hippo!'

But once out of the pool, Connolly continued to disturb the equilibrium: 'It would be OK without Cyril who complains of mosquitoes, food and climate, and only wants royalty and money; now he has met the Snowdons he dreams of being invited on the Aga's yacht saying wistfully, "but if I was, I might be expected to act charades on water skis"!'

For Maurice Bowra, the Sardinian jaunt proved most unsatisfactory. His final verdict on Princess Margaret was unequivocal. She was, he said, 'a tremendous blood-sucker, and, like her sister, a bit of a sour puss'. Contemplating the advance of old age, he consoled himself with a list of things he need never do again: 'Sardinia heads the list. Royalty comes jolly nearly as high.' To Noel Annan, he even complained that the Princess had given him mumps.

As for Sardinia, he thought it 'a horrible place. Very ugly. No mountains, no olive trees, no cypresses, but lumps of rock and scrub. On this is planted a top bogus town, which would just do as the stage setting for *Carmen* in Costa Rica.' It was populated, he complained, by 'the English rich – Princess Margaret, American queens, lots of Austrians with Australian passports, Roman duchesses complaining about the disappearance of the British Empire. Not again.'

The 'American queens' to whom he referred were, it transpires, the caustic novelist and essayist Gore Vidal and his boyfriend Howard Austen, who happened to be staying next door with Diana Phipps.

All in all, Vidal didn't enjoy his time there either, describing it as 'a terrible place, made worse by the quarrelling Snowdons'. In a nightclub on her birthday, the Princess and Snowdon had what Vidal described as 'a splendid row ... they're both nice separately but together hell'. Snowdon had spent his time pursuing his old hobby of flicking lit cigarettes at his wife, before going off to dance with Diana Phipps, leaving Margaret with Vidal.

'Margaret said, "Let's dance." I said, "I don't dance."'

The next day their paths crossed again, over lunch with Ann Fleming, who Vidal felt was 'a witty, rather nasty woman'.

Princess Margaret said, 'I want to apologize to you for our behaviour last night. It was intolerable and I've been trying to write a letter of apology all day. Thank God we met at lunch and I can say it.' Vidal accepted her apology. 'She's well brought up,' he concluded. Shortly afterwards, reading the diaries of the duc de Saint-Simon, it occurred to him that 'only the French master of social cynicism could have done the royal bickering justice'.

53

At the start of the following year, 1968, the Tynans, Ken and Kathleen, threw a dinner party for eight at their house in Thurloe Square, SW7. The other guests were Princess Margaret and Lord Snowdon, Harold Pinter and his wife Vivien Merchant, and Peter Cook and his wife Wendy Snowden.

The evening got off to a shaky start when Kenneth Tynan attempted to present Vivien Merchant to Princess Margaret. Keen to parade her anti-Establishment credentials, Merchant simply carried on talking to Peter Cook. 'I put out my hand, which was refused, so I sort of drew it up as if it were meant for another direction,' Princess Margaret told her biographer.

And so to dinner, where Merchant, still in an uncooperative mood, found that she had been placed next to Lord Snowdon, who had recently photographed her playing Lady Macbeth at Stratford. 'Of course, the only reason we *artistes* let you take our pictures is because you are married to *her*!' she said, stabbing her finger in the direction of Princess Margaret. 'Hereabouts,' recalled Kenneth Tynan, 'Harold began to drink steadily. Indeed, everyone did. Princess M. was awkwardly unruffled, but every word had registered on that watchful little psyche.'

After dinner they all sat down to watch some blue movies, in line with Tynan's desire to be at the helm of the permissive society. Prior to the showing, he had taken the trouble to warn Snowdon that 'some pretty blue material' awaited them. 'It would be good for M,' Snowdon replied, graciously.

The first few films were English, and comparatively mild. 'The English bits were amateurish and charming, with odd flashes of nipple and pubic bush, and the American stuff with fish-eye lens and zoom was so technically self-conscious that the occasional bits of explicit sex passed almost unnoticed – e.g. a fast zoom along an erect prick looked like a flash zoom up a factory chimney,' Tynan wrote in his diary. 'But when the Genet started the atmosphere began to freeze.'

The Jean Genet film was *Un chant d'amour* (1950), set in a French prison and featuring cigarettes and penises in roughly equal proportions. Two years before the dinner party, a court in California had sat through the film twice before concluding that it 'explicitly and vividly revealed acts of masturbation, oral copulation, the infamous crime against nature, voyeurism, nudity, sadism, masochism and sex', and furthermore, that it was 'calculated to promote homosexuality, perversion and morbid sex practices'. The ban was upheld by the US Supreme Court, and the film was still banned in the UK when Princess Margaret and her fellow guests sat down to watch what Tynan described as its 'many quite unmistakeable shots of cocks – cocks limp and stiff, cocks being waved, brandished, massaged or waggled – intercut with lyrical fantasy sequences as the convicts imagine themselves frolicking in vernal undergrowth'.

A barrier had been crossed, and everyone seemed at a loss as to how to get back. Instead, they just stared blankly at the screen, trusting that the moment would pass. On an earlier occasion, Princess Margaret had made, in Kathleen Tynan's words, 'small squeaking noises of disapproval' when forced to endure a film about bullfighting. But now there was nothing but an icy hush. 'Silence became gelid in the room,' recalled Tynan. And then, at last, salvation: 'Suddenly, the inspired Peter Cook came to the rescue ... He supplied a commentary, treating the movie as if it were a long commercial for Cadbury's Milk Flake Chocolate and brilliantly seizing on the similarity between Genet's woodland fantasies and the sylvan capering that inevitably accompanies, on TV, the sale of anything from cigarettes to Rolls-Royces. Within five minutes we were all helplessly rocking with laughter, Princess M. included. It was a performance of genius … I hugged Peter for the funniest improvisations I have ever heard in my life.'

Order having been restored, the guests departed with a spring in their step, though the spring in Harold Pinter's step proved erratic. Having made his farewells, he tumbled all the way downstairs.

54

Throughout her life, Princess Margaret's entrances into bohemia tended to set everyone on edge. Anti-monarchists in particular would react in a strange way to her presence, either becoming more obsequious or more aggressive, or – catastrophically – a rapidly alternating mix of the two. On the way to a gala dinner for the film *My Fair Lady* in January 1965, the Hollywood mogul Jack Warner gave his curvaceous young escort – who had changed her name to 'Lady Scarborough' for the occasion – a rapid tutorial in one of the most basic rules of royal etiquette. 'Don't say shit in front of the Princess,' he said.

In fact, the self-styled Lady Scarborough behaved impeccably in the Princess's presence, while more seasoned members of society failed to catch the right tone. Lady Diana Cooper – never the Princess's greatest fan – pointedly refused to curtsey, then came up later to apologise.

'Oh, but I'm sure you did curtsey,' replied the Princess.

'No – ramrod!'

My Fair Lady's costume designer, Cecil Beaton, looked on aghast as the actress Rachel Roberts, 'a bit tight', tottered up to the Princess and said, more than once, 'I don't know what I call you,' without waiting for a reply. Her husband, Rex Harrison, who played Professor Henry Higgins, that stickler for correct manners, attempted to butt in: 'You call her Ma'am!' but Roberts appeared not to hear, and kept repeating the same question, over and over again. Eventually, both Princess Margaret and Rex Harrison began chanting the same reply – 'You call her Ma'am! You call her Ma'am!' – while Roberts persisted in yelling, 'I don't know what I call you! I don't know what I call you!'

55

As the sixties gave way to the seventies, so respect gave way to rebellion, and the chances of disturbance increased.

The songwriter Leslie Bricusse recalls sitting in a Mayfair restaurant with his wife and the actor Laurence Harvey, Harvey's girlfriend, the model Paulene Stone, and the comedian Dudley Moore.

Across from us, Peter Sellers was having dinner with Princess Margaret, Tony Snowdon, and Bryan and Nanette Forbes. Great hilarity was issuing from both tables, ours the more raucous on account of Dudley's outrageousness. He had perfected the super-slurred drunken voice that he was later to use to Oscar-nominated acclaim in the film *Arthur*, and he was on a deadly Dudley roll that had us convulsed with laughter throughout the meal. The more we laughed, the more outrageous he became. We finished dinner ahead of the others, and went by to say hello as we left. I detected a slight envy that they hadn't been at our table, having the fun we'd been having. Dudley, drunk with success at his surefire humour, was on a high. He just wouldn't give up. He lurched over to their table, playing it drunker than ever, gave Princess Margaret a sweeping courtly bow and slurred, 'G'd evenin' your Royal Highness … I s'pose a blow-job is out of the question?'

In 1977, at a party thrown by Lady Rothermere, Princess Margaret took to the stage to a huge round of applause, seized the microphone, and instructed the band to play a selection of tunes by Cole Porter. She then burst into song, in a voice that was, according to Lady Caroline Blackwood, 'very off-key'.

Egged on by the spirited cheering of the well-behaved, the Princess launched into a raucous version of 'Let's Do It', winking and wiggling her hips. But before long, the sound of jeering and booing could be heard from the back of the ballroom. It emanated from the painter Francis Bacon, who had been brought along, uninvited, by his fellow painter Lucian Freud.

The Princess faltered, then rushed off stage, scarlet-faced, to a phalanx of flustered ladies-in-waiting. Uncertain what to do next, the band stopped playing. 'It was that dreadful man, Francis Bacon,' says a red-faced partygoer. 'He calls himself a painter but he does the most frightful paintings. I just don't understand how a creature like him was allowed to get in. It's really quite disgraceful.'

But Bacon was unrepentant. 'Her singing was really too awful,' he explained years later. 'Someone had to stop her. I don't think people should perform if they can't do it properly.'

56

Born in an age of deference, the Princess was to die in an age of egalitarianism. Attempting to straddle the two, wanting to be treated as both equal and superior, and vacillating, from one moment to the next, between the easy-going and the hoity-toity, her behaviour often led to tears before bedtime.

Writing to Maya Angelou on 30 April 1992, Jessica Mitford, the most radical of the Mitford sisters, recalled one such awkward moment. She and her American husband, Bob Treuhaft, had been invited to dinner at Edna O'Brien's house with 'all sorts of actors, etc.'. After dinner, 'a new crowd came, Gore Vidal & followers, plus Princess M'.

Things got off to a bad start. Why wouldn't they? Jessica was by nature unaccommodating, particularly towards members of the Royal Family. 'I rather loathe the Royals, esp. Princess M', she confessed – or boasted – to Angelou earlier in the same letter.

On entering O'Brien's drawing room, the Princess had 'plunked herself next to me on a small love-seat in the drawing room. "How's Debo?" she asked in her silly little voice ... So I muttered, "I suppose she's all right," edging away'. At this point, Bob joined them. A radical lawyer whose clients included the Black Panthers, he had never shown any inclination to fall in with the manners and customs of the English upper classes.

'Bob comes over, so I say, "This is my husband Bob Treuhaft."

'"Typical English introduction!" says Bob. "What's your name?"'

He clearly didn't know who she was, or if he did, he wasn't saying. This would have discombobulated the Princess.

'Princess M comes over all royal & says, "Decca, please present your husband to me."'

But Jessica was never one to fall in line. '"I can't think why you can't simply SAY your name," says I, so she calls over a sort of Gold Stick character to do it right. "May I present Mr Treuhaft?" Such bosh, when she shows up with the Gore Vidal heavy drinking, heavy drugging set.'

57

The distinguished literary biographer Michael Holroyd found himself sitting next to Princess Margaret at a dinner party. She began by imitating Edna O'Brien's breathy Irish accent. She then launched into what he took to be another impersonation, and he laughed dutifully, even though he couldn't quite identify it. 'If I may say so, Ma'am,' he purred, 'I think that's your funniest yet.' At that point there was a sudden silence: the Princess had been speaking in her own voice.

'What happened then?' Holroyd was asked, when he recounted his *faux pas* to the Princess's biographer, Tim Heald.

'I seem to remember that she spent rather a lot of time talking to the person on her left.'

58

It is 29 May 1984. Princess Margaret is the guest of honour at the Sony Radio Awards at the London Hilton Hotel. Among those lined up to greet her is Boy George, who is at the peak of his fame.

In February he won the Grammy Award for Best New Artist, and together with his group, Culture Club, Brit Awards for Best British Single ('Karma Chameleon') and Best British Group. He has recently been judged the most famous person in Britain by *Tatler* magazine, just above HM the Queen at number two. Princess Margaret's name features nowhere in the top one hundred: the rapid growth in the celebrity population over the previous ten years or so has diminished her own fame, which has been overtaken even within the Royal Family, by, among others, Princess Diana, Princess Michael of Kent, and Prince William, who is just short of his second birthday.

Princess Margaret is wearing a green and white print dress. Towering over her is Boy George, well over six foot, in black sequins under a shocking-pink overcoat. The contrast could not be more extreme, though in their liberal application of make-up – heavy eye-liner, blusher, bright red lipstick – the two have something in common. Nevertheless, they look uneasy.

Princess Margaret dispenses a brief handshake to Boy George before moving on. A few minutes later, she is asked to pose with him for a more formal photograph. 'I don't know who he is,' the Princess is overheard telling an aide. 'But he looks like an over-made-up tart. I don't want to be photographed with him.'

Her remark causes a stir. At first, Boy George appears unbothered. 'It's her royal prerogative if she doesn't want to talk to me,' he tells reporters. 'I'm just a peasant.' Later in the evening he is escorted to the door by the hotel's head of security, having been apprehended in the ladies' toilet.

The following day, a spokesman at Kensington Palace issues a denial that the Princess ever uttered the offending words, implausibly suggesting that she had been referring to his make-up resembling 'commedia dell'arte'.* In response, Boy George grows more combative, saying, 'If I had been rude to her, I would apologise.' Later, a spokesman for Culture Club explains that this did not in fact mean that Boy George was demanding an apology.

Boy George is a garrulous character, unused to turning the other cheek. Asked by a reporter what he thinks of Princess Margaret's supposed snub, he replies, 'I don't think I'm special, but I do object to having been called a tart. It's a damn cheek. I bring more money into this country than she does. Princess Margaret went to school for elocution and I come from the gutter, which just goes to show you can't buy manners.'

Once he gets going, he finds it hard to stop. 'She's not a happy person,' he adds. 'It shows in her face.'

A week later, a new waxwork of Boy George is unveiled in Madame Tussaud's amidst much hoo-ha. Princess Margaret's waxwork, which

---

* The same spokesman, Lord Napier, was also responsible for issuing a denial that Princess Margaret had referred to 'Irish pigs' during a fund-raising tour of the United States in October 1979; she had, he insisted, been talking of Irish jigs. In his *Private Eye* diary, Auberon Waugh, a natural contrarian, noted that, far from causing upset by her remark, 'all over the country people are raising their glasses to toast the Bonnie Princess'. However, this seemed to annoy him. 'For the last fifty-six years,' he wrote, stealthily adding seven years to her age, 'this woman has been flouncing around embarrassing everybody with her rudeness, self-importance and general air of peevish boredom. Now it looks as if everything will be forgiven for the sake of one *bon mot*.'

once occupied pride of place, could be seen tucked in somewhere towards the back on the far right of an extensive Royal Family group, two along from Captain Mark Phillips.

59

Of all her friends in the world of the arts, it was the acerbic Gore Vidal, of all people, who remained most loyal to the Princess. They enjoyed each other's camp, dismissive wit, and each fostered the other's innate sense of grandeur. Margaret was, wrote Vidal's friend and biographer Jay Parini, 'an important figure in his mind if not his life ... a bold reminder to himself that he was important, and that he moved in the highest social circles'.

To honour Vidal's fiftieth birthday, on 3 October 1975 his friend Diana Phipps presented him with a collage of his most illustrious friends, with the occasional deadly enemy thrown in for good measure. She had constructed it by cutting out headshots and sticking them onto an illustrated scene of debauchery in ancient Rome. Apart from Vidal himself, those depicted included Graham Greene, J.K. Galbraith, Lady Diana Cooper, Robert Kennedy and Jackie Kennedy, along with Vidal's old rivals William F. Buckley (lying vanquished beneath Vidal's left foot) and Norman Mailer (kneeling in obeisance). But in the most prominent position, standing on a staircase above a semi-naked Vidal, was Her Royal Highness the Princess Margaret, Countess of Snowdon.

Vidal threw a fiftieth birthday party at Mark's Club in Mayfair for fifty people ('50 for 50,' in the words of his partner Howard Austen). Fame seems to have been the principal qualification for an invitation: the guests included Ryan O'Neal, Tennessee Williams, Kenneth Tynan, Claire Bloom, Tom Driberg, Peter Bogdanovich, Jonathan Miller and

Lady Diana Cooper. Lady Antonia Fraser brought her new boyfriend, Harold Pinter; Lee Remick happened to be in London, so was sent a last-minute invitation. But his real catch was HRH the Princess Margaret. As Parini puts it: 'Gore was happy with the dinner. He didn't like turning fifty. Who does? But he and Tennessee got to talk, and he really liked Pinter. That Princess Margaret came mattered to him a lot. (So much for Jackie [Onassis] and her sister, Lee: this was real royalty.)'

Vidal placed the Princess on his right during dinner, and was glued to her throughout the reception beforehand. 'I looked across the room and saw Gore with Princess Margaret on one side of him and Tennessee Williams on the other,' recalled the English writer John Bowen. 'She had a long cigarette with a holder. Tennessee Williams just giggled at her.'

After dinner, Kenneth Tynan gave a speech, addressing his fellow guests as 'Comrades', since Vidal's birthday celebrations happened to coincide with the last day of the Labour Party Conference in Blackpool. Clive James followed this with an ode to Vidal, which, according to Tynan, was 'delivered (because of nerves) too fast, but much appreciated'. After the party, Tynan and his wife dropped Princess Margaret back at Kensington Palace before returning home, 'tipsily to fuck, for the first time in many weeks'.

The next day, Tynan attended what he called a 'post-party lunch' at Marguerite Littman's house. Tennessee Williams entered, 'blandly euphoric on speed', and immediately started complaining to his hostess. 'You did a terrible thing to me last night. You know what she did? She told me to sit beside Princess Margaret and give her a bit of a giggle – that's what she said. I don't know Princess Margaret, and anyway I expect she's quite a stupid person – so how could I give her a giggle?'

Tynan asked Williams what he had said to the Princess. Accounts of his reply differ slightly, but here is Tynan's former wife Elaine Dundy's:

TENNESSEE: I'm afraid we can't talk to each other, Ma'am, because we
live in such different worlds.

MARGARET: What world do you live in?

TENNESSEE: Are you acquainted with the opera *La Bohème*, Ma'am?
That's my world.

Though Tennessee Williams was not to know, some seven years previously Princess Margaret had told Cecil Beaton that she 'loathed' his plays. 'I hate squalor! Tennessee Williams makes me feel ill!'

Vidal first met her in Rome in 1965, having been introduced by their mutual friend Judy Montagu. 'Like so many good-looking women, Princess Margaret likes plain-looking women like Judy,' he said some years later.

He immediately warmed to her. 'The Princess arrived with her husband and turned out to be quite splendid, droll, with at least three manners, all beguiling,' he wrote to his cousin Louis Auchincloss. 'One: gracious lady visiting the troops. Two: bitchy young matron with a cold eye for contemporaries. Three: a splendid Edith Evans delivery (Q. Victoria with slow measured accents): "We are not partial to heights" she intoned gravely over a chicken wing, "not partial at all." That took care of Switzerland.'

At this first meeting, the two of them gossiped about President Kennedy's visit to Buckingham Palace four years previously: Vidal's stepfather had gone on to marry Jackie Kennedy's mother. He always liked to trumpet the family link.

The guest list for the wedding had, he told Margaret, been subject to intense negotiation, the Queen having vetoed Jackie Kennedy's sister Princess Lee Radziwill, because she was on her second marriage, and her husband Prince Stanislaw Radziwill, because he was on his third. Jackie, he said, had in turn threatened to veto the entire occasion, forcing the Queen to relent. But, as Jackie told Vidal (or so he claimed), and Vidal now passed on to Princess Margaret, 'The Queen had her revenge': President Kennedy had said he would like to meet the

Duchess of Kent, and Jackie had wanted to meet Princess Margaret – but neither had been invited.

When Vidal told the Princess of these to-ings and fro-ings, the Princess 'nodded thoughtfully'.

'That could've been true – I know I rang my sister, furious at not being invited, and she said, "Ah, I thought since you were pregnant you wouldn't want to bother!" Too maddening!'

Vidal informed Auchincloss that the Snowdons were both 'renowned cadgers', adding that 'She admitted as much when I said how much I liked the Romans because they are lovely to be with but, like cats, when one was gone that was that.' The Princess told him that people often accused her of this, adding, '"and I suppose it's true. But there isn't time. How many people do you write letters to? Regularly?" I said very few ... "You see," she said triumphantly, "I write none!"'

In 2009, seven years after her death and three years before his own, Vidal published *Snapshots in History's Glare*, a picture book that included a photograph of the Princess, cigarette in her right hand, glass in her left, on the balcony of La Rondinaia, Vidal's Italian clifftop villa. 'Princess Margaret on a trip to visit us on the Amalfi Coast,' reads the extended caption. 'In the foreground is her son, Lord Linley. Today he is, deservedly, the most celebrated cabinetmaker in England.'

He praised the Princess for letting Linley do what he wanted, rather than forcing him along a traditional royal path. He did not underplay his own influence in these matters. 'I ... take some credit for my having persuaded her to forget about fashionable schools or, indeed, Oxbridge itself, to be followed by the military.' He was clearly unaware that Bedales, where Lord Linley was educated, has long been one of the most fashionable schools in Britain: alumni include Daniel Day-Lewis, Cara Delevingne, Minnie Driver, Gyles Brandreth and Lily Allen.

Also in the book is an informal group shot taken at Vidal's house on the Princess's trip to Hollywood in 1978. 'Like many British royals, she was fascinated by the place,' observed Vidal. In the front row is what he refers to as 'a batch of Tynan children'. Behind them stands the

Princess, sandwiched between the film director Tony Richardson and the mustachioed Jack Nicholson. Vidal pokes his head between Nicholson and the Princess, and appears to be whispering something in her ear.

The juxtaposition of the Princess and Jack Nicholson, she in a flowery, low-cut frock and a string of pearls, he in a double-breasted suit and tie, a white handkerchief in his breast pocket, is particularly bizarre. He was soon to start filming *The Shining* with Stanley Kubrick, in which he played a writer who turns homicidal. For now, he stands still, his left hand in his jacket pocket, as though about to pull out a gun.

In 1983, Princess Margaret invited Vidal to a house party at Royal Lodge. 'You can easily recognise it,' she said. 'It is very pink.' There were, he reported, 'three or four other houseguests', but, in an unprecedented fit of discretion, he failed to name them. It was a bright hot summer weekend. They all 'swam in an ancient pool full of drowning bees'.

On the Saturday evening they were due at a lavish birthday party in Ascot complete with an orchestra and a Ferris wheel. Though they were both keen gossips, Princess Margaret failed to mention that it was she who had negotiated her sister's acceptance of the invitation, having made it clear to her hostess that she would invite the Queen only on condition that Princess Michael was not invited.

Vidal registered Princess Margaret's easy-going approach to punctuality. 'I should note that no one is supposed to attend an event after the Queen's arrival but PM and I, at the Lodge, lingered over gin and tonics.'

According to Vidal, not always the most reliable witness,* when they finally arrived at the party, 'the Queen frowned at her sister'. Princess Margaret said, 'How's it going?' to which the Queen replied, 'We have shaken many hands.' Vidal interpreted this as a curt nod to the number of Americans present: 'the sovereign is not supposed to be touched by subjects: males incline their heads in a bow, females curtsy'.

As Princess Margaret presented Vidal to the Queen, 'I did the nod.' The Queen said, 'You are staying at the lodge. Which room?' Vidal replied that he thought it was called the Blue Bedroom. 'Suddenly, the Queen's girlish voice was replaced by the voice of Lady Bracknell: "My room!" she boomed. Then she fled across the lawn.'

Vidal's acidic view of the Queen might be put down to rivalry. 'The trouble with Gore,' Margaret once observed, 'is that he wants my sister's job.'

---

* In his final decade, Vidal's *aperçus* became more and more crackpot. In different essays, he argued that Frank Sinatra was a charming man who had no connection with the Mafia; that there was a media conspiracy to demonise Oklahoma bomber Timothy McVeigh, who was simply an innocent young man with an exaggerated sense of justice; that there is 'overwhelming' evidence that the 1995 Oklahoma bombing was part of a plot by the US government to get President Clinton to sign an anti-terrorism act; that Anthony Hopkins is just 'a solid, workmanlike English repertory actor'; that 90 per cent of all American paper currency contains drug residue; that Clinton was innocent of any sexual congress with Monica Lewinsky, who had been put up to it by the American tobacco industry; and that the Soviet Union had never been any danger to anyone. In his dotage, Vidal was doomed to become the victim of his own paranoid theories. One day he woke up insisting that he was the victim of radioactivity that had drifted to Italy from Chernobyl. The truth was less dramatic: he had a hangover. He saw increasing numbers of enemies everywhere. A few months before he died in 2012, he phoned his friend and biographer Jay Parini in a panic. 'Get the next plane to LA at once. I need help. There are Somali pirates in my swimming pool.'

After the party, Princess Margaret and her guests returned to Royal Lodge. According to Vidal, Princess Margaret started reading aloud from Vidal's latest novel, *Duluth*. 'Some of the descriptions were very graphic but the several young men who had come back to the lodge with the house party were, happily, clueless.'

Closing the book, the Princess told its author, 'I don't know what there is in me that is so low and base that I love this book.'

Four years after her death, Vidal declared that the Princess had been 'far too intelligent for her station in life', adding that 'she often had a bad press, the usual fate of wits in a literal society'. He claimed that she had once told him the reason for her unpopularity: 'It was inevitable; when there are two sisters and one is the Queen who must be the source of honour and all that is good while the other must be the focus of the most creative malice, the evil sister.'

60

The language sounds more like his, but the sentiment was undoubtedly hers. Margaret thought the world cruel for seeing her as the negative version of her sister, yet it was also how she came to define herself. The journalist and author Selina Hastings feels this self-image had been shaped in childhood. 'On one side she was given an inflated sense of her own value, while on the other her confidence was continually undermined by comparisons with her sister; she was very spoilt and indulged and made to feel a very special person indeed, while simultaneously being given clearly to understand that it was her sister who was important.'

The abdication of their uncle King Edward VIII had ensured that Lilibet would one day be Queen. Lilibet was then ten years old, Margaret six. But courtiers were already speaking of providence: the crown would, they felt, be going to the better sister.

'She was a wicked little girl,' one courtier said of Margaret, and others agreed. 'There were moments when I'd have given anything to have given her the hell of a slap,' an unnamed courtier told the biographer of King George VI. To the sisters' cousin Margaret Rhodes, Lilibet was always the sensible one: polite, thoughtful, well-behaved: 'Princess Margaret was the naughty one. She was always more larky. She used to tease the servants. There was a wonderful old page and, as he carried the plates around the dining room, Margaret used to stare at him, trying to make him laugh. But she never got herself reprimanded. She got away with everything.'

Selina Hastings thinks her character was at least partly shaped by her ever-increasing distance from the throne. 'At each royal birth, the new Order of Succession appeared in *The Times*, Margaret's position moving down from second to third to fourth with monotonous regularity, like a game of Snakes and Ladders, all snake and no ladder.'

Perhaps as a consequence, she set great store by protocol, pulling rank as others might fiddle with their necklace or bite their fingernails. Lucinda Lambton remembers Princess Margaret upbraiding her when she was a child. 'I was nine or ten and sat on the sofa, and she came over with cartoon imperiousness and she said, "One does not sit before Royalty sits."'

Her antennae for transgressions were unusually sensitive, quivering into action at the slightest opportunity. 'I detested Queen Mary,' she told Gore Vidal. 'She was rude to all of us except Lilibet, who was going to be Queen. Of course, she had an inferiority complex. We were Royal, and she was not.' Unlike her, Queen Mary had been born a Serene Highness, not a Royal Highness. The difference, invisible to most, was monumental to Princess Margaret, who treasured the definite article in Her Royal Highness *the* Princess Margaret. Lacking that 'the', her grandmother was in some sense below the salt.

Margaret had been born to the King-Emperor at a time when the map of the world was still largely pink. Her sense of entitlement, never modest, grew bigger and bigger with each passing year, gathering weight and speed as the British Empire grew smaller and smaller, and her role in it smaller still.

She remained conscious of her image as the one who wasn't, and to some extent played on it: the one who wasn't the Queen; the one who wasn't taught constitutional history because she wasn't the one who'd be needing it; the one who wasn't in the first coach, and wouldn't ever be first onto the Buckingham Palace balcony; the one who wasn't given the important duties, but was obliged to make do with the also-rans: the naming of the more out-of-the-way council building, school, hospital or regiment, the state visit to the duller country, the patronage of the more obscure charity, the glad-handing of the smaller fry – the deputies, the vices, the second-in-commands. Her most devoted friends praised her stoicism for assuming the role of lightning rod. 'For nearly five decades,' said Reinaldo Herrera, 'she bore with great dignity the criticism and envy that people dared not show the Queen.'

Did she envy her elder sister? According to Crawfie, the young Elizabeth once complained, 'Margaret always wants what I've got' – but this is a traditional sibling complaint. It seems more probable that, deep down, what Margaret really wanted from Elizabeth was approval.

On her desk in Kensington Palace she had a telephone with a direct line to the Queen in Buckingham Palace. Sitting next to her at a dinner party, the novelist and historian A.N. Wilson found himself tongue-tied.

'I could think of absolutely nothing to say to her, and I heard myself asking: "Are you one of those millions of people who have dreams about the Queen?"

'Her reply was as candid as it was revealing. Yes, she said, and it was always the same dream. She dreamed that she was disapproved of, she knew she had done something truly awful, something that transgressed everything that she had been brought up to believe, something which had made the Queen angry. Usually, in the dreams, it was nothing specific; but she could not rest until she had heard her sister's voice in waking life. Since the Princess kept later hours than her elder sister and sovereign, she would often, when she woke up midmorning and reached for the telephone, find that the Queen was already at work with secretaries, politicians or her boxes. All Margaret needed to hear was the voice: "Hello." "Hello." They would then hang up and the day could proceed without the black cloud of being "in disgrace" to depress the Queen's vivacious but inwardly troubled younger sister.'

Immediately after the Queen's coronation ceremony, Anne Tennant had spotted Margaret looking tearful. 'Oh, Ma'am, you look so sad,' she said.

'I've lost my father, and I've lost my sister,' replied Margaret, adding, 'She will be busy. Our lives will change.' For all their Martha-and-Mary differences, they had much in common, not least their uniquely peculiar childhood. But once Elizabeth became Queen, the gap between them grew wider, and harder to bridge. Though they were in constant touch, the Queen knew when to keep her head down. 'How's Margaret's mood?' she asked one of her sister's friends before lunch at Royal Lodge. 'Shall I venture out on the terrace?'

As Margaret grew older, the Queen was alert to her loneliness and vulnerability. Sheltering at Balmoral, Margaret seemed, according to one member of the household, 'almost like a poor relation. The Queen felt very sorry for her.'

61

In middle age, hurt by life, Margaret retreated into camp, becoming a nightclub burlesque of her sister. But she was never camp in the same way that the Queen Mother was camp. Her camp was not arch or sentimental. It did not strive to be inclusive, or merry, or to render the world as a romp. She didn't twinkle or sparkle. She would never say 'Such fun' as though she meant it; she would take pains to inject the phrase with a dash of generalised irony. Nor was she camp in the service of something beyond herself. She had no wish to draw others in, and refused to offer them the illusion, however fleeting, of parity. Being thought 'real' or 'down to earth' is not what she wanted.

She was of royalty, yet divorced from it; royalty set at an oblique angle, royalty through the looking glass, royalty as pastiche. At a fancy-dress party on Mustique she wore a Valkyrie outfit, hired for her by Colin Tennant from a Los Angeles costumier, and in it she mimed an aria from *The Ring*. For her fiftieth birthday, the Tennants gave her a gold-embroidered dress from India. 'I've always LONGED to have a dress like that,' she said. 'It's what a REAL princess would wear.' She was royalty as Hokey-Cokey, one-foot-out, one-foot-in; royalty as real yet unreal; royalty as real as you want it to be, as the mood takes you.

She was cabaret camp, Ma'am Ca'amp: she was Noël Coward, cigarette holders, blusher, Jean Cocteau, winking, sighing, dark glasses, Bet Lynch, charades, Watteau, colourful cocktails at midday, ballet, silk,

hoity-toity, dismissive overstatement, arriving late, entering with a flourish, exiting with a flounce, pausing for effect, making a scene.

Ma'am Ca'amp is having a drink in a cut-glass tumbler delivered to you in the swimming pool and then ordering your hostess to bring the tumbler into the pool, even though she is fully clothed. Ma'am Ca'amp is her hosts' compliance in these antics. Ma'am Ca'amp enjoys inverting expectations: to those expecting grace, it presents *hauteur*; to those wanting empathy, it delivers distance. To those in need of tradition, it offers modernity. To those in need of modernity, it offers tradition.

It is languid, bored, world-weary, detached, bored, fidgety, demanding, entitled, disgruntled, bored. It carries the seeds of its own sadness and scatters them around like confetti. It looks in the mirror for protracted periods of time, but avoids exchanging glances with itself. It is disappointment hiding behind the shield of *hauteur*, keeping pity at bay. 'I have never known an unhappier woman,' says John Julius Norwich after her death.

It is pantomime as tragedy, and tragedy as pantomime. It is *Cinderella* in reverse. It is hope dashed, happiness mislaid, life mishandled. Nothing is as thrilling as they said it would be: no one is as amusing, as clever, as attractive or as interesting. The sun never shines as bright as it used to, and even the fiercest thunderstorm lacks any real sense of drama or pizzazz. As the curtain falls, Group Captain Charming has left her for someone more suitable and has gone to live in France, and Buttons, in his zip-up jumpsuit, has taken up with a wearying succession of younger lovers. When Cinderella dies, her little glass slipper is put up for auction, a memento of days of hope and innocence. The catalogue entry reads: 'Only worn once.'

62

December 1991
Friends take Princess Margaret to see *The Madness of George III* by Alan Bennett. In the interval, she smokes and sips nervously from a glass of Famous Grouse.

'Do you think it's hereditary?' she asks.

63

'She and Tony were a glamorous couple,' says the journalist Drusilla Beyfus, who was part of their circle. 'But there was a halo of anxiety about the way things would go. Because quite soon it was apparent they weren't getting on very well.'

The breakdown of the Snowdon marriage calls to mind Patrick Hamilton's famous play (and film) *Gaslight*, in which the villain, Jack Manningham, tries to convince his wife Bella that she is insane by subjecting her to a series of fiendish ploys. He hides items in her work-basket, then suggests she must have stolen them; he removes a picture from the wall, and tells her she must have taken it; he makes the lights go dim, then says she is imagining it; when she hears footsteps in the flat above, he assures her the flat is empty; he shows her his watch-chain, from which his watch has disappeared, and then finds it in her handbag. Eventually, she becomes hysterical. This is Jack and Bella, but it might as easily be Tony and Margaret.

After three years of marriage Snowdon had grown restless, spending as much time away from home as he possibly could. In turn, Margaret grew more and more possessive, frantically phoning to find out where he was before bursting into tears when told he was elsewhere. Snowdon refused to let her come with him on his photographic assignments, and, once safely away, wouldn't bother to contact her. She kept phoning him at work; he would instruct his assistant to tell her he was mid-shot. Through a succession of phone calls, she would trace him to a restaurant and turn up unannounced. His biographer writes of 'Margaret's almost hysterical possessiveness'. The closer she wanted to be, the more distant he became. He welcomed trips abroad.

He was a busy bee, designing clocks, furniture, ski-wear, theatre sets. At the investiture of the Prince of Wales at Caernarvon in 1969, he designed both the thrones and the audience chairs, the Perspex canopy, Prince Charles's crown (complete with a golden orb made out of a ping-pong ball) and his own uniform as 'Constable of the Castle': the tight, zip-fastened affair in the style of Pierre Cardin, with a roll-collared jacket and skinny trousers, which first earned him the nick-name of 'Buttons'.

Princess Margaret lacked her husband's drive, waking late in the day, only to find herself with nothing to do. Her servants took care of all the household chores, leaving her with a succession of time-killing hobbies, such as washing her collection of seashells* and putting her spaniel Rowley in the bath and giving him a shampoo, then drying him with her hairdryer. 'I've told them I have to wash Rowley because he wouldn't like it if anyone else did,' she explained. Once or twice she tried to emulate her husband's capacity for design, but with limited success. For a while, she glued matchboxes onto tumblers so that she could strike matches while drinking, but it was a craze that never caught on.

By 1963, Tony was already exhibiting Manningham tendencies. On holiday in Greece with Stavros Niarchos, the Princess asked her husband what she should wear to a barbecue party for her birthday that evening. 'Oh, I think that ballgown you wore last week,' said Snowdon casually. She went along with his suggestion. When she arrived downstairs in her ballgown she found that all the other guests were wearing jeans and sandals. Snowdon knew full well that his

---

* She liked to keep things clean, even as a young woman. Late in life, she informed one visitor to Kensington Palace that before the Clean Air Act of 1956 'I had to wipe every single leaf of my camellias by hand.'

fingerprints would remain undetected by all but her: his wife's reputation for inappropriate grandeur preceded her, and facilitated his own cunning ruses.

Home alone, they sniped and bickered. Each of their friends has a story to tell of their acid rows. Snowdon would shut himself away in his studio, telling her, 'Never come in here without knocking!' When she asked him if he'd be in for lunch, he pretended not to hear. In turn, the Princess yelled that she wasn't prepared to entertain his friends, and slammed the door with such force that a mirror shattered. He would flaunt his flirtations with other women, and she would react with fury. At a dance, he spent too much time with a younger woman. The Princess interrupted them, and asked the woman if she was enjoying herself.

'Very much so, Ma'am,' she replied.

'That's enough, then, for one evening. Now run along home.'

Even when they went on holiday together, Snowdon would do his best to avoid her, often in the showiest way possible: he liked an audience. Staying with friends in Rome, he climbed out of a window and onto the roof. 'It's the only place I can get away from her,' he explained. In the winter of 1965 he lost his temper with Margaret after she insisted on accompanying him on a skiing trip. 'She's fucked up my holiday,' he complained to friends.

His revenge on Margaret for being Margaret was deliberate and sly. Knowing her hatred of being kept waiting, he dragged out the skiing so that it overran. His group returned late for lunch to find the Princess furious, but they couldn't see why. True to plan, their sympathy for the poor put-upon husband grew as their respect for his demanding wife diminished. In this, Snowdon was just like Jack Manningham. Back home, he took to leaving nasty notes on her desk, including one headed 'Twenty Four Reasons Why I Hate You', which particularly upset her. 'I can't think of twenty-four reasons to hate ANYBODY,' she said to a friend. On another occasion he left a note in her glovebox saying 'You look like a Jewish manicurist,' and on another, a note tucked into her bedside book, saying simply, 'I hate you.'

He was skilled at keeping his audience onside by taking care to conceal his workings: his mischief was delivered by sleight of hand. The rest of the Royal Family, particularly her sister and mother, considered him charming. Margaret accused Tony of being 'oily' towards them. Years of experience had taught them that she was in the habit of being capricious and demanding. Tony played on this history, goading and enticing his wife into temper tantrums in front of them, while quietly slipping into the role of long-suffering victim. 'He could be fiendishly cruel,' observed a friend.

Before a grand party or a public engagement, he would make a point of reducing the Princess to tears, ensuring that she would appear puffy-faced and red-eyed on arrival. When they were due to set off for official appointments he would keep her waiting, knowing that her reputation for tardiness preceded her. On their way, he would open the window of their car wide, so that the wind would blast her perfect hairdo out of shape. According to their chauffeur, John Larkin, a furious row would then ensue, with the Princess shouting, 'Put that window up!' and Snowdon refusing to do so. A *Private Eye* cover from the period shows the couple beaming in the back of a chauffeur-driven car. 'What's all this about us rowing in public?' asks the Princess. 'Shut up you fat bitch and keep smiling,' replies her husband. Like so many *Private Eye* covers, it touched on the truth.

In 1966, Snowdon managed to persuade Princess Margaret to seek psychiatric help. He booked an appointment for her with Dr Peter Dally, a distinguished consultant psychiatrist attached to Westminster Hospital. A pioneer in the treatment of anorexia nervosa, Dr Dally was also a writer, the future author of a psychological portrait of Elizabeth Barrett Browning (1989) and *The Marriage of Heaven and Hell: Manic Depression and the Life of Virginia Woolf* (1999).

'Tony sent me to him,' Margaret told a friend. 'He said it would be the answer. But I only lasted one session – I didn't like it at all. Perfectly useless!'

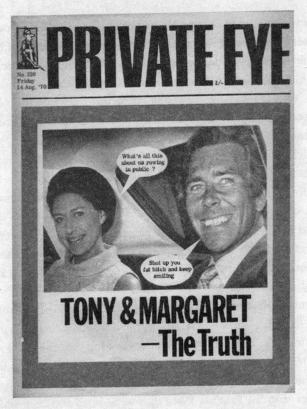

She never went back. Perhaps her sole treatment was hampered by royal protocol, which dictates that it is the royals who ask the questions, not those to whom they are presented. Possibly the Princess regarded Dr Dally's most tentative enquiry – 'Now, what would you like to talk about?' – as an impertinence.

Yet somehow the hour must have been filled. Did she talk about her mother and father? About her relationship with her elder sibling? And what was it about the session that she particularly disliked? Did she go to Dr Dally, or did he come to her? What was she wearing? Did she inform Dr Dally before she left him (or he left her) that she did not intend to continue her treatment, or did she dither and make excuses, telling his secretary that she didn't have her diary to hand?

Biography is at the mercy of information, and information about the Royal Family is seldom there when you want it. Or rather, there is a wealth of information, but most of it is window-dressing: the shop itself is shut, visible only through the front window, its private offices firmly under lock and key.

This is what makes biography the most sheepish and constrained of the arts, and the least like life; and royal biography doubly so.

64

At the annual Royal Variety Performance, a small selection of the Royal Family sits in the Royal Box while a bewildering array of different acts – jugglers, singers, ventriloquists, dancers, comedians – take to the stage for a few minutes at a time.

Once the show is over, the performers line up onstage as the Royal Family members conduct a whistle-stop walk. The effect is said to be almost hallucinogenic, as though all the celebrities of any given year had been thrown into a pot, boiled down and merged in a particularly gooey sort of celebrity marmalade.

Take, for instance, the Royal Variety Performance of 7 November 1949, which was held at the London Coliseum 'in the presence of His Majesty King George VI, Her Majesty Queen Elizabeth, HRH Princess Elizabeth and HRH Princess Margaret'. Within the space of a couple of hours, the Royal Family had witnessed, among many others, Noele Gordon singing songs from *Brigadoon*, Michael Bentine performing a string of impersonations and Maurice Chevalier singing 'Louise' and 'Valentine'. Also on the bill was the comedian Johnny Lockwood, who hit his nose against the revolving stage while singing 'When I Go Into My Dance', and was forced to continue his rendition with a handkerchief pressed to his face in a vain attempt to staunch a heavy nosebleed. For the finale, the HM Royal Marines Band and the Sea Cadet Corps took to the stage to play a medley of military marches.

Backstage, the nineteen-year-old Princess Margaret, wearing an off-white tulle dress patterned with diamanté, cut with wide cape shoulders, exchanged pleasantries with many of the performers, among them the Australian acrobatic troupe the Seven Ashtons, the comedy dancers Elsa and Waldo, and Borrah Minevitch's Harmonica Rascals.

Nineteen years later, on 18 November 1968, she was backstage at another Royal Variety Performance, shaking hands with, among others, Engelbert Humperdinck, Mike Yarwood, Sacha Distel, Manitas de Plata, the Czechoslovakian State Song and Dance Ensemble, Ted Rogers, Des O'Connor (who had hosted the evening), Arthur Askey, Ron Moody, Val Doonican, Lionel Blair, Petula Clark and Frankie Howerd.

This photograph* shows her exchanging pleasantries with Petula Clark.† Frankie Howerd is beaming at the Queen Mother, who is just out of shot. Meanwhile, the three Supremes – Diana Ross, Mary Wilson and Cindy Birdsong – all in tight white sparkly dresses, are getting ready to be presented. Cindy Birdsong can be seen taking a sideways glance at Princess Margaret. She has what can only be described as a sceptical look on her face.

The Supremes' performance had taken an unexpectedly radical turn – quite a rarity in a Royal Variety Performance. Halfway through their rendition of 'Somewhere' from *West Side Story*, Diana Ross had embarked on a spoken tribute to Dr Martin Luther King, who had been assassinated seven months before. 'There's a place for us,' she said, as the music continued to play. 'A place for all of us. Black and white, Jew and gentile, Catholic and Protestant. Let our efforts be determined as those of Dr Martin Luther King, who had a dream that all God's

---

* The same photograph cropped up ten years later, on the cover of *Private Eye*, at the time of the Princess's affair with Roddy Llewellyn, with Frankie Howerd saying, 'Isn't the Queen with you?' and the Princess replying, 'No, he had to go to the recording studio.'

† Ten years later, Petula was to sing a duet of the song 'L'Avventura' on French television with the Princess's lover Roddy Llewellyn.

children … could join hands and sing. There's a place for us, black and white … and the world of Martin Luther King and his ideals.'

The audience, more used to tapping their toes, greeted her speech at first with a baffled silence, followed by perhaps equally baffled applause. 'There was a two-minute standing ovation, and the Royal Family cheered wildly,' recalled Mary Wilson, with a touch of wishful thinking, in her autobiography *Dream Girl*. Once the Supremes had left the stage, Frankie Howerd came on and received a lot of laughs when he said, 'I'm the surprise … I thought you might like a bit of relief, *after all that drama!*' To close the show, the Supremes returned to the stage with the rest of the cast. Facing the Royal Box, they sang 'God Save the Queen'.

Mary Wilson was to recall the evening with mixed emotions. Had she been snubbed by Princess Margaret? 'Though we had enjoyed doing the show, because we were meeting royalty and had memorized all the protocol, we weren't exactly loose. Everything was quite proper and formal; we knew not to speak until spoken to, and not to address a royal, and so on. We stood in line, with Diana first, then me, then Cindy. Princess Margaret walked up to me, extended her hand, then – so quietly that no one else could hear – she whispered in her prim, high-pitched voice, "Is that a wig you're wearing, Mary?" I did all I could to suppress a giggle. When I realized that she was very serious about it I thought how bizarre it was that a member of the Royal Family could be so candid. Here I'd grown up in the projects and I had more sense than to ask someone a question like that. But then I thought how great it was to have these experiences, and how glad I was to be a Supreme.'

65

It is 19 December 1976. Princess Margaret has just attended *Christmas Supersonic* at the Theatre Royal, Drury Lane, a charity concert organised by the *Daily Mirror* Pop Club. She is looking delightedly at the compere, Russell Harty, as he introduces her to the line of stars – Marc Bolan, Twiggy, Gary Glitter. A few minutes ago they were joining Marti Caine and Guys and Dolls for a rousing finale of 'We Wish You a Merry Christmas'.

Twiggy is smiling at a witticism being made by Harty. She has clearly chosen to forgive and forget the Princess's dinner-party dismissal of her name ('How unfortunate')* some years ago.

Apart from Twiggy, everyone in the photograph is now either dead or in prison. Nine months after it was taken, Marc Bolan – real name Mark Feld – died in a car crash near his home in Barnes. At the age of seventy, Gary Glitter – real name Paul Gadd – was found guilty at Southwark Crown Court of one count of attempted rape, four counts of indecent assault, and one count of unlawful sexual intercourse with a girl under the age of thirteen. On 27 February 2015 he received the maximum sentence of sixteen years in prison.

Russell Harty died from liver failure caused by hepatitis C in 1988, at the age of fifty-three. Visiting him on his deathbed at St James's University Hospital in Leeds, his old friend Alan Bennett found him 'festooned with wires and equipment, a tracheotomy tube in his throat, monitored, ventilated'. Before long, he realised that Harty was trying to tell him something. The nurse, an experienced lip-reader, thought he might be saying 'Sherry,' but Harty shook his head impatiently. Attempting to calm him down, the nurse disconnected Harty from his machine, removed his tracheotomy tube and pressed a pad over his throat, so that they could at last hear what he had been trying to say.

'Ned Sherrin had supper with Princess Margaret last week,' he said, 'and she asked how I was. Twice.'

Harty died a few weeks later. Forty years before, in his schoolboy diary, he had taken the trouble to note down the news that HRH the Princess Margaret was suffering from a slight cold.

---

* See page 15.

66

In January 2017, Princess Margaret makes an unexpected appearance in my kitchen in Suffolk. She is much prettier than I have always imagined her to be, and friendlier too. She mentions that my last book has just been remaindered, and is now selling for £3.75. But she says it in a very kindly, unbitchy way, with no intent to cause offence.

After a short time, I remember to ask her what she wants to drink.

'When I was last here, you gave me a Flimsy, so I might have a Coloured Flimsy, if you have one?' she says.

I go blank. I have no idea what a Flimsy is. But I don't want to admit it to the Princess. I quietly ask my wife what a Coloured Flimsy is. She says it might be another name for a Dubonnet.

I go downstairs to see, as all the drinks are now in my library on the ground floor of our house. Princess Margaret follows me down. Just as we are about to go into the library together, I panic: if she follows me in, she is going to see all my work related to her laid out over the table and the floor. What to do? I feel boxed in. I have no alternative but to say, 'I'm terribly sorry, but you can't come in.'

Princess Margaret looks momentarily put out, but she seems to take it well, even though I haven't offered any sort of explanation.

But the question of her drink is still not settled. I decide that honesty is the best strategy.

'I'm sorry,' I say, 'but I can't remember what exactly a "Flimsy" is. Is it a Dubonnet?' While I am saying this, I remember that she's recently given up alcohol.

'Oh, don't worry,' she says, perfectly politely. 'Just give me water.'

The next minute, she is in the library, perusing the Willie Rushton cartoons on my wall, and making approving comments about them. At this point, I am struck by another wave of panic, much the same as the one before, but freshly experienced: she's bound to see all the books and papers about herself scattered around the room. And then what will I do? I wake up in terror.

Once I have woken up, I realise that one of my Willie Rushton cartoons is a caricature of Princess Margaret lying on the ground looking very tarty, brandishing a glass in one hand and a cigarette in the other.

67

Robert Brown, an accountant from Jersey, believes himself to be the illegitimate son of Princess Margaret.

Brown is registered as having been born in Nairobi on 5 January 1955, though the birth was not officially registered until 2 February of the same year. His parents are registered as Douglas and Cynthia Brown, who are both now dead.

Brown thinks that, in its later stage, the Princess's pregnancy was covered up by body doubles; he was then moved to Kenya, for adoption by Cynthia Brown, who had been a model for Hardy Amies. He believes that his true father may have been Princess Margaret's lover Robin Douglas-Home, who committed suicide in 1968.

For some time, Brown has harboured an instinctive conviction that he was not the natural son of the Browns, who had always been more distant from him than from their other children, his supposed siblings. Douglas and Cynthia Brown would sometimes forget his birthday, and never discussed his birth with him. His first idea was that he was related to King Edward VIII; he then wondered if Prince Philip might be his father.

'Cynthia gave me my birth certificate in my early twenties in a rather stiff, matter-of-fact way – a pure statement of fact in a slightly stressed monotone. It struck me as odd at the time – on her part devoid of emotion, slightly embarrassed, and her manner did not invite discussion,' he says. 'Odd for a mother, but maybe not in the circumstances, given she would have played a part, if only of silence, in the registration of the birth.'

Since Princess Margaret's death in 2002, Brown has fought to obtain secret court papers relating to her will. He thinks that these documents will show that Buckingham Palace, the attorney general and a senior judge conspired to cover up the Princess's last testament, in which, he suspects, details of his birth were included. In an early court hearing, lawyers for the Royal Family dismissed him as 'a fantasist seeking to feed his private obsession'. In 2007, Geoffrey Robertson QC told the court that Brown was 'a perfectly rational man who seeks peace of mind', but Sir Mark Porter, president of the Family Division, described Brown's claim as 'imaginary and baseless'.

Brown has a childhood memory of meeting a woman he now believes to have been Princess Margaret. 'The woman told me to stand on a tree-trunk and repeat, "I'm the king of the castle, you're the dirty rascal" again and again. It was meant to be fun, but it wasn't. There was a poignant subtext to it. I had a gut feeling that there was a royal connection, even though my logical side said there must be some other explanation.' Princess Margaret paid an official visit to Kenya in October 1956, when Brown would have been a year and nine months old.

'I can't get it out of my head that I am right,' Brown told a reporter from the *Guardian* in 2012. 'I can understand that people are sceptical because it seems to be childhood fantasy stuff, but it is not like that with me … Hopefully I am not a nutcase. I am either right or I am wrong.'

An obviously intelligent and articulate man, who bears more than a passing resemblance to Princess Margaret, Brown was initially in two minds about pursuing his case. 'It took me ages to do anything about it because though my instinctual side suggested that it was correct, and my emotions said it was correct, my rational side said that's nuts, how could they have covered up a pregnancy, it's the stuff of fantasy, there must be some other explanation for the memories that you have.'

Critics of his theory point out that Princess Margaret attended a dress show in London on 1 December 1955, and a performance of *Cinderella on Ice* at Earl's Court a week later. Had she been eight months pregnant, it would, they say, have been evident. On 21 December she attended the Royal Family's annual staff party at Buckingham Palace, and led the dancing with Cyril Dickman, a Palace footman. Lady Rosemary Muir recalled Princess Margaret attending her son Alexander's christening at Woodstock on 8 January. 'There was no evidence she had just given birth. I should know, having just done so myself ... These claims are absolute poppycock.'

In January 1992, the seventy-seven-year-old Peter Townsend was visited at his home outside Paris by a man who introduced himself as Philip Thomas. 'The purpose of his unannounced visit was to inform me that he had reason to believe that he was the son of HRH Princess Margaret and that I might well be his father!' Townsend explained in a letter to Sir Martin Gilliat, the Queen Mother's private secretary.

Townsend told Thomas that he would never discuss the Princess 'on any account', but he offered him a glass of wine, and the two men had a conversation about Welsh rugby. When Thomas got in touch with him again a year later, Townsend contacted his solicitor. 'Silly as this may be,' he wrote, 'I cannot resist the following observations: considering that (as he confirms) he was born in Swansea on 25 April 1956, it is not likely that P.M., whom he claims to be his mother, would (as he also confirms) have made an official visit to Port Talbot on 26 April 1956.'

68

Given time, neurologists may well establish a firm connection between mental illness and the writing of books about the Royal Family. But which comes first? Are mad men driven to write about royalty? Or does writing about royalty drive men mad?

The authors of royal books divide into fawners and psychos. The fawners employ the adjectives 'radiant', 'gracious', 'vivacious', 'jubilant' 'delightful' and 'enchanting' with unusual frequency. They coo over the most banal royal remark, treating it as proof of sanctity, but are seldom able to decide whether the royal in question is praiseworthy for being so exceptional, or for being so unexceptional. Ever since the television documentary *The Royal Family* was first screened in 1969, the trend has been towards praising the unexceptional. Despite it all, the biographers seem to say, They are just like Us. They chat, they squabble, they breakfast, they barbecue: praise them! praise them!

Royal biographers relish detailing the gorgeous ordinariness of the Royal Family. In other biographies, anecdotes are employed to highlight idiosyncrasies; in royal biographies, they are more likely to be there to celebrate the commonplace; the punch-line is that there is no punch-line.

Witness this paragraph from Charles Higham and Roy Moseley's *Elizabeth and Philip: The Untold Story*:

The Queen and Prince Philip drove themselves to the polo ground. Philip drove a station wagon, the Queen her favourite Rover. Sometimes, instead of changing into polo gear at the castle, Prince Philip was seen changing, quite uncomfortably, in his automobile, sitting sideways, the door open, pulling his breeches on. Then he would stand up to fasten the belt.

And so it goes on:

One wet day, the Queen was seen driving her car quite fast to the back of the tent. The Queen Mother was seated beside her, with a tartan rug rolled up in her arms, along with various magazines. The Queen pulled up sharply, jumped out of the Rover, walked briskly up to a white-coated attendant, and asked about the pitch and whether the rain had damaged the grass or would threaten the horses. The Queen Mother was left behind to get out of the car and make her own way to the spectator seats. On another occasion, the passenger door refused to open, and –

Enough! For royal biographers, there is no division between the interesting and the uninteresting; in fact, the less interesting anything is, the more they are interested. The assumption behind this assiduous chronicling of royal normality is that there is something inherently special, almost other-worldly, about it. Even when the veteran royal oleaginist Godfrey Talbot gushes over the Queen Mother's 'effortless smile' in his *BBC Book of Royal Memories*, he seems to be suggesting that such supreme effortlessness could not have come about without supreme effort.

Rare is the royal biography that fails to quote Walter Bagehot's line, 'Its mystery is its life. We must not let in daylight upon magic.' But, through his nervousness, Bagehot seems to acknowledge that the mystery of monarchy is no mystery at all, but rather a neat illusion, the magic no more than a conjuring trick. After decades of daylight, one is forced to ask two questions. If they are so ordinary, why are they so special? And, if they are so special, why are they so ordinary?

In many royal biographies, the humdrum is peppered with intimations of the divine. Ingrid Seward's *Sarah*, a pioneering biography of Sarah, Duchess of York, written before the first of the Duchess's numerous falls from grace, is packed with chummy, girl-next-door detail: her father, Major Ron, likes watching repeats of *The Two Ronnies*; giant teddies 'jostle for position' on the sofas of the Yorks' new house; her husband Andrew is 'very good with children and loves just being at home with his wife and two baby girls'; and 'like the Queen and the Queen Mother, Sarah loves brooches'. Yet there are also constant reminders ('The Duchess of York exudes energy; she fills a room with her presence') that this is no ordinary human being.

The psychopaths, on the other hand, blame the Royal Family for all that is wrong with the world, and attribute diabolic motives to everything they do. In this way, they too invest them with superhuman powers.

In her day, the Queen Mother attracted many more fawners than psychos. Penelope Mortimer's 1986 biography of her now seems at the vanguard of dottiness. Mortimer describes Her Majesty in the war years as looking 'remarkably plain', before going on to condemn her as a sex vixen: 'Sexuality was her most formidable characteristic. This doesn't mean that she invited anyone to bed. On the contrary. High moral principles, by inhibiting activity, produce an enormous reserve of sexual power. It was this power that transformed her husband from an inarticulate nobody ... she is the most successful sex-symbol that British royalty has ever known.'

In other instances, royal biographers are beset by split personalities, their inner sycophant battling with their inner psychopath. Anthony Holden spent the first half of his career genuflecting to the Prince of Wales ('Prince Charles has more natural intelligence than most previous heirs apparent, and a more conscientious spirit than a nation has any right to expect'), before executing what journalists term a 'reverse ferret' and spending the second half of his career pulling the Prince of Wales to pieces, complaining that, among other misdemeanours, he 'used his unelected office to bankrupt British architects'. Even Hugo Vickers, one of the most reliable royal biographers, can sometimes seem conflicted. He concluded *Debrett's Book of the Royal Wedding* (1981) with the judgement, 'He [Prince Charles] is indeed fortunate to have found in Lady Diana Spencer somebody who is, in his words, "pretty special".' Yet in his biography of the Queen Mother (2005), he reveals that he was simultaneously detailing his beady misgivings about that very same royal wedding in his private diary: 'The Royal Wedding,' he wrote, 'is no more romantic than a picnic amid the wasps.'

Royal biographers who are either authorised or semi-authorised end up in hock to their masters and mistresses. The acknowledgements in Anne de Courcy's 2008 biography of Lord Snowdon begin: 'I would like to express my great gratitude to Lord Snowdon. He was the perfect biographical subject, not only because of his brilliant talent, campaigning work for others, colourful life, complex and interesting personality, and kindness giving up hours of his time to lengthy taped interviews but because he never once attempted to influence what I wrote. It only remains to add not only my admiration but also my affection.'

De Courcy acknowledges that 'The material in this book is primarily based on many hours of talk with Lord Snowdon, who also gave me full and unfettered access to his files and archives.' At the back of the book, she offers brief source notes for each chapter: 'Most of the material in this book, unless otherwise stated, comes from Tony himself, as the result of taped interviews and of the access to his files that he generously gave me.'

Though de Courcy offers an extremely thorough (and not entirely starry-eyed) account of Snowdon's life and career, more than one reviewer felt that her affection for her subject was sometimes in danger of slipping into infatuation. Others disagreed. 'How refreshing to read a biography in which the author is half in love with her subject,' wrote Richard Davenport-Hines in the *Sunday Times*. 'There are none of the usual patronising putdowns, envious backbiting or mean-spirited cavilling in Anne de Courcy's portrait of the Earl of Snowdon.'

On page 155, de Courcy offers her account of the end of Princess Margaret's affair with Robin Douglas-Home, who committed suicide eighteen months after they broke up. Apparently, in March 1967, having been told by Snowdon to call off the affair,

> the Princess telephoned Douglas-Home and told him she would never be able to see him again. To Tony she said, 'He wasn't nearly as good a lover as you, darling' (a phrase that she would use again to her husband several times in the future).

It doesn't take Sherlock Holmes to trace the source of this information. It could only have been Tony or Margaret, and by the time the book was published, Margaret had been dead six years. History is written by the victor.

69

Tony's simmering enmity meant that Colin Tennant saw precious little of Princess Margaret over the early years of her marriage; and whenever they did bump into each other, the wedding gift would pass unmentioned. But the deterioration of her marriage prompted a revival in the old friendship. Dining with the Tennants in 1968, she asked whether the plot of land on Mustique was still on offer, and if so, did it include a house? Caught on the back foot, Tennant answered yes to both questions. Deftly, the Princess had just managed to negotiate herself a free home.

By the end of the dinner she had invited herself to stay on the island. Before she arrived, Tennant staked out a suitable patch of land. Wearing a trouser suit as protection from the mosquitoes, the Princess surveyed it approvingly. Oddly enough, it would be the first and last piece of land she ever owned.

She immediately set about claiming more: when Tennant's back was turned, she pulled up his stakes and replanted them further afield, awarding herself more acreage. Realising her ploy, Tennant waited until her back was turned and then returned the stakes to their original holes. This *pas de deux* continued for a while, back and forth, but Margaret proved the more determined, and finished her stay with a full ten acres. Finally she persuaded Tennant that Tony's uncle, the theatre designer Oliver Messel, would be just the person to design a house, for two reasons: a) she would gain a suitably glamorous home, and b) the involvement of his beloved uncle might jolt Tony into joining her on Mustique. As things turned out, Tony never revisited the island, and spent his time complaining to Margaret that Tennant was cynically using her to promote it.*

For his part, Tennant affected to miss Tony. 'I was sorry T could not bear me, because he was perfect for PM,' he wrote in notes for an auto-biography he died before completing. 'An occasional drop of his Angostura into our Gin Fizz would have jazzed up our *Jolie Eaux*.'

Margaret finally moved into her house, the aforesaid 'Les Jolies Eaux', in 1973. She furnished it mainly with free gifts hoovered up during her annual visits to the Ideal Home Exhibition. Her tableware was donated by successive porcelain factories, parting presents for official visits. 'The whole place was really terribly plain,' recalled Tennant. 'There was a sofa facing the sea with a comfortable armchair on either side with a basketry kind of coffee table in front. There was no evidence at all of her being a Royal person other than a rather small reproduction of the picture of The Queen by Annigoni which hung beside her desk.'

There were, however, clues elsewhere, not least in Tennant's frantic preparations for her twice-yearly visits. 'He collapsed with exhaustion when Princess Margaret left the island,' recalls Nicholas Courtney. 'He put every ounce of energy into making it fun for her.' And few conventional tourists arrive with a royal protection officer and a lady-in-waiting dancing attendance.

The Princess's timetable on Mustique was unvarying. Rising at 11 a.m., she would take a cup of coffee with her lady-in-waiting. On one occasion the lady-in-waiting in question, her cousin Jean Wills, tried to slip out for a quick walk before their coffee appointment, only to be caught red-handed and, according to Tennant, 'soundly berated'.

---

* Tennant certainly recognised that the popularity of the island among the jet set was bound up with her presence on it. He once declared that he lived 'by the three Ps – the people, the Press and the Princess', so he tried to remain on the best possible terms with all three. There were other benefits to his royal association: he would sometimes be allowed to join his wife, the Princess's lady-in-waiting, on the more carefree royal tours.

Margaret would then make her way to the island's hotel, the Cotton House, for a cigarette and a pick-me-up, thence to the beach, where she would swim a very slow breaststroke, her head held high, as though the sea itself might try to take advantage, while a member of her court swam alongside her, employing side-stroke so the Princess could see his or her face. To minimise the irritation of sand sticking to the Princess's feet as she got out of the sea, Colin Tennant would make sure that a basin of fresh water was to hand.

On the beach, she cut an imposing figure, or figurine. 'She stood erect but lacked height,' recalled Tennant, 'but had an hourglass figure with a lumpy bosom. All day she wore a whaleboned thronged garment, laced at the back with a short, frilled skirt of her own design. It appeared to be armour-plated.'

And so to lunch, for which she would join a group for a picnic on the beach, a table having been laid before their arrival. This picnic generally consisted of chicken in Hellmann's mayonnaise topped off with a salad, though sausages were sometimes served, in the interests of variety.

In the evening, the Princess would change into what a friend describes as 'one of her kaftany things'. Dinner was invariably at the Cotton House, sometimes to musical accompaniment by a dance band from St Vincent, the table decorated with flowers ordered by Tennant, flown in from Trinidad. 'It may look like frivolity,' he observed, 'but making these visits a success takes constant imagination.' If the Princess chose to dine at home, the meal would be cooked by a Mrs Lane, helped by her daughter, who went by the name of Cloreen. The dinner menu was unchanging. The first course consisted of shrimp cocktail in a pink sauce served in a V-shaped glass. The Princess was under the impression that the pink sauce was a closely guarded native secret, handed down from generation to generation. Which it was, in a sense: they made it from Hellmann's with a dash of Heinz tomato ketchup. Then came chicken or lamb in a watery gravy, with ice cream to follow.

How risqué was the Princess's life on Mustique? By all accounts, it was a curious combination of the jaunty and the ceremonial, the tone pitched somewhere between a lunch party at Balmoral and a hen party on Ibiza, any sauciness underpinned by deference, so that things rarely got out of hand. Anyone who overstepped the mark could expect a swift tongue-lashing from the Princess.

Buxom in her floral swimsuit, tipsy in the foreign sun, her adherence to protocol remained doggedly intact. Those who arrived too late or left too early could expect to be taken down a peg or two. On one occasion, Raquel Welch arrived for lunch halfway through pudding, beaming blithely at her hostess, as if under the illusion that she had done nothing wrong. It must have resembled one of those moments in *Goodfellas* when a podgy henchman, his life already hanging by a thread, carries on joking away while his fellow stooges hold their breath, knowing that this time he has gone too far. In response, the Princess took a good long slug on her cigarette holder, exhaled slowly, and then stared pointedly at her wristwatch.

The sun shone brightly on Mustique, but there was always the risk of frost.

70

Princess Margaret's biographers are unsure what to think about John Bindon. Who was he? What did he get up to? Can he be trusted? How far did he go?

Tim Heald introduces him as 'the least appealing' of the 'doubtful characters' attracted to Mustique in the 1970s. In a footnote, he offers this brief pen-portrait: 'John Bindon (1943–1992). Violent criminal of exhibitionist disposition who visited Mustique and claimed to have had an affaire [sic] with Princess Margaret.'

Theo Aronson follows suit, introducing Bindon as a sure sign of the way in which Mustique in the 1970s was 'beginning to act as a magnet for some of society's more disreputable elements'. Bindon was, he continues, 'an East Ender with a criminal record who visited the island on a couple of occasions. He briefly met the Princess, who was said to be amused by his cockney rhyming slang and his hilarious stories of his time in gaol.'

Nigel Dempster followed suit, describing him as 'an East Ender with a criminal record'. Bindon had, he says, 'been twice to Mustique, and had been boasting in Brixton Jail while on remand awaiting trial that he was an intimate of the Princess, and had photographs of them together to prove his relationship'.

John Dennis 'Biffo' Bindon was the son of a taxi driver. He was born in 1943, in Fulham, a good few miles from the East End. His first ten years went comparatively smoothly, but at the age of eleven he was charged with malicious damage. A few years later he was convicted of possession of live ammunition and sent to borstal.

Aged twenty-five, he appeared to have come good, having been presented with the Queen's Award for Bravery for diving into the Thames near Putney in a failed attempt to rescue a drowning man. However, Bindon was later heard boasting that he had pushed the man off Putney Bridge, and had dived in to save him only when he spotted a policeman coming.

Dividing his time between the antiques trade and 'security', Bindon happened to enter a pub while Ken Loach was filming *Poor Cow* in 1967, and found himself with a walk-on role. He went on to act in *Performance*, *Quadrophenia*, *The Mackintosh Man* and various episodes of *Hazell*, *The Sweeney* and *Softly, Softly*. His knack for playing thugs was boosted by the fact that he was one.

In 1978 he was charged with killing a violent gangster called Johnny Darke in a fight outside a pub in Putney. Once again, he successfully played the philanthropic card, convincing the jury that he had rushed to the defence of a man who had been knifed in the face by the deceased. Bindon thought the jury was swayed by the testimony of the actor Bob Hoskins, who appeared as a character witness. 'When Bob walked in, the jury knew I was OK.' He was acquitted.

In 1982, he pleaded guilty to employing a section of pavement as an offensive weapon; he explained that he had been upset when his victim, a man he described as 'short and weedy', accidentally bumped into him during his birthday celebrations. Two years later he was given a two-month suspended sentence for holding a carving knife to the face of a detective constable. In 1985 he was cleared of causing damage to an Earl's Court restaurant, and in 1988 he was cleared again, this time of threatening to petrol-bomb the home of a mother of three.

Despite this packed CV, John Bindon is now probably best remembered for his party piece with his penis. The biographers of Princess Margaret disagree on the specifics, but agree on the broad essentials.

Noel Botham clearly states that Bindon's 'unique cabaret turn' involved 'balancing three half-pint glasses on his erect penis'. Tim Heald is vaguer as to the number, believes it to have been more of a party trick than a cabaret turn, and is convinced it involved dangling rather than balancing: Bindon was, he says 'best known for a party trick that involved hanging beer tankards from his erect penis'.

Theo Aronson, on the other hand, fails to mention either glasses or tankards, simply saying that 'Bindon was apparently very proud of his "enormous penis" which he would display in the palm of his hand.' There was talk on the island that he had even once 'flashed it for Princess Margaret'.

Either way, it's all a far cry from the comings and goings at Balmoral. Royal biographers are a sensitive bunch, unused to totting up pint mugs on penises. On the other hand, beyond the world of royal biography, accounts also differ: *Brewer's Dictionary of Rogues and Villains* claims Bindon entertained Princess Margaret 'by balancing six glasses of beer on his penis', while his obituarist in the *Daily Telegraph* argued that 'He was justly famed for a party trick which entailed the balancing of as many as six half-pint mugs on one part of his anatomy.' In *Confessions of a King's Road Cowboy*, Johnny Cigarini, a contemporary of Bindon, confidently states that 'It was like a hose. His party trick in pubs was to put empty pint glasses on it and put his penis through the handles,' and goes on to estimate the final count as 'ten at one time, or something ridiculous'.

Christine Keeler, best known for her key role in the Profumo scandal, used to live two doors down the road from John Bindon in Seymour Place, Fulham. She remembers him fondly, referring to him as Biffo, 'because he was so bear-like'.

'Biffo's party trick,' she recalls, 'was to balance five half pints of beer on his penis. It attracted much attention.' Her numbers tally with those provided by Bindon's own biographer, Wensley Clarkson, though the two disagree as to method. On page 26 of his book *Bindon* (2007), Clarkson claims that the penis in question was twelve inches long, and that for forty years Bindon's 'favourite party trick' was to 'hang five half-pint beer glasses' from it.*

In his *Private Eye* diary for 15 November 1979, Auberon Waugh dismissed as 'ludicrous' and 'preposterous' the claim made in that week's *Daily Star* by 'Princess Margaret's friend John Bindon, the excitable actor', that 'when he had an erection he could balance five half-pint beer mugs on it'. The *Daily Star* article had been illustrated with five beer mugs.

Waugh added that he had been assured by 'sources close to Princess Margaret (N. Dempster)' that this estimate was 'wholly inaccurate. When Bindon was staying with Princess Margaret in Mustique, he never managed to balance more than one small sherry schooner in this way'. Waugh went on to express his fear that younger, more impressionable readers of the *Star* might be tempted into painful experimentation, 'in some cases involving serious damage'.

By now, this field of research is growing as complex as the Schleswig-Holstein Question, each expert contradicting the next. Time, then, for a handy chart:

BOTHAM: 3 half-pint glasses (balancing)
BREWER'S DICTIONARY: 6 glasses of beer (balancing)
CLARKSON: 5 half-pint glasses (hanging)
DAILY TELEGRAPH: 6 half-pint glasses (balancing)
HEALD: Unspecified number of 'tankards' (hanging)
KEELER: 5 half-pint glasses (balancing)
CIGARINI: 10 pint glasses (hanging)
WAUGH: 1 small sherry schooner (balancing)

Such vastly different accounts of such a comparatively minor detail in the history of the twentieth century might lead some to question the

---

* 'He would also sometimes dip his penis in people's glasses while saying, "He needs a drink!"' states Clarkson, adding that 'he never lost his outrageous sense of humour'.

very nature of biography. If no one – not even those who witnessed it – can agree on John Bindon's party piece, then what on earth can they agree on? Bindon is, after all, a pretty recent figure, having passed away in 1993 (or 1992 according to Heald) from either liver cancer (Clarkson) or an Aids-related illness (Cigarini). His stunt was witnessed by so many people on so many occasions that it might be said to have been his calling card. Yet no one can agree on exactly what it was.

Will we ever get to the bottom of what happened between John Bindon and Princess Margaret in the mid-1970s on the island of Mustique? Even the Princess's most fervent apologists agree that a meeting took place. There is, after all, this photograph to prove it: the Princess, her hair swept back, sitting at a sun-soaked picnic table in an extremely low-cut strapless swimsuit, and next to her, Bindon clad in an orange T-shirt bearing the legend 'Enjoy Cocaine'.

Bindon had been invited to Mustique by his vivacious young friend Dana Gillespie,* who had herself been invited by Lionel Bart,† who was a friend of Princess Margaret. 'I thought she was pulling my plonker until I realised she meant it,' Bindon told friends. The two of them had flown to Barbados before taking a boat to Mustique, 'the sort of tropical paradise I'd only seen in the Bounty ads on telly. There weren't a lot of people around – it ain't Southend.'

Soon after Bindon's arrival, the island's owner, Colin Tennant, took him to one side and instructed him on how to behave in front of the Princess. 'He gave me some tips on what to do, like "Don't talk to her until she talks to you."'

Before long, Bindon was invited to the Cotton House, where he was presented to the Princess: 'I remember thinking what nice skin she had.' They sat down to dinner. 'It was like the last great bastion of the Empire. Everyone was in evening dress and dickie bows. It was all white tablecloths, black waiters and loads of silver to puzzle you – which knife and fork to use.'

They found they had a surprising amount in common, and spoke of P.G. Wodehouse, acting and show business. Bindon was impressed. 'She seemed very much her own girl, not daft at all.' Conversation flowed, the Princess expressing an interest in Cockney rhyming slang. 'Sometimes she'd laugh and I had to explain what I was saying, like "Gay and hearty or Moriarty means party, Ma'am," and "Apples and pears is stairs."'

'She asked me, "What's a wally? Is it the same as a toby, that word you used earlier?" When I said yes, she said, "How silly, two words for

---

* Actress and singer. Born Richenda Antoinette de Winterstein Gillespie, 30 March 1949. British junior water-skiing champion, 1962. Created the role of Mary Magdalene in the original West End production of *Jesus Christ Superstar* (1972).

† Born Lionel Begleiter (1930–99). Composer, lyricist and playwright of, among other things, the musical *Oliver!* and the Cliff Richard song 'Living Doll', which he claimed to have written in six minutes flat. Though he was said to have earned £16 a minute from *Oliver!* in the sixties, he spent all his money, and was declared bankrupt in 1972, for which Princess Margaret called him a 'silly bugger'.

the same thing." … I think she liked me 'cos I nattered away quite happily.'

Bindon stayed on Mustique for three weeks, and entered the social swing. 'Her beach parties weren't exactly a snack on the sands. A fleet of cars would set all the guests down, plus the maids, tables, crockery, silver and glass. PM would be in a strapless costume or loose kaftan with her cigarette in one hand and a drink in the other.' Bindon, too, opted for the casual look. One day he borrowed Dana Gillespie's 'Enjoy Cocaine' T-shirt, which is how he came to be wearing it in the famous photograph.

According to him, the Princess would 'let her hair down' at Colin Tennant's evening parties, joining in the singing of saucy calypsos. But all gaiety was underpinned by etiquette. 'I asked what I should call her,' recalled Dana Gillespie, 'and she said, "Ma'am, just like a Christian name."'

Bindon followed suit, though Gillespie felt he was given more leeway than the others. 'At one point I remember John was talking to her and telling her funny stories, although respectfully calling her "Ma'am". Then he started singing, "Marks and Spencer's, she gets her knickers at Marks and Spencer's." It was hilarious, and John had broken the ice brilliantly, as usual.'

How far did they go? Bindon liked to make a show of refusing to talk about it, perhaps to give the impression that there was something to talk about.

Bindon's biographer, Wensley Clarkson,* thinks Bindon might have had a fling with the Princess, but, given the choice, even the most strait-laced biographers exert a bias towards consummation. Dana Gillespie apparently told Clarkson, 'Bindon was discreet. He would never have told if something did happen between them.' But at the

---

* His other books include biographies of Kenneth Noye, Fred West, the Great Train Robber Charlie Wilson and 'legendary south London criminal Jimmy Moody', as well as *Sexy Beasts: The Real Inside Story of the Hatton Garden Mob* and *Hitmen: True Stories of Street Executions*.

same time he says she was 'reluctant to talk in any more detail', which suggests there was more detail about which to talk. Or, like so many biographers, is Clarkson trying to make a mountain out of a molehill?

One of Bindon's girlfriends on Mustique apparently 'broke a thirty-year silence' to tell Clarkson 'what really happened' between Bindon and the Princess. Bindon supposedly swore this unnamed woman to silence, 'but admitted that he'd slept with her on Mustique just a couple of days before we met. I don't know why he told me. I guess he thought that because I was a local girl I'd never end up telling anyone important ...'

Another friend told Clarkson that Bindon 'let slip' to him that the Princess 'regularly' sent a car round to pick him up for 'love trysts' in Kensington Palace, 'but he was very nervous about mentioning it ... This is the first time I've told anyone.' There is a strong element of Chinese whispers about these passages: the ex-boyfriend of a former girlfriend of Bindon tells Clarkson that she told him that Bindon told her that he had indeed slept with Princess Margaret, but 'He kept it very quiet. He didn't shout about it. He told his girlfriend he'd be locked up for life if he started talking about it.'

On New Year's Eve 1975, Colin Tennant threw a party for everyone on the island. Guests included Mick Jagger, Jerry Hall and Bryan Ferry, as well as Dana Gillespie, Vicki Hodge* and John Bindon. 'It was a magic evening,' recalled Hodge. 'Colin spared no expense and we all enjoyed ourselves. The Princess joined in everything. When she sang, she had a lovely clear voice.' Bindon and the Princess joined in the dancing of The Gay Gordons and The Lancers.

Later, at a beach table, someone said to Bindon, 'Ma'am knows about your advantage in life and would really like to see it.' Bindon got up,

---

* Actress and model (1946–). Daughter of Sir John Rowland Hodge. Films include *The Stud* and *Confessions of a Sex Maniac*. Romantically linked with Ringo Starr, HRH Prince Andrew, Elliott Gould, Rod Stewart, Yul Brynner and David Bailey, among others.

and proceeded to walk down the beach with Margaret and her lady-in-waiting. According to Clarkson, 'He stopped about twenty yards from the lunch party, unzipped his flies and took out his flaccid penis which hung a full twelve inches down the side of one leg. Vicki Hodge and others watched from a distance as the princess examined it rather like a fossil. Everyone gasped. Bindon had a smile on his face but said nothing. After a few minutes, they all returned to the table. "I've seen bigger," said the lady-in-waiting.' Another report, passed on by Terrence Stamp, suggests that the lady-in-waiting was rather more specific, saying, 'I've seen bigger in Malaya.'

But there is a school of thought that regards this story as a smoke-screen. 'That was all bollocks to disguise the fact that John had been seeing Margaret in London,' an anonymous friend of Bindon told Clarkson. 'She already knew all about his tackle.'

71

After leaving Shrewsbury school, Roddy Llewellyn was deemed too short, at five foot nine inches, to join a Guards regiment. Instead he went to work at one of his father's factories in Newport, dipping the push-buttons for telephones into electroplating vats.

Coming into a modest inheritance of £3,000 from his grandfather, he said goodbye to the factory at the age of twenty-one, and took to the road as the co-partner of a mobile discothèque, 'Elevation Entertainment'.

It proved a flop, so he became an assistant at the College of Arms, supplementing his £15-a-week salary with a part-time job as a sales assistant at the fashionable DM Gallery in Fulham Road. For several months he lived with the interior decorator and man-about-town Nicky Haslam, but he left following a row.

Haslam claims that Roddy always nursed an ambition to meet Princess Margaret. 'He told me, as our friendship advanced, how he longed to meet Princess Margaret, whose marriage was now reportedly on the skids … It seemed a more interesting ambition than Lloyd's or the Foreign Office, and one that I might be able to nudge him toward. And the fact that Roddy, like Tony, was small, red-blonde, slim and Welsh made this fantasy possible.'

He mentioned Roddy's dream to Violet Wyndham, who in turn mentioned it to her cousin Colin Tennant, who happened to be having Princess Margaret to stay at The Glen, his castle in Scotland. 'She couldn't bear sitting next to women, and Colin hadn't got a spare man, so there was a bit of a crisis,' recalls a friend. Consequently, Violet Wyndham got in touch with Haslam: 'Colin hasn't got a spare man. I thought of you first, but how about darling Roddy? Do you know where I can find him?'

On 5 September 1973, Roddy arrived at 1 p.m. sharp, as instructed, at the Café Royal in Edinburgh. Colin Tennant was already there, sitting next to Princess Margaret, who was sipping a gin and tonic. Roddy was dressed in an old sweater and a high-collared shirt. Tennant, who had never set eyes on him before, later said he 'could see at once that he was what you would call "just the ticket"'.

Roddy sat down beside the Princess. She asked after his father, whom she had known for some twenty-odd years. 'It was obvious that something happened as soon as Princess Margaret saw Roddy,' said Tennant. 'She was taken with him immediately and devoured him through luncheon. It was a great relief.' After lunch, Margaret took Roddy shopping for swimming trunks. They picked a pair emblazoned with the Union Jack, and then travelled back to The Glen, huddled together in the back of Tennant's mini-bus.

For both, it appears to have been love at first sight: by the end of that first evening they were sitting together at the piano singing 'The bells are ringing, for me and my gal.' Seeing them there, Anne Tennant's immediate thought was, 'Heavens, what have I done?'

The next day, Roddy told Anne that he thought Princess Margaret had the most beautiful eyes. 'Don't tell me, tell her!' she replied. Roddy followed this advice, and it did the trick. Years later, Colin Tennant confessed to having hidden behind an arch on the main landing at The Glen that night. His stealth had been rewarded with a glimpse of toing-and-froing. 'By that evening, the tower was rocking,' recalls a friend.

Returning to the South Kensington flat he shared with his brother Dai, Roddy declared that he had just had the most wonderful week of his life; he was in love with the sister of the Queen. 'I was amazed for obvious reasons,' recalled Dai. 'But it was clearly true because she started telephoning him at the flat. How it happened, God knows, but it did and I was very pleased for him. He'd been through a very depressing time. Now he had a chance to build a new life with, of all people, Princess Margaret.'

Dai recounted all this in a great many interviews he gave over the next five years. This was, after all, the 1970s: the boundaries that had previously existed between the private and the public, between friendship and commerce, discretion and self-promotion, were fast becoming blurred. Dai Llewellyn was just one of many people, the Princess and Roddy among them, who in this brave new world of openness and candour were finding it increasingly hard to keep their lips buttoned.

That winter, Roddy moved out of his brother's flat and, with £19,000 given to him by his parents, bought a basement flat in Fulham. On her first visit, Princess Margaret was surprised by quite how small it was.* She had, she observed, known royal servants with more spacious accommodation. We know she said this, because she was in the habit of passing on such details to Nigel Dempster of the *Daily Mail*, often described as 'the doyen of gossip columnists', who was in due course to write her biography.

In March 1974, Roddy flew to Mustique. Together he and the Princess sang, sunbathed and played Scrabble; Roddy, always a keen gardener, had a go at planting shrubs and vegetables in the sandy soil. It was, he told his brother, 'almost like a honeymoon'. Back in Britain, Lord Snowdon tipped off a gossip column that his wife had gone abroad, leaving him to shiver back in the UK.

Though Snowdon was far from faithful, he was rattled by his wife's new friendship, and took to placing banana skins in its way. Knowing

---

* Older members of the Royal Family can still reveal themselves as surprisingly out-of-date as regards home interiors. Only a few years ago, the Queen went for a meal for the first time with neighbours near Sandringham. A few weeks later, she saw their son in London. 'So unusual, to have your dining room as part of your kitchen,' she said.

that Roddy was on Mustique, but knowing that Margaret didn't know he knew, he sent a telegram to her to sound the alarm – bogus, but effective – that he might just be dropping by:

> POSSIBLE ASSIGNMENT IN MEXICO MAY DROP IN ON WAY
> OUT SO LOOKING FORWARD TO SEEING YOU WILL CABLE
> DETAILS LATER FONDEST LOVE TONY

A couple of months later, Nicky Haslam was on the receiving end of numerous calls from both Margaret and Tony. 'The telephone at the studio crackled with breathy, infatuated yet imperious messages for Roddy, or late-night commands along the lines of "Get your friend out of my wife's bed" for me.'

As the Princess's relationship with Roddy blossomed, Haslam noticed her becoming increasingly standoffish towards him. 'When I asked one of the Princess's ladies-in-waiting why her boss was now rather cold … the answer was probably because I'd had a close friendship with Roddy before Margaret had. Oh dear, I thought. Wait till she finds out about my earlier one with Tony.'

Meanwhile, Roddy, always short of cash, had been refused a pay rise of £2 a week from the College of Arms. Learning of his plight, Colin Tennant pulled strings, and within weeks Roddy had become the personal assistant to Algy Cluff, who was making a fast fortune from North Sea oil. Sadly, a brief stint managing a mobile disco offered a poor grounding in the ins and outs of the international oil business. 'It was obvious to everyone at Cluff's that I didn't have a clue what was happening,' Roddy explained. 'I was whisked around the City all day by Rolls and occasionally asked to produce pieces of paper.'

In emotional turmoil – 'She had vamped him, and he couldn't quite manage it,' says a friend – he packed a suitcase, went to Heathrow airport and caught the first available plane, regardless of its destination. As it happened, it took him to Guernsey, a starchy, uneventful island upon which a single night proved more than enough. The next day he flew back to Heathrow, and from there to Istanbul. On the plane he got into conversation with a travel agent in the next seat, and told him that he was having an affair with a married woman, that it had all got too much for him, that the sex had become a problem, that he was growing a beard as a disguise, and that he was vaguely planning to go to India. Roddy was the trusting, chatty type, much given to sharing confidences.

He spent the next three weeks travelling around Turkey in a bus. Upon his return to London he found his desk at Cluff Resources occupied by someone more single-minded in his pursuit of oil. Meanwhile, Princess Margaret, in a similar state of disequilibrium, had taken a handful of sleeping pills, not quite dangerous, but sufficiently powerful to force her to cancel official engagements in Wolverhampton. A Kensington Palace spokesman explained that Her Royal Highness was suffering from 'a severe cold'.

* * *

At the start of 1975, Roddy remained unsettled. On a whim he flew to Barbados with a friend, who described him as being 'on a permanent high, behaving very irrationally, drinking rum and hardly eating anything'. At one point, he touched down on the island of Mustique. But it was bad timing, to say the least: Princess Margaret was having her parents-in-law to stay. Back in Barbados, Roddy was prescribed tranquillisers, and then bundled onto a plane back to London. The tranquillisers released his remaining inhibitions. On the flight, he walked up and down the aisle brandishing a Sunday newspaper, pointing to a photograph of himself and the Princess and telling perfect strangers, 'Look, that's me, that's my picture!' On his return to London he was admitted to Charing Cross Hospital, where he stayed for three weeks.

Meanwhile, back in Kensington Palace, Princess Margaret was growing increasingly distressed by her husband's affair with Lucy Lindsay-Hogg, whose flat was just around the corner in Kensington Square. 'There he was, living in my house, thinking he could have a lovely affair. I asked him for a separation but he laughed in my face. I would only know he was back at night when I heard him banging about in the bathroom – it was all hours. And he was drinking a lot of vodka in the morning, a bottle of wine at lunch and he even used to take a bottle up to his room afterwards. He was like an alcoholic. He was becoming a virtual stranger and we would meet on the stairs and growl at each other. And I had to go on behaving as if nothing was happening.'

How do we know all this? Where did it come from? It is in fact a direct quote from the Princess herself, talking to Nigel Dempster, who was by now the principal exporter of Kensington spice to the world beyond. Margaret first encountered him at a dinner party in 1971, where he had amused her by telling her how he had gained a recent scoop involving a bachelor bishop and a buxom young lady. With his eagle eye, he had spotted a 40D cup brassière on the clerical washing-line.

The Princess always liked to be kept up to date with the indiscretions of others.

Throughout the 1970s, and beyond, Princess Margaret remained in regular touch with Dempster. She became, in playground slang, a tell-tale-tit, feeding him stories to cast her enemies in an unflattering light. In this she was not alone: family feuds within Kensington Palace were often fought in the pages of the *Daily Mail* or the *Daily Express*. An acquaintance of Dempster refused to believe him when he claimed that key members of the Royal Family were among his regular sources. Dempster invited him to sit in his office for a morning. Sure enough, within the space of a couple of hours, calls came through from both Princess Margaret and another princess, who were at that time not speaking to one another.

Some years later, as the seventies gave way to the eighties, Dempster presented Princess Margaret with a seventeen-page synopsis of a proposed biography. They spent two hours polishing it up together, the Princess making helpful corrections and suggestions. In his gossip columns, Dempster always followed the tradition of attributing her quotes to 'a close friend' or 'a source close to the Palace', but the finished book was full of direct quotes attributed to her. 'She was eager to make sure that it was accurate, because she has never had a chance to put forth her case before,' Dempster explained to the *New York Times* on the book's publication in 1981. 'Princess Margaret figures that she has paid her dues, and that now it is time for her to get on with the next phase of her new life.' Her compulsion to talk to the press, and to settle scores, prefigured Princess Diana's by a dozen years, yet it did nothing to soften her condemnation of Diana when Andrew Morton's *Diana: Her True Story* appeared, out of the blue, in June 1992.

In the early summer of 1975 – a time when albums by Tangerine Dream, Steeleye Span, Pink Floyd and Mike Oldfield were high in the charts – Roddy Llewellyn was invited to put up £1,000 to join an unusually blue-chip commune based on Surrendell Farm near Malmesbury. The communards reckoned they could add to their agricultural income by opening a restaurant in Bath. In the event the farm was to have its electricity and phone cut off, and the restaurant, 'Parsenn Sally', was to close, having accrued debts of £28,000. But while that summer lasted, the dream of a hippy paradise remained intact.

Back with Roddy, Princess Margaret enjoyed the relaxed atmosphere of the commune, with its unexpected touch of glamour: the up-and-coming young actress Helen Mirren was sometimes a fellow guest. Margaret even helped with the farm's garden; she had always been a dab hand with the secateurs, snipping away with gay abandon at the burgeoning undergrowth. The ethos of Surrendell was free and easy. On one occasion Margaret gave the American singer John Phillips,* of the Mamas and the Papas, a lift down to the farm, and their friendship endured. 'She and John got on like a house on fire,' said Genevieve Waite, Phillips's long-time partner. At a party at Colin Tennant's Scottish castle they sang 'Chattanooga Choo Choo' together, and later, at Kensington Palace, a jaunty medley of Cole Porter songs.

---

* In a crowded field, Phillips (1935–2001) was possibly the most debauched person ever to have formed a friendship with a member of the Royal Family. After his death, his daughter Mackenzie claimed in her autobiography *High on Arrival* that he had subjected her to a ten-year incestuous relationship. He himself confessed in his autobiography, *Papa John*, that at one period in his life he was injecting himself with heroin every quarter of an hour. Moreover, his golden retriever Trelawny once 'gobbled up a bag full of mescaline caps and then ran in circles for three days without stopping ... then he just stared at himself in the mirror for twelve hours'.

72

For two and a half years the Princess's office at Kensington Palace was able to dismiss rumours of an affair with Roddy Llewellyn as so much gossip and tittle-tattle. Partly thanks to Colin Tennant's beady eye, anyone looking remotely journalistic was turned away from Mustique. This meant that the press had no firm evidence of an affair. But in February 1976 a New Zealand journalist managed to slip through the net, and photographed the pair sitting at the beach bar together, the Princess in her floral swimsuit. From then on, Margaret and Roddy were sitting ducks, perfect targets for finger-wagging from the politicians, tut-tuttery from opinionators, and tomfoolery from satirists.

'I suppose young Roddy Llewellyn knows what he is doing galli-vanting around the tropical island of Mustique with a foreign lady old enough to be his mother,' wrote Auberon Waugh in his *Private Eye* diary on 22 February 1976. '... I am sure that Marje Proops would agree with me when I suggest that a prolonged association between people of very different age groups seldom comes to much good. But if Roddy is too shy to write to either of us for advice he should go for a quiet word with Group Captain Peter Townsend in the French village near Rambouillet where he has retired and where he is famous for his scarred and hunted look.'

Those in search of less sophisticated comedy could find it in every bar and on every street corner. 'Have you heard that Roddy Llewellyn's

311

taken up acting?' went one of the jokes doing the rounds at that time. 'He's got a small part in Charlie's Aunt.'

From the Labour benches in Parliament, the veteran republican Willie Hamilton called on the chancellor of the exchequer, Denis Healey, to withdraw the Princess's income. 'Even when she is here, a lot of her so-called engagements are audiences which last perhaps a couple of minutes. There are charity balls and premieres which are really entertainment, yet which are called official engagements.'

That August, Princess Margaret and Roddy went to a raucous house party at The Glen. Their fellow guests included John Phillips, Bianca Jagger and Prince Rupert Loewenstein.* The weekend culminated in an amateur concert performance for friends and neighbours, at which Princess Margaret dressed up in a slinky black dress, a feather boa and a curly blonde wig, and pretended to be Sophie Tucker, performing her risqué 'Red Hot Mama' routine.

Anne Tennant took photographs, then placed the negatives in a drawer for safekeeping. But they were purloined by her son Charlie, a heroin addict; through a dodgy third party he sold them to the *Daily Mail* for £7,000, of which only £100 found its way back to Charlie.

Photographs of the Princess and Roddy were at a premium. At one time or another, various members of the Tennant family had struggled, not always successfully, with the temptation of putting them to good use. One such photograph had been taken when Mustique had been infected by the incautious 1970s craze for streaking. 'Colin went through a short "streaking" period and would drop his trunks at the earliest opportunity,' recalled his friend and biographer Nicholas

---

* Full name Rupert Louis Ferdinand Frederick Constantine Lofredo Leopold Herbert Maximilian Hubert John Henry zu Loewenstein-Wertheim-Freudenberg (1933–2014), banker and financial adviser. Best known for his highly successful management of the business interests of the Rolling Stones for nearly forty years. In 2005, Jagger, Richards and Watts earned £81.3 million while paying tax at 1.6 per cent.

Courtney. At a picnic on the beach, Tennant had turned to the Princess. 'Would you mind awfully, Ma'am, if I were to remove my swimming trunks?'

'So long as I don't have to look at IT,' replied the Princess, ring-fencing the final word with a withering emphasis. But her squeamishness did nothing to deter Tennant, who stripped naked and persuaded Roddy Llewellyn and Courtney to follow suit. The Princess herself remained firmly in her carefully upholstered floral chintz swimming costume.

Tennant borrowed Llewellyn's camera and took a snap of the Princess with the stark-naked Llewellyn and Courtney on either side of her, the skirts of her swimming costume enveloping, or at least obscuring, her two companions' private parts. In turn, the Princess took photographs of the three naked men performing comical poses together.

Tennant took care to remove the film from Roddy's camera. He wanted to prevent it from falling into the wrong hands, without realising that the wrong hands were none other than his own. Rather than destroy the negatives, he arranged for them to be developed by his local chemist in Scotland; he then squirrelled the prints away in the bottom drawer of his desk.

Years later, in her published diaries, Tennant's arty half-sister Emma revealed that she had been plotting to steal either these photographs, or others in a similarly fruity vein. With the proceeds, she hoped to finance an avant-garde literary magazine called, coincidentally, *Bananas*. Timing her arrival at The Glen for an hour when everybody would be out at the swimming pool, she stole her way through the hall and into the drawing room, where she uncovered her sister-in-law's photograph albums in their usual safe place. Sifting through them, she found the recent snaps of Mustique. 'Palm trees of course, one or two of them set at picturesque angles to show we are really in the Caribbean here – without them one could imagine a house party in the south of England on a hot day. Upper-class families are sprawled on wicker chairs, one lordling actually hurling what seems to be a bread roll in a picture of Basil's Bar ... Women, dukes' daughters and ex-wives, in huge hats as if at Ascot ...'

Eventually, she chanced upon the most coveted photograph of all, 'and I deliver it from the confines of four little grey tucks in the stiff grey paper. I thrust Princess Margaret – there's no time to see if she's actually naked, but the picture gives at first glance that impression – into my shirt, open-necked on this fine summer's day. Roddy Llewellyn comes into my bosom, too: he's very much in focus, attentive, even loving, clearly an amorous couple is what this holiday snap announces.'

At this point, Colin came into the room. Quick as a flash, Emma returned the album to its place, and stood upright. 'I feel the purloined photo cut into my flesh, anchored by the top of my bra, and I wonder, for the first time as I am ashamed to own, whether it will really fetch the money needed to start up a literary magazine. However, I can hardly fish it out now, the consequences being too extreme even to imagine.' Back in London, 'glamorous friends ... advise me crisply on the subject of selling P.M. in *semi-flagrante*'. The journalist James Fox told her that *Paris Match* paid best.

But she had too many qualms to be able to follow through on her dastardly plan. Paralysed by conscience, she stowed the offending photograph in a volume by Diderot. A week or two later, she learned that her sister-in-law had noticed the disappearance of the photograph, and had called in the Peebles police. All the staff were now being cross-questioned. Deciding that her escapade had gone far enough, Emma attempted to flush the offending photograph down the lavatory, but it kept bobbing to the surface, so she fished it out, locked the bathroom door, employed a pair of nail scissors to cut it into pieces, and then tried to flush them all down again. Alas, 'the faces and other portions of Princess Margaret and her companion floated determinedly through repeated flushings. Finally, maddened and punished by their resolve never to go down, I had to pick out the pieces and wrap them in old newspaper before consigning them dangerously to the bin.'*

Some time later, in February 1976, a selection of Mustique photographs appeared in the *News of the World*. In some of them Roddy was wearing the very same Union Jack swimming trunks he had bought with Princess Margaret on their first shopping trip together. True to form, Willie Hamilton demanded in the House of Commons that the Princess be 'sacked'. A week later, the same photographs were published again, this time in full colour, in *Paris Match*. 'Few believed Colin when he said that he had nothing to do with the sale,' observes Courtney in his biography.

Their publication accelerated the Snowdons' separation. Even within the confines of Kensington Palace, the Princess's embarrassment presented Tony with a golden opportunity: he was now perfectly placed to portray himself as the wronged party. He declared that he felt humiliated, that his position was 'quite intolerable', and that a separation was the only possible solution. 'Lord Snowdon,' Margaret was to tell Nigel Dempster years later, 'was devilish cunning.'

The day after the photographs appeared in the *News of the World* – a Monday – Snowdon summoned the Princess's private secretary, Lord Napier, and showed him the newspaper. 'What's going on?'

Though Snowdon proved adept at playing the part of the startled cuckold, Napier remained unconvinced. Everyone in Britain, and many further afield, had been aware for months that Princess Margaret had been having a fling with Roddy Llewellyn. Nor was Snowdon

---

* A more dramatic theft gave rise to the 2007 film *The Bank Job*, which is predicated on the hypothesis that sexually compromising photographs of Princess Margaret were at the centre of a raid on Lloyd's Bank in Baker Street in 1971. The robbers had rented a leather-goods shop two doors down. Over the course of three weeks, they dug a tunnel forty feet long. The photographs had apparently been placed in the bank by Michael X, a criminal originally from the Caribbean, who was later hanged for murder in Trinidad. Though half a million pounds were indeed stolen from the bank, the film is more speculative in suggesting that the raid was organised by MI5, purely to suppress the photographs. The Heath government stopped further investigation of the raid by issuing a D-Notice, consequently fanning this rumour.

CRAIG BROWN

blameless in that department: he himself was in the middle of his long affair with Lucy Lindsay-Hogg, whom he was eventually to marry. Napier told Snowdon to stop being so ridiculous.

At this point Snowdon buzzed his secretary, Dorothy Everard.* 'Dotty, we're leaving.' Then he turned to Napier. 'We'll be out by the end of the week.'

This left Lord Napier with the tricky task of telling Princess Margaret, who was still on Mustique. Aware that the phone line was leaky, he couched what he said in a wary mixture of code and euphemism.

'Ma'am, I have been talking to ROBERT. He has given in his notice. He will be leaving by the end of the week.'

Unfortunately, the Princess did not catch his drift. 'Have you taken leave of your senses? What ARE you talking about?'

Napier repeated what he had to say, extra slowly: 'ROBERT – has – given – in – his – notice. He – will – be – out – by – the – end – of – the – week.'

At this point, the Princess suddenly clocked that Robert was her husband's third name. 'Oh, I SEE! Thank you, Nigel. I think that's the best news you've ever given me.'

* By a curious coincidence, 'Everard' was also the name of the close friend often mentioned onstage by the comedian Larry Grayson (1923–95). Dorothy Everard was perhaps best known for playing Pass the Parcel and dancing The Gay Gordons.

316

73

Tony found temporary accommodation in a small basement flat in West Halkin Street belonging to Jeremy Fry, his original choice of best man, and the supposed father of Snowdon's illegitimate daughter. Margaret returned from Mustique on 2 March, her head wrapped in a turquoise scarf and dark glasses. A fortnight later, on 17 March, the *Daily Express* revealed that the royal couple were to separate. It was a busy time for news: on that same day, the prime minister, Harold Wilson, resigned, and the trial began at Exeter Crown Court of Mr Andrew 'Gino' Newton on charges of possessing a firearm with intent to endanger life. The life in question was that of Mr Norman Scott, the former male model who had, as luck would have it, once enjoyed a close friendship with Snowdon's second choice of best man, the leader of the Liberal Party, Jeremy Thorpe.

Two days later, Kensington Palace issued a statement saying that the couple had 'agreed mutually to live apart'. This, in turn, found Auberon Waugh 'thrown into gloom and despair', though the source of his misery was less the content of the statement than its phrasing:

'Wrong or redundant uses of "mutual" are a well known trap, as Fowler points out. In this case, the use is not so much incorrect as otiose,' he pointed out. 'Every agreement between two people is mutual – is it not? – or there would be no agreement.' He condemned the announcement as an example of 'New Proletarian Fine Writing, the English of John Lennon and Dave Spart'. The Royal Family, he continued, 'has always shunned the world of letters, but at least until now it has had the good manners to make sure its English was respectable. If it can't do better than this, we should send them all straight back to Germany.'

The news travelled around the world, and even affected President Idi Amin of Uganda, who managed to pluck a message for all mankind from the ruins of the royal marriage: 'I hope it will be a lesson to all of us men not to marry ladies in a very high position,' he said. On a photographic assignment in Sydney, Snowdon, looking desperately upset, delivered an emotional interview on television. But Princess Margaret remained unmoved. 'I have never seen such good acting,' she said.

A month later, Auberon Waugh confessed to being 'seriously worried' about Princess Margaret's newly solitary state, fearing that 'there may be no men left with enough heart for the job'. He had, he said, suggested to the Queen that she might place an advertisement in the personal columns of *Private Eye*, but Her Majesty had been hesitant, feeling that 'this might cheapen the monarchy'.

But then Waugh had a brainwave. 'What about asking the Victoria and George Cross Association to Windsor? Surely, among their number we can find an unattached male who would not flinch from what has been described as the most gruelling job in Britain?'

More conventional journalists remained busy with their wallets, placing temptation in the path of anyone with the slightest knowledge of the unhappy couple. The *Daily Express* offered Roddy's commune £6,000 for a group photograph, to be handed over in cash, in a brown paper bag. 'I said, why not?' recalled Roddy. 'So we all piled into the van and went back to the farm where we agreed to this photograph. Like a fool, I only kept £500 for myself and put the rest into the restaurant, which was in trouble. It was a silly gesture, but the sort of thing one does in a commune, I suppose.'

74

Like many innocents, Roddy was easily swayed. If a potential scoop was tactfully packaged as a bit of a laugh, he would happily go along with it, often with unfortunate results. In April, he turned up at Tramp nightclub in Jermyn Street wearing a T-shirt with the logo 'Roddy for PM'. Towards the end of 1977 he was approached by a Turkish leather merchant called Victor Melik with the offer of a recording contract. He leapt at it, explaining, 'I've got a list of things I want to do in life, and one of them is to sing a record.' Melik had high hopes that Roddy's earnings could run to £250,000. 'If we can find the right song for him and produce a hit,' he told the press, 'then the sky's the limit ... We think Roddy has a very good voice and has a great future. He will sing ballads in the John Denver style. I don't think he is cashing in on his fame through Princess Margaret.'

Having signed the contract, Roddy appointed a public relations adviser whose list of clients included a number of reassuring names from the world of light entertainment: Des O'Connor, Mike Yarwood, Norman Wisdom. Carefully-picked interviewers listened sympathetically as Roddy tried to explain how he had come to record a pop song. 'I consulted the Princess before taking up the offer to make records and she likes the idea of my becoming a pop singer. We are always singing together. One of our favourites is "The Bells Are Ringing" ... My musical career is my first priority. I know I've been quite a fickle character in the past and hopefully I can settle down to singing.'

Roddy's debut was on French television, in a duet with Petula Clark. On the first two takes, he had sprung to his feet a touch too soon; in the third, the champagne flute he handed to Clark was clearly empty. But the fourth take was considered good enough to transmit. It can still be viewed on YouTube: Roddy may look a little awkward in his fancy dinner jacket and fashionable flares, nervously jogging his leg up and down while miming to 'L'Avventura' in French ('When you kiss me, everything under the sun is new ... The adventure is to sleep every night in your arms'), but he doesn't do too badly, all things considered.

At the end of February 1978 he flew to Mustique for a holiday, but was 'badly run down', and went to hospital in Barbados. 'His faeces were pitch-black,' records Nigel Dempster, with off-putting omniscience, in his semi-authorised biography. Princess Margaret's regular visits to Roddy's bedside generated further headlines, and the headlines generated further comment, which in turn generated further headlines. 'Here she is, going away with her boyfriend to a paradise island while we are being asked to tighten our belts,' spluttered the Labour MP Dennis Canavan. Willie Hamilton was equally incensed: 'If she thumbs her nose at taxpayers by flying off to Mustique to see this pop-singer chap, she shouldn't expect the workers of this country to pay for it.'

On his return to England, Roddy responded to their critics. 'I would like to see Willie Hamilton or any of the others do all her jobs in the marvellous way that she does. People love the Monarchy and appreciate with their whole hearts the job she does. I shall go on seeing Princess Margaret when and where I want ... I am a loyal and obedient servant of the Queen.'

But Hamilton was no lapdog: a few words of reproof only encouraged him to sink his teeth deeper into the bone. 'For anybody to say seriously that Princess Margaret works hard is absurd nonsense. She has had eight public engagements to date this year and that is in three months. In that time she has drawn about £14,000 – not bad for eight performances. The Royal Family themselves must be very disturbed by the defence coming from this quarter. I think this is the last thing they would want.'

And so the tuttathon continued, each action sparking yet another reaction from politicians, columnists and readers: tut-tuts followed by more tut-tuts, then tut-tuts at the tut-tuts, tut-tuts at the tut-tuts at the tut-tuts, and so on, and so forth, *ad infinitum*. Church leaders now joined in this Tuttelujah Chorus. The Bishop of Truro, Dr Graham Leonard, condemned the Princess's holiday with Roddy as 'foolish' and called for her immediate resignation from public life.

Meanwhile, Roddy, the put-upon anti-hero of a picaresque novel, wide-eyed and feckless, sheepish and gallivanting, opportunist and victim, was finding more and more offers strewn across his path, each promising something for nothing, or if not for nothing, then for not very much: an advance on a gardening book, *Town Gardens*, for Lord Weidenfeld; a monthly retainer of £1,000 from his manager, Claude Wolff; a weekly retainer of £150 to oversee the pots and plants at Bennett, a new nightclub in Battersea; and the chance to judge the Miss Great Britain beauty contest in Morecambe, alongside fellow judges the show jumper Harvey Smith, the knockabout comedian Harry Worth, the snooker champion Ray Reardon and the singer and comedienne Marti Caine. He also undertook a series of interviews in which whatever he said always came back to the one topic he was struggling so hard to avoid.

'Staying with one woman indefinitely is out of the question. I'm far too selfish,' he told *Woman's World*. 'I couldn't bear to have a wife who snored or slept with the window open when I wanted it closed or did anything I didn't want her to. And I have no desire to have children … I'm a yokel at heart. I don't really like London much, though I must admit I love visiting for two or three days, being terribly naughty and then disappearing again.'

These chatty outpourings didn't help the Princess. 'Such a pity Princess Margaret is threatening to let down the royal family,' the liberal broadcaster Ludovic Kennedy said to his old friend, the British ambassador to France Nico Henderson. 'His reactions are those of Mr Liberal Everyman,' Henderson noted in his diary.

At the end of April, Roddy was advised to make himself scarce. Accordingly he flew to Tangier, a city which for decades had pulsed with the hullabaloo of people making themselves scarce. On 19 May 1978, the reason for his scarcity became evident. From Kensington Palace came the official announcement: 'Her Royal Highness The Princess Margaret, Countess of Snowdon, and the Earl of Snowdon, after two years of separation have agreed that their marriage should formally be ended ...'

Within minutes, Roddy had been traced to Tangier, and asked for a comment, which he duly delivered with his usual level of chattiness. 'I am saying categorically that I will never marry Princess Margaret. Circumstances – personal reasons – would prevent it. I don't consider myself in any way responsible for the divorce. Of course I hope to see her again. One always likes to see one's friends.'

His album, *Roddy*, was finally launched in September 1978, amidst much fanfare, at Tramp nightclub. But it failed to take off. Having promised to make it their Record of the Week, Radio 2 dropped it in favour of *Bobby Goldsboro's Greatest Hits*. Plans for an appearance on *The Morecambe and Wise Show* also came to nothing. Sales proved disappointing: in a fortnight, only thirteen copies had sold at London's largest record store, HMV, compared to 460 copies of the soundtrack of *Grease*. 'This album is not setting the world on fire,' confessed its producer, Tony Eyers.*

Things began to unravel. Llewellyn accused the owner of Bennett nightclub of exploiting his good name. 'All I did was shove a few plants in a few pots, yet the world was made to believe I was director for publicity purposes.' In turn, the owner suggested that it was Roddy

---

* Eyers' more successful work included 'I Love to Love (But My Baby Loves to Dance)' by Tina Charles, 'Paddy McGinty's Goat' by Val Doonican, and 'Little Arrows' by Leapy Lee.

who had been doing the exploiting. 'Originally Roddy was just going to landscape the garden. Later, it was agreed that he would pose for photographs and supervise membership and be paid £7,500 a year. He even told us he would bring Princess Margaret to the club.'

In the midst of these shenanigans, Princess Margaret was unflappable. Through it all, her devotion to Roddy remained unshaken. 'Sometimes I think he is the only man to have ever treated Princess Margaret properly,' observed Colin Tennant decades later. 'For instance, they were playing gin rummy one day with Roddy keeping the score. Princess Margaret asked what it was, he passed over the pad, and when she turned the page, there was a message he had written: "You are looking very beautiful today."'

For all his undoubted sweetness, Roddy was a loose cannon. Soon after Princess Margaret's Civil List allowance had been raised by £5,000 to £64,000 to take inflation into account, he ran into a spot of bother with the law. Upon leaving a party at Regine's nightclub in celebration of Shirley Bassey's twenty-five years in show business, he pranged an undercover police car with his Ford Transit. 'After the accident,' reported a police spokesman, 'the van continued and the police car, a general-purpose unmarked red Chrysler Hunter, which had not been badly damaged, pursued it and stopped it in Kensington High Street near Kensington Palace Gardens.'

Roddy's Ford Transit finally came to a standstill after hitting a bollard. He pleaded innocent, or at least ignorant. 'I wasn't drunk at all, which was so silly,' he said. 'I had no idea I had touched another car. I did feel a bump or something, but nothing of importance, and drove on. Then, suddenly, I found I was being chased by half the police force of London.' He was breathalysed, and found to be 80 per cent over the limit.

From time to time the Princess and Roddy attended events together, but only if absolute discretion was assured. On a visit to London in July 1979, Andy Warhol spotted the two of them together at a party in the Savoy Hotel. 'We were upstairs and we didn't know the party was upstairs and downstairs,' he recorded in his diary. 'The downstairs party had Princess Margaret and Halston,* Liza† and everybody, and when we finally realised we were missing it, we went downstairs. Halston was nervous, but his party was terrific, had the best time. Victor‡ wanted me to meet Princess Margaret, and I didn't but I got two pictures. Victor got two photos of Princess Margaret and Roddy Llewellyn. They didn't want to be seen together and they wanted to take his film away but Fred§ said not to, that Victor was with Halston. Left the party about 4:00 went to Liza's room. She was wearing a really beautiful see-through fabric dress with her hair brushed back like her mother used to wear it … It was a wig but I couldn't tell.'

In Fleet Street and beyond, the asking price for details of Princess Margaret's racy affair with a younger man continued to rise. In January 1980, Roddy's older brother Dai accepted £30,000 from the *News of the World*. He was, he explained, in 'a very vulnerable position', heavily in debt. 'I've written Pa and Roddy notes telling them I've been a naughty boy and asking their forgiveness, but I had to go through with it. The money will pay off all my debts and give me a fresh start – it's as simple as that.'

In retrospect, the Llewellyn brothers may be seen as novice surfers on the waves of indiscretion that swept the British Isles in the decades to follow. Roddy gave interviews in which he condemned Dai's 'gross betrayal'. 'If you write a load of tripe like that and describe your brother as a pansy, surely you must expect to run into flak? I said, David, you've

---

* Roy Halston Frowick (1932–90), American fashion designer, commonly known by his middle name.

† Liza Minnelli (1946–), American entertainer best-known for her role in *Cabaret* (1972).

‡ Victor Hugo (1948–), Venezuelan boyfriend of Halston. His surname was believed to be a pun on his 'huge-o' private parts.

§ Fred Hughes (1943–2001), Warhol's business manager.

cooked yourself here. You should get out of England. But of course he took no notice.' Even the brothers' complaints about indiscretions were hopelessly indiscreet.

In turn, Dai poured out his heart to society's father confessor, Nigel Dempster, in the sanctuary of the *Daily Mail*: 'That's the trouble with Roddy. He badmouths Pa and me to Princess Margaret and she is taken in by his side of the story ... I've never let Roddy down, yet I've hardly known an instance when I've helped him and he hasn't kicked me in the teeth ... With Roddy, it's always been, "Look at me, look at me." He's never been part of the set that I have, just hanging around the edges and resenting it. I have no interest in his friends – they are the most awful bunch of hippies and pooves and I can't stand them. They sit around all evening talking about each other's neuroses.'

In November 1980, Princess Margaret was given a belated fiftieth birthday party at the Ritz Hotel. The owners – the Trafalgar House Group, of which Margaret's old friend Jocelyn Stevens was deputy chairman – had offered exceptionally favourable terms, mindful of the publicity the event would induce.

It was Roddy Llewellyn who had come up with the idea of a party in the Princess's honour, but many of her more traditional friends had been reluctant to throw their hats in the ring, anxious to avoid getting on the wrong side of the Queen by associating their names with his. There was always a hint of Vito Corleone about Her Majesty – or, to put it another way, she is singularly blessed with what Evelyn Waugh once called 'the sly, sharp instinct for self-preservation that passes for wisdom among the rich'. Unable to rally everyone, Roddy dropped out. At this point, a committee made up largely of traditionalists took over the arrangements.

Was Roddy to be invited? The committee was divided. Her Royal Highness wanted him, but Her Majesty did not. One of Margaret's oldest friends, Dominic Elliott, sided with the Queen, which made Margaret so livid that she told him she never wanted to see him again.

At this, Elliott resigned from the committee, and refused to come to the party.

Eventually, a compromise was reached: Roddy would not be among the forty invited to dinner at the Ritz, but he would be permitted to pop in afterwards, along with 140 others, for drinks and dancing.

But who was to give Roddy dinner? It was decided that the Tennants should forgo their invitation to the first part of the evening in order to look after him. Understandably, this upset them. 'We feel just like the servants, being invited in after dinner,' Lady Anne complained to a friend. In other families, it would have seemed extraordinary that an elder sister could dictate who was coming to her younger sister's fiftieth birthday party; and odder still that the younger sister should go along with it. But this was the British Royal Family, and even on her birthday, Margaret's personal wishes were subordinate to its continued prosperity.

For his own thirty-third birthday in October 1980, Roddy accepted an offer from the up-and-coming Northern club-owner Peter Stringfellow of a free party at the newly opened Stringfellow's night-club ('the epitome of fine dining, service and certainly the most beautiful girls you will ever have the pleasure of meeting'). There he happened to meet a travel writer called Tania Soskin. They soon became an item. For a while he kept the news from Princess Margaret, but she began to sense that something was not quite right. 'I forced the story out of him eventually,' she told Nigel Dempster. 'He told me he was in love and wanted to marry. I had absolutely no idea it had been going on.'

Within six months, Roddy and Tania had become engaged. Princess Margaret seems to have taken the news with exceptional grace, even throwing a lunch party for them in celebration. 'I'm really very happy for him,' she enthused to Dempster. 'Anyway, I couldn't have afforded him much longer.'

Roddy Llewellyn and Tania Soskin were married on 11 July 1981. Just over a fortnight later, cheering crowds gathered in London to celebrate the wedding of HRH the Prince of Wales and Lady Diana Spencer. For the first time in years, it seemed as though, on the strength of a simple love story, the Royal Family had regained the loyalty and support of its people; from this day forward, nothing could possibly go wrong.

75

The director of the National Theatre, Richard Eyre, goes to the opening of the new Andrew Lloyd Webber musical *Aspects of Love* with Max and Jane Rayne and Princess Margaret, who arrives with Norman St John Stevas. The Princess of Wales is also there. Eyre studies the two Princesses.

> Princess Di appears with her friends and, one gathers, her lover, giving us the opportunity to compare and contrast two princesses at close quarters. Princess Margaret gestures emphatically and rather self-consciously, keen to establish the persona of a 'jolly' girl, but if it weren't for the sharp English upper-class voice, you'd say she looks like a Maltese landlady: small, frowning, drawn and unhealthy. Diana is pretty but not beautiful, tall, slightly awkward and faintly pitiable. Margaret talks to me about opera: 'Can't stand it. A lot of frightfully boring people standing still onstage and yelling.'

Eyre asks her about Alan Bennett's new play, *A Question of Attribution*, which features Sir Anthony Blunt and the Queen. 'She's quite tart about it. She didn't approve of putting the head of state on stage, but would like to watch it from the wings. She's wary of "Bennett", she says.'

76

'I've always adored Margot,' Princess Diana told her friend James Colthurst, before things took a turn for the worse. 'I love her to bits and she's been wonderful to me from day one.'

At the party in Buckingham Palace to celebrate Diana's wedding, Margaret walked around with a balloon jauntily attached to her tiara. Diana used to greet Margaret by throwing her arms around her neck; she was one of the handful outside the immediate family permitted to address her as 'Margot'.

This encouraged Diana to imagine that her friendship was boundless, and that as her marriage disintegrated, Margaret would take her side, and be happy to listen to her waspish comments about Charles. Instead, Margaret grew increasingly prone to avoid her.

When it became clear that Diana had been the principal source for the revelations in Andrew Morton's book *Diana: Her True Story*,* Princess Margaret sent her a furious note of reproof. Around this time, Margaret complained about her next-door neighbour to a friend: 'Poor Lilibet and Charles have done everything they can to get rid of the wretched girl, but she just won't go.'

On the evening of the Prince of Wales's forty-seventh birthday,

---

* In his book-of-the-book, published after Diana's death, Morton makes it clear that the Princess of Wales's participation in *Diana: Her True Story* was total. She was the organ-grinder, he the monkey; she even made last-minute changes to the blurb.

Diana confided to twenty-three million viewers that there was a family conspiracy against her. 'I was the separated wife of the Prince of Wales. I was a problem, full stop. Never happened before. What do we do with her? She won't go quietly, that's the problem. I'll fight to the end, because I believe that I have a role to fulfil, and I've got two children to bring up.'

'You really believe that it was out of jealousy that they wanted to undermine you?' asked her interviewer, Martin Bashir.

'I think it was out of fear,' replied the Princess. 'Because here was a strong woman doing her bit, and where was she getting her strength from to continue?'*

For Margaret, this was the final straw. Her wrath was fierce and unstoppable. When the programme came to an end, she went around her Kensington Palace apartment turning over every magazine with the Princess of Wales on its cover. The next day, she made it clear to her children that they were never again to be friends with the woman she called 'that wretched girl'.†

To send a fellow resident of Kensington Palace to Coventry is not easy, as the chances of an encounter are so high. Nevertheless, Princess Margaret proved well up to the task, cutting Diana dead whenever their paths crossed.‡ Her son, Viscount Linley, liked to spend his afternoons tinkering with a sports car, but he would obediently dart behind the garage wall rather than risk a greeting from the *persona non grata*. 'He went out of his way to avoid her,' recalled Margaret's chauffeur,

---

* Twenty years on, watching the programme on YouTube is a spooky business. Diana looks like a vengeful ghost, her huge dark panda eyes looming reproachfully out of her ashen face as her damning words pour forth. Self-pity of this magnitude takes on a power in death denied it in life. 'And all who heard should see her there! And all should cry, Beware! Beware! Her flashing eyes, her floating hair!'

† The same sort of reaction was replicated in Clarence House. The Queen Mother refused to hear Diana's name mentioned. After her death, the Queen Mother dutifully dressed in black, but would never utter her name.

‡ She had already put in quite a bit of practice. She once boasted to a friend that she'd never spoken to Princess Michael of Kent, and never intended to.

David Griffin. When Diana bought something for Margaret's daughter Lady Sarah's first baby in July 1996, she gave the parcel to Griffin to deliver, rather than risk presenting it to her personally.

Diana's death did little to diminish Margaret's animosity. It might even have served to increase it, or at least turned her triumphalist, for death belongs to that district of Coventry from which no one returns. 'She didn't like any of the emotionalism one bit,' recalled Anne Tennant. 'She said the hysteria was rather like Diana herself. It was as if when she died she got everyone to be as hysterical as she was.'

Alone among the Royal Family, Margaret argued that Diana's corpse should not be allowed to rest in the Royal Chapel, nor be honoured with a royal funeral. On the day of the funeral, all the other members of the Royal Family bowed their heads as the coffin passed, but Margaret offered it only the most cursory of nods, almost as though she were warding off a fly. She was furious, too, about the mass of flowers outside Kensington Palace, complaining that they would have to double-dig the ground to get all the wax out. Later, she led the opposition to a move to replace the statue of King William III outside Kensington Palace with one of the late Princess of Wales.

'I'm not having that woman outside my bedroom window,' she said.

77

Margaret also made clear what she thought of the bubbly Sarah, Duchess of York, after a newspaper had published photographs of her lying topless on a sun-lounger on the Côte d'Azur with her big toe being sucked by her financial adviser.

Yet it had all begun so well. The Duchess of York's autobiographical account of the moment she exchanged wedding vows in July 1986 sounds a triumphant note, almost as though she had just come from the back of the field to reach the final of the hundred-yard Windsor sprint:

> In a trice, I had become Princess Andrew and the Duchess of York, as
> well as the Countess of Inverness and Baroness of Killyleagh. In the
> order of royal precedence I now outranked Anne and Margaret;
> among the women I stood fourth, behind the Queen, the Queen
> Mother, and the Princess of Wales.
>
> While we signed the marriage books, I replaced the flowers that
> had anchored my veil with a diamond tiara for my return trip down
> the aisle. It was my time to be Cinderella. I had stepped up as the
> country girl, now I would walk back as a Princess.

But her triumph was to be short-lived. In 1992 a newspaper carried photographs of her topless with her 'financial adviser' John Bryan. The main photograph, published throughout the known world, had a surreal quality about it, the bald head of the businessman looking uncannily like another big toe.

On the morning of the publication of the *Daily Mirror* exclusive – 'FERGIE'S STOLEN KISSES' – the Duchess was staying at Balmoral. Forewarned, she took breakfast in her bedroom, creeping down to apologise to the Queen at 9.30 a.m. The Queen, she recalled, was 'furious'. At dinner that evening, she felt that everyone was staring at her. 'I *knew* they must be seeing me topless, or being nuzzled by a bald American. The courtiers eyed me sneakily, discreetly. The butlers and footmen gaped, and I felt naked in their sight … I felt disgust in that dining room and a queasy fascination, as if they were looking at a burn victim.'

Down in Kensington Palace, Princess Margaret took the publication of the Duchess's topless photographs particularly hard. 'She was more furious than I have ever seen her,' noted one visitor. 'And that is saying something.' Over the telephone, Margaret impressed her fury on the Queen, who dutifully passed it on to the Duchess.

On her return to Kensington Palace, the Duchess attempted to assuage any unpleasantness by sending Margaret a bouquet of mixed spring flowers, accompanied by a note of apology. They failed to do the trick. A handwritten letter arrived from Princess Margaret. It did not beat around the bush:

> Not once have you hung your head in embarrassment even for a
> minute after those disgraceful photographs. You have done more to
> bring shame on the Family than you could ever have imagined.
> Clearly you have never considered the damage you are doing to us all.
> How dare you discredit us like this and how dare you send me those
> flowers.

The letter was leaked to the newspapers. Was Princess Margaret responsible for the leak? Given the circumstances, it is unlikely to have been the Duchess.

From that day on, their relationship, never warm, turned freezing cold. Princess Margaret told friends that she had chided the Queen for still bothering with the fallen Duchess. But a quarter of a century on, Fergie seems to have recovered her bounce. In a later volume of auto-biography, *Finding Sarah: A Duchess's Journey to Find Herself*,* she passes on the secret of a happy life: one simply repeats the mantra 'I love myself more than I ever imagined possible and others love me too,' twenty-five times a day.

In an interview to promote an accompanying TV series on the Oprah Channel, she took the trouble to recite her daily inventory of the parts of her body she had learned to love. 'I love my hands and my wrists and ankles. I've got a really good waist and a great pair of bosoms. Plus the pins aren't bad.'

By the time of this notably upbeat broadcast, Princess Margaret had been dead for well over a decade.

---

* The Duchess of York has published numerous volumes, among them distillations of her hard-won wisdom: *What I Know Now, Reinventing Yourself with the Duchess of York, Moments, Dining with the Duchess* and *Dieting with the Duchess*. Beneath a photograph of a pink flower in a forest on the back cover of *Finding Sarah: A Duchess's Journey to Find Herself* is a brief checklist headed 'Wisdom from the Duchess'. It includes 'Be open', 'Make time for quiet reflection and listen to your heart', and 'Face your fears'. It ends with the less reassuring 'Free your mind and your bottom will follow'.

78

6 July 1975

Princess Margaret attends the second night of *Bow Down*, a musical production by Harrison Birtwistle and Tony Harrison, at the Cottesloe Theatre.

'A fairly disastrous evening,' writes Peter Hall in his diary. 'Princess Margaret was very affronted by the whole thing, and afterwards said she didn't think she should have been invited. This surprised me, though *Bow Down* is certainly strong, cruel and somewhat upsetting.'

20 July 1975

A fortnight later, Peter Hall is walking across the Buckingham Palace reception rooms at the Queen's Jubilee Party when he hears a voice crying 'Cuckoo!' It is Her Royal Highness the Princess Margaret.

We paid our respects and chatted away. In the background the band of the Coldstream Guards were playing selections from Gilbert and Sullivan. The Princess invited me to choose the next piece of music. I said I would like something by Harrison Birtwistle. She didn't find that funny and went into a long pout about her evening at Harry's *Bow Down*. I, with enormous smiles, told her what frightful trouble her dislike of the production had caused us because what she thought had so disturbed the chairman. I then moved further through the crush and met Max Rayne. He asked me if I'd seen her. 'Who?' I asked. 'The Princess,' he said. 'I'm keeping well away from her.'

14 March 1990
Her Royal Highness attends a preview of Stephen Sondheim's *Sunday in the Park with George* at the National Theatre. The National's artistic director, Richard Eyre, is obliged to stand in the foyer to await her arrival.

As she comes in she announces to me quite loudly that she can't STAND Sondheim. She demonstrates this quite conspicuously throughout the evening. She raps me, quite painfully, and only half jokingly, at the end of the National Anthem, which Jeremy Sams has rearranged in a slightly arch fashion. She shifts restlessly during the show. At the interval grim comedy getting her a drink. Ice! Whisky! Water! and more whisky. She wasn't hard work after the show. She talked to me about public speaking, which she hates. She said that Reagan enjoyed it; he knew he was a bad actor but was properly trained. Mary* was very touched by Princess Mgt saying that she'd liked Christopher Soames.† I didn't tell Mary that she'd also said that she hadn't liked Churchill, who had no time for her and her sister when they were children and she'd found him rude and self-interested.

---

* Mary Soames (1922–2014), Winston Churchill's youngest daughter, wife of Christopher Soames.

† Christopher Soames (1920–87), politician and diplomat.

79

The journalist and biographer Selina Hastings first met Princess Margaret at a dinner in the country with Prince Rupert Loewenstein.

'I then had a boyfriend called Derek Hart who had done some work with Tony – he was on television, on the *Tonight* programme with Cliff Michelmore, and he and Tony were quite good friends partly because they'd won a libel against the *Daily Express*.

'Then, through Tony, Derek became a very close friend – but nothing else – with Princess Margaret. He was very protective of her and she would often come to him when she was very unhappy about something. Sometimes she would ring up at two or three in the morning when she'd had quite a few glasses, in floods of tears complaining: "So-and-so's just called me a cunt," or something like that.

'Derek became much closer to her when her marriage was breaking up. Occasionally the three of us used to have dinner in a little restaurant in Notting Hill called Chez Moi. We sat in an alcove screened from the rest of the diners. Princess Margaret always said she wasn't going to have anything and then, just as Derek was about to call for the bill, she'd say, "Oh, I think I'll have a little Dover sole!"

'She once invited us for the weekend to stay at Royal Lodge. It was in the summer and it was boiling hot. She was terribly sweet, and she was so nice to me because she couldn't have had the faintest interest in me. She had organised the archivist at Windsor Castle to show me whatever I wanted to see in the archive. She was always … not cosy, but always very, very nice. I was so touched that she had gone to the trouble to organise something that would interest me. She was more intelligent than a lot of people give her credit for: she used to go once a week to the V&A and she'd just concentrate on one object. When she went to New York, she knew exactly what she wanted to see, and she'd go to galleries and museums. Once when she visited New York, her host asked her what she would like to do, thinking that she'd want to go to Bloomingdale's or Saks. Instead she chose to be taken to the Pierpont Morgan Library to look at the medieval missals. It turned out she knew almost as much about them as the curator did. The others aren't like that. When Princess Anne went there for the first time, I was told that all she wanted was a set of hunting table-mats.

'We were going to drive from Royal Lodge to the Castle. She was wearing some peep-toe sandals and as she got into the car she said, "Selina, I've got some chewing gum on my shoe!" So I had to get out and go round to the other side and pull the chewing gum off. Things were different then. If you're brought up to have everything done for you, well, that's just what you come to expect.

'We then went to Windsor Castle and the archivist was there and we looked at all sorts of things, and it was wonderful, and Princess Margaret took us round the private apartment, and it was riveting. It was boiling hot and she said, "I think we should have a swim!" so we went to the huge indoor swimming pool and there was the wooden polo pony on which Prince Philip practised his swipes, and I said, "I'm awfully sorry Ma'am, I don't have a costume." And she said, "Oh, you can have one of Lilibet's!"

'It was a very frilly corseted costume, but anyway, I did struggle into it. PM didn't want to swim because it would spoil her hair, and so she said, "We'll walk up and down," and so as she and I walked up and down the shallow end, I remember she said, "Selina, do you ever use Carmen rollers?" and I said, "Well, yes, Ma'am, as a matter of fact I do," and she said, "But where do you buy them from?" and I said, "Boots, Ma'am," and she said, "No! How TOO fascinating!"

'Part of her longed to take part in ordinary life, yet without understanding what ordinary life was – like Lord Curzon who, accused of knowing nothing of the common man, jumped on a bus, then ordered it to take him to No. 1 Carlton House Terrace. She once told someone that she knew more than was generally supposed about the working classes, because, you see, she had always been surrounded by servants. She looked at the world outside between the bars of her extremely comfortable cage. She was inquisitive and she was courageous, and sometimes she ventured halfway out. But the moment it looked as though there may be difficulties, back she flew into her cage, slamming the door behind her.

'There was an absolutely horrific evening in 1982. Elizabeth Taylor had come over to play in *Little Foxes*,* and Princess Margaret took Derek Hart and me and Jeremy Fry and a couple of other people to see it. Princess Margaret didn't go backstage afterwards. We all went back to Kensington Palace for dinner and Elizabeth Taylor was going to join us at Kensington Palace after she had got out of her costume, done her make-up and so on.

'The drawing room at Kensington Palace is long and narrow, with the doors at one end and the drinks down the other. So we were all up the other end, talking, when suddenly ET appeared in the most ill-advised dress: she was very fat then and it was made of scarlet T-shirt material, so everything plunged, and her spare tyre, I remember noticing, was just a little bit bigger than her bust. Her dress was very short and she had high-heel sandals on and her legs were very big. She stood in the doorway and Princess Margaret just went on talking, ignoring her. Eventually Jeremy Fry said, "Oh Ma'am, Elizabeth Taylor has just arrived!" And Princess Margaret sighed and said, "Oh, well I suppose somebody had better offer her a drink!"

---

* The production attracted poor reviews. One critic declared that Taylor had made 'an entrance worthy of Miss Piggy, trailing mauve lingerie'. Another described her voice as 'a needle screeching across an old 78 record'. A third called her Regina 'as threatening as a pink blancmange'.

'And so someone got her a drink and returned to the group. Elizabeth Taylor was just left standing there, and so, with my well-brought-up manners, I went up to her and I remember saying something idiotic and then I said, "That costume you were wearing in the second act was so beautiful, did you have any say in what you wore?" and she said, "Did I have any say in what I wore?! You bet your sweet bippy I had a say in what I wore!"

'After a very awkward half-hour we went down to have dinner. It was a fairly long table and the man on my left immediately turned to talk to Princess Margaret and the man on my right, ignoring Elizabeth Taylor, began talking to the man on her other side, so she and I had no one to talk to. And so I leaned forward and, with my very good manners, I started talking to her.

'Years before, when I'd been at Oxford, she and Richard Burton had come to do *Dr Faustus* at the Playhouse and so I said, ingratiatingly, that the production was absolutely wonderful and she said, "Oh wow, did you see that, oh I'm so glad!" and she began talking about it. Then, on my bare shoulder – I was wearing a strapless evening dress – I felt a sting like a wasp and I turned round and there was Princess Margaret's fingernail. "Selina," she said, "has nobody ever told you it's rude to talk across the table?"

'And then, finally, this very awkward meal ended and the ladies were taken out by PM to her bedroom. At the bottom of the bed there was a chaise longue in which had been laid out her underwear for the next day – corsets, a petticoat – but Elizabeth Taylor flung herself on the chaise. At this point, Princess Margaret turned round and said: "You're lying on my underwear!"

'"Well, that's a kind of funny place to keep your underwear!"

'And it went on getting worse and worse. When we finally rejoined the men, Princess Margaret started reciting the play and Elizabeth Taylor said, "That's my part!" and Princess Margaret said, "No, I can do it!"

'She had it by heart, it was amazing, and then she started to play the piano. Eventually at about 2 a.m., Princess Margaret looked at Elizabeth

Taylor and said in a very loud voice, "Is anyone going to take her home – or we'll have to find a sleeping bag?!"

'Derek Hart said, "I've got a car." So he and I drove Elizabeth Taylor back to Claridge's or the Connaught. Later we were told that Princess Margaret had been out in California six months before and the Queen of Hollywood had snubbed Princess Margaret – she hadn't curtseyed or something – and so this was Princess Margaret's well-planned revenge. That was a friendship that was never going to work.

'It was one of the few times apparently that Elizabeth Taylor didn't have a man in her life. Someone said they felt sorry for her because there was no one to back her up: normally she'd have turned up with a boyfriend or walker. But she didn't seem particularly fazed, I have to say.'

The source of the feud between Princess Margaret and Elizabeth Taylor remains obscure. Speaking on *The Jonathan Ross Show* in March 2016, Carrie Fisher claimed that her father, Eddie Fisher, who was Elizabeth Taylor's fourth husband, had once had an affair with Princess Margaret, so this may have contributed to it.*

Then again, in a private conversation with the playwright Emlyn Williams in 1967, Princess Margaret described Elizabeth Taylor as 'a common little thing'.† A stranger to discretion, Williams repeated her remark to all and sundry; word may well have got back to the victim.

The following year, after Richard Burton presented Taylor with the

---

* 'I met Princess Margaret once,' she told Ross. 'I did. I really did. Well, they did *The Empire Strikes Back* and they did it over here. So we all went [to the premiere] with Alec Guinness, Harrison [Ford] and with Mark [Hamill] and as she was coming down the line I mentioned to my co-stars that my father had had sex with Princess Margaret. In a beautiful way they made love. Anyway, I did mention this. I am going to get in a lot of trouble for this! After the movie, we went over to the Savoy where the party was and Harrison had arrived at the party prior to my arrival and also before Princess Margaret had arrived as well. He came up to me and said, "Well, clearly your father will sleep with anybody." He was joking. It was funny.'

† Williams added that, from his point of view, the Princess was 'a ridiculous tiny creature in pink with an enormous cigarette holder'.

huge Krupp Diamond, Princess Margaret remarked to a friend that it was 'the most vulgar thing I've ever seen'. Taylor heard of this slight. A while later, the two women met at a party. Taylor was wearing the diamond, and asked Margaret if she would like to try it on. Margaret slipped it on her finger. 'Doesn't look so vulgar now, does it?' observed Taylor. This did nothing to assuage the friction between the two women.

In Gstaad on Monday, 20 October 1969, Richard Burton complained to his diary about having to fly to London the following day 'to see Princess Margaret again at the opening night of Staircase', adding that she is 'infinitely boringly uncomfortable to be around'. At a film premiere in her presence, he had told the audience, 'My name is really Richard Jenkins and up there is a lady whose name is Maggie Jones.' It was a joke she had not enjoyed.

On another occasion, Elizabeth Taylor committed the cardinal sin of keeping Princess Margaret waiting. 'I did my utmost to get Liz to her appointments on time,' recalled her butler, Raymond Vignale. 'She would say, "I kept the Queen of England waiting for twenty minutes, Princess Margaret thirty minutes, and President Tito an hour. They can damn well wait for me for a few minutes at a meaningless dinner party."'

80

At home in Los Angeles, Christopher Isherwood was struggling to write a book about the Buddha, but kept finding himself interrupted by thoughts of Princess Margaret.

He was due to meet the Princess at a party Kenneth Tynan was throwing that evening, Friday, 13 October 1978. Fearful lest his guests say the wrong thing, Tynan had issued instructions to both Isherwood and George Cukor to address the Princess as 'Ma'am', a skill that came easier to the British expatriate than to the American: 'George is working himself up into a nervous cramp, like a young actor with only one line to say; he feels sure he'll get it wrong and call her Mum or Mom or something.'

The evening came close to going pear-shaped. In an effort to cut down on costs, the cash-strapped Tynans had decided on soul food served by a hip, cut-price caterer. When it looked as if the caterer was not going to materialise, Tynan vowed to go to the bathroom and kill himself. Fortunately the caterer arrived in the nick of time, and Tynan was soon back on form greeting his guests, who included Paul Newman and Joanne Woodward, Joan Didion and her husband John Gregory Dunne, Gene Kelly, Sidney Poitier, Ryan and Tatum O'Neal, David Hockney and Neil Simon.

The Princess proved even more of a catch in America than in Great Britain. 'It was quite a sight to see Hollywood royalty scrambling over each other's backs to get to real royalty,' noted Tynan's daughter

Tracy. 'People were shoving each other aside to get the princess's attention.'

Isherwood played it cool. 'Meeting Princess Margaret was hardly a dance. We only got her in very short hops, and although Ken Tynan honored me by putting me at her table, I hardly got to tell her more than that I had been at a school which produced three archbishops of Canterbury in a row* – that was all the royal talk I knew; and Neil Simon's wit, as he sat opposite me, was altogether silenced.'

Isherwood's final verdict was that the Princess 'seemed quite a common little thing, fairly good-humored but no doubt quite capable of rapping your knuckles'.

Ten days later, the Hollywood agent Sue Mengers arranged a party in honour of Princess Margaret at her home in Beverly Hills. Security was intense, with helicopters circling above and police everywhere. Every guest was carefully checked.

Princess Margaret arrived in a black and silver dress by Dior with a diamond necklace and earrings left to her by her grandmother, Queen Mary.

'I already knew Princess Margaret, so I was considered socially safe enough to be seated at her right hand at the dinner table,' recalled Michael Caine, who over the years had become what he called 'a sort of British Social Ambassador whenever royalty or the aristocracy came to visit us'. The others on the Princess's table were Barbra Streisand, Robin Williams, Nick Nolte, Danny Kaye, Joni Mitchell, Steve McQueen ('high on coke' according to his ex-wife Ali MacGraw, who was also there), Neil Diamond, Gene Hackman, Peter Falk, Barry Diller, Jack Nicholson, Anjelica Huston, Clint Eastwood and – by royal request – Barry Manilow. Scattered across the remaining half a dozen tables were Sean Connery, Farrah Fawcett-Majors and John Travolta. This was, in many ways, the Princess's perfect environment. It was said of the Duke of Windsor that what he liked best was to meet new people

---

* Repton: Archbishops Temple, Fisher and Ramsey.

for not more than ten minutes at a time, and this weakness applied to her too.

Sue Mengers had placed the fashionable governor of California, Jerry Brown, to the Princess's left. It was clear from the start that he was not going to stand on ceremony. He had mastered the first lesson of royal etiquette – the correct form of address – but considered further deference unnecessary.

'Good evening, Your Highness,' he said. 'I just dropped by to say hello. I have another appointment so I'm only staying for the first course.'

This did not go down well. Caine noticed that throughout Brown's little introductory speech the Princess maintained a rigid smile, but once he had finished, 'she just turned her back on him without a word and engaged me in conversation until he left'.

The Princess was served her meal first, and then Governor Brown was served his. At this point the governor's girlfriend, the singer Linda Ronstadt, walked over to the table in a white cotton mini-dress and little red boots, put one hand on the governor's shoulder and the other on the Princess's shoulder, peered closely at their plates and said, 'What are we having to start?' She then took a piece of food off Brown's plate and popped it into her mouth.

'I have seen people shrug many times,' recalls Caine. 'But the Princess's shoulder shrugged that night like a punch from a boxer and with almost the same effect on Miss Ronstadt. She almost overbalanced and fell on the floor. The Princess never again during the evening acknowledged Jerry Brown's presence, nor his departure when he finally left.'

Once Governor Brown had gone, the atmosphere perked up, though there was a bit of a blip when Jack Nicholson allegedly leaned over and offered the Princess some of his cocaine, 'in a bid to get to know her better'. The Princess declined his invitation, but took it in good heart. She remained at the party until 12.30 a.m., dancing with John Travolta, among others. Before she left, she told Michael Caine how much she had enjoyed herself, adding, 'But I didn't like that dreadful man at all.'

Like many an over-conscientious hostess, Sue Mengers failed to enjoy her own party; nerves had clearly got the better of her. 'Every time Princess Margaret looked my way I curtseyed. I was curtseying all night! She thought I was an idiot.'

81

The most unlikely figures lost their nerve in the presence of Princess Margaret. Marlon Brando once asked Kenneth Tynan to arrange an introduction. Accordingly, Tynan took them for a dinner *à trois* at Parkes restaurant in Beauchamp Place, Knightsbridge.

'For the only time in my experience I saw him over-awed, literally unable to address her except through me: "Would you ask Princess Margaret what she thinks of ..." etc.

'HRH said next day on the phone that this wasn't an uncommon reaction. "People just clam up. I'm told it's like going on television for the first time."'

Her sister, both more forbidding and more cautious, takes active steps to prevent over-excitement. Guests entering Buckingham Palace are discreetly asked if they would care to spend a penny before being presented.

82

I had a friend at school called Michael, who was the second son of a lord. His brother William was two or three years above. The two brothers were in many ways different: Michael was quite sporty and disorganised, whereas William was more bookish and dutiful, eventually becoming house captain. But they were both extremely nice, with a shyness and diffidence rare in public school boys; they were both much given to blushing.

In our final two years, Michael would sometimes invite friends to stay at one of his family homes. By the time I left school I think I had stayed in them all, or nearly all: a town house in Chelsea, a holiday house in France, a castle in Yorkshire, a stately home in Norfolk. Later, when watching *Brideshead Revisited* on television, I couldn't help thinking of Michael's family, though they were in fact substantially better off than the Marchmains, and would probably have regarded them as middle-class. Their homes were strewn with the sort of masterpieces we both studied for History of Art A-Level: a Rembrandt painting was displayed on an easel in one of the drawing rooms, and forgotten corridors at the top of the house were virtually wallpapered with Dutch landscapes by Ruisdael.

The grandeur of their houses was offset by the reticence of the family itself. They tended to speak to one another with such courtesy that a passer-by might have assumed they had only just met.

In the hallway of their grandest home the family kept a large leather-bound visitors' book, in which, at the end of their stay, guests would be asked to write their names. Here and there a photograph would be stuck in the book, to commemorate a family event or a special celebration.

'Would you all be sure to sign your names in the book before you go?' Michael's mother asked over breakfast on the last morning of one of our stays.

When it came to writing my name, I nosily leafed through the rest of the book. One quite recent page was devoted to a single signature, three times the size of anyone else's: 'Margaret'. Below it was a colour photograph, about nine inches by five inches, of Princess Margaret standing in the same hallway, looking towards the camera. She was wearing a light-blue dress, her customary vivid make-up, and a fixed smile. Standing next to her, looking a little awkward, but no more awkward than usual, was Michael's elder brother William, in a tweed jacket, collared shirt and the type of trousers that would later come to be known as chinos.

As photographs of Princess Margaret go, it seemed at first glance unexceptional. She had not been caught off-guard; in fact she looked very much on duty, as though her smile would not last a split-second beyond the click of the shutter. From her point of view it must have been just another photo.

Yet even the most fleeting look at the photograph revealed something very bizarre indeed, something unheard-of in royal photographs, something so outrageous and out-of-place that it was, quite literally, unspeakable.

At the moment the shutter clicked, the natural downward trajectory of the fabric of William's trousers was being sent askew by a bluff diagonal: this most bashful of young men was clearly struggling unsuccessfully to contain an erection, an erection that he could no more hope to disguise than the mayor of Paris might hope to disguise the presence of the Eiffel Tower.

As everyone who has ever been an adolescent boy can attest, at that age – and William would then have been around eighteen – erections pop up, of their own accord, without warning, at frequent yet distressingly random intervals, and with a stubborn disregard for the propriety of their possessor. It is, of course, perfectly possible that William found himself sexually aroused by the proximity of HRH Princess Margaret, who was, even at that relatively late stage, still regarded, at least in the more stately circles, as something of a firecracker. But for those of us in the younger generation, these were racy days – at school, posters of Raquel Welch striding out of the sea in her fur bikini and Sylvia Kristel as Emmanuelle lounging topless on her peacock chair were all the rage – and, even for a fairly conventional adolescent, the sight of the portly Princess Margaret in a formal blue dress with handbag and pearls seems unlikely to have pressed the right buttons, or popped the wrong ones.

A more likely scenario would have found William being called by his mother when his erection was already in progress, as it were. He would then have found himself unable to come up with a suitable excuse for a cover-up – you can't really say 'Hang on! I'll just finish this paragraph!' when you're being called for a photograph with Her Royal Highness – and simply hoping that the Princess would keep looking straight ahead, his mother would concentrate on focusing her camera, so no one would notice, and the photo in question would be from the waist up.

So what happened when the royal photograph arrived back, full-length, from the chemist? Perhaps William's mother simply glanced at it, checking that neither William nor Princess Margaret had their eyes closed, or was pulling a funny face, before pasting it into the visitors' book. Or did her glance stray below their waists? Is a mother genetically predisposed to blank out the shadow of a son's erection? Or did she notice that something was awry, but decide to go ahead and paste the whole photograph in regardless – lock, stock and, as it were, barrel?

And what of William himself? Did he – does he – wince whenever he saw the photograph stuck in pride of place in the visitors' book? Or did he too fail to notice the sundial protrusion? Or was he – and this is frankly the least likely of the possible scenarios – secretly rather proud of having maintained an erection in these most unarousing of circumstances?

Had they been a more bohemian family, they might have stuck the photograph in the book simply to *épater le bourgeois*. There is a story I have often heard, a sort of royal urban myth, I suppose, that demonstrates this sort of behaviour, and the love/hate, push-me/pull-you tug between deference and disdain. Princess Margaret – or, sometimes, the Queen – is staying the night with a family somewhere. At one point she goes to the loo, and unwittingly leaves behind what in technical parlance is known as a 'floater'. After she has left, the family fish the floater out of the loo, and place it in one of those rubber-sealed jars usually reserved for pickling eggs or onions, or bottling marmalade. For years to come, they apparently bring out the jar on social occasions, explaining its provenance to hoots of delight from their friends.

Whether true or not, this is a singular story about bohemia and snobbery. They only bother to preserve the turd because they believe it to be special: after all, it belongs – or belonged (at what point does a turd cease to be the property of the person who brought it into the world?) – to the sister of the Queen. On the other hand, their only purpose in showing it off is to demonstrate the absurdity of the very same snobbery that found them fishing it out of the loo in the first place.

But Michael and William's family were not of this brash, guffawing sort. They would not have found anything in the slightest bit amusing about a photograph of their eldest son displaying an erection beside the Queen's sister.

They had left a large space in their book for a photograph of William and Princess Margaret, and they had no alternative detumescent photograph up their sleeves to put in its place. Granted, it would have looked odd to just leave a gap, but why didn't his mother simply get a pair of scissors and cut the two of them off at their waists?

Or perhaps she simply didn't look at the photograph long enough to notice her son's erection, and stuck it in the album without a second glance. Other members of the family may well have clocked it, but I suspect they would have found it far more embarrassing to raise an objection and have the photo removed than to say nothing and let it remain where it was. And so it stayed there, a monument – eccentric, yes, but also rather touching – to the reticence of the English upper classes.

83

1 December 1992
Princess Margaret attends a preview of *Carousel* at the National Theatre. After meeting the cast, she is escorted to the front door by Richard Eyre, who makes a note of their brief conversation.

ME: I'm glad you enjoyed the show.
SHE: I didn't. I can't bear the piece.

84

What became of Crawfie?

The last time we set eyes on her, all those years ago, she had just married George Buthlay in Dunfermline, having put off the marriage for sixteen years to ensure the future wellbeing of her royal charges.

The next phase of her story begins with Crawfie's fateful decision to publish a memoir of her days as the royal governess. Some authors blame this on the avarice of her new husband. 'There is no question that Buthlay was a bad influence on Crawfie,' writes Hugo Vickers in his sharp biography, *Elizabeth, the Queen Mother.* 'We can but speculate how this thirty-eight-year-old spinster adapted to married life with such a man. He was a philanderer, both before and after the marriage, he manipulated her and fuelled her anger. Prodded by him, she became irritated by her pay, felt that her pension was inadequate, was unhappy with the meagre wedding presents she had received from the Royal Family, and even became dissatisfied with the CVO she was given on retirement in January 1949, apparently feeling a DCVO would have been more appropriate.'

In March 1949, shortly after Crawfie had retired with her husband to a grace-and-favour cottage at Kensington Palace, she asked her old employer to approve her plan to write a series of articles for an American magazine about her time as governess of the two little Princesses. In April, Queen Elizabeth posted her reply in a letter marked 'Private':

My Dear Crawfie,

I am so sorry to have been so long in giving you my views about the questions you asked me, but, you know they were extremely difficult to answer especially as I fear that the answers are still the same as I gave you when you came to see me. I do feel, most definitely, that you should not write and sign articles about the children, as people in positions of confidence with us must be utterly oyster, and if you, the moment you finished teaching Margaret, started writing about her and Lilibet, well, we should never feel confidence in anyone again. I know you understand this, because you have been so wonderfully discreet all the years you were with us …

At this point the Queen's letter changes gear, moving, with the discreetest of little jolts, from supplication to threat.

Also, you would lose all your friends, because such a thing has never been done or even contemplated amongst the people who serve us so loyally, and I do hope that you will put all the American temptations aside very firmly. Having been with us in our family life for so long, you must be prepared to be attacked by journalists to give away private and confidential things, and I know that your good sense & loyal affection will guide you well. I do feel most strongly that you must resist the allure of American money & persistent editors, & say No No No to offers of dollars for articles about something as private & as precious as our family.

In June, Crawfie began to write her pieces with the aid of Dorothy Black,* a prolific novelist who also found the time to write a column

---

* Dorothy Delius Allan Black (1890–1977) was the niece of the composer Frederick Delius. Her mother Clare wrote a memoir of him: *Frederick Delius: Memories of My Brother*. Dorothy herself wrote ninety-eight novels, among them *Romance – The Loveliest Thing* (1925), *Someday I'll Find You* (1934), *Never Leave Me* (1941), *My Love Belongs to Me* (1942), *Two for Mirth* (1942), *Alone Am I* (1944), *The Gay Adventure* (1945), *Well Done, Belinda!* (1952), *Her*

for the *Ladies' Home Journal*. By August the work was completed and sent to America, where it was edited to suit the magazine's readership. 'I hope you will trust Beatrice and me to take fullest advantage of your rich material in a way which will give it the broadest possible appeal,' wrote Bruce Gould.*

The finished version was then delivered, via Nancy Astor, to the Queen, in the hope of gaining her approval, as well as her permission to reproduce facsimile copies of letters sent to her by various members of the Royal Family, including the little Princesses. Crawfie was confident that everything would go according to plan, and that 'the Queen will not only agree but also write a preface in her own handwriting'.

As it turned out, the Queen was furious: 'We have worried greatly over this matter, and can only think that our late & completely trusted governess has gone off her head, because she promised in writing that she would not publish any story about our daughters, and this development has made us very sad …'

Through her private secretary, she expressed her disapproval of the 'repugnant' project, and called for a minimum of thirteen alterations to the text. These included a story that, having drawn 'Royal Flush' during a game of charades, the Duchess of Kent had mimed pulling a lavatory chain. Crawfie made the requested changes, and by so doing, convinced herself that the entire manuscript now had royal approval. This was wishful thinking. The Queen's fury was never to subside.

The cold-shouldering of Crawfie now began in earnest. At Christmas no card arrived from the Queen, and though Queen Mary managed one, it was accompanied by no present. Before long Crawfie and her husband were, in the unequivocal words of one courtier, 'shunned by colleagues from top to bottom'. In her turn, Crawfie retreated into a

---

Heart Was in the Highlands (1955), *Forsaking All Others* (1956), *Paradise for Two* (1963), *O Come, My Love* (1967), *Love Endureth* (1968) and *Love Belongs to Everyone* (1972). At the age of eighty-four she published her last three novels, *Where Love Is, From Faraway* and *It Had to Be You*.

* Co-editor, with his wife Beatrice, of the magazine.

sort of siege mentality, becoming increasingly indignant at the way she had been treated. In a letter to Bruce Gould, signed by her but probably composed by her more belligerent husband, she described the Queen's refusal to send a Christmas card as 'absolutely childish':

> I have no fear of what might be called 'consequences' because I have adhered to the terms of my understanding with the Queen, and if she decides to be unfriendly, or worse, she will be the loser. If any action on Her Majesty's part is brought to bear on me to my detriment, I shall not hesitate to expose it in the Press if necessary, and if an attempt should be made to eject me from this house and/or deprive me of my pension, I shall fight in Court and have the facts made public if I am driven to do so.

During the period of serialisation, the *Ladies' Home Journal* added 500,000 copies to its circulation, which now reached two million. The book version of *The Little Princesses* hit the number one position in the American non-fiction charts. With the $80,000 they gained from the deal, Crawfie and her husband acquired a substantial house in Aberdeen, 60 Rubislaw Den South, which is nowadays valued at just under a million pounds.

With her ties to the Palace entirely severed, Crawfie may have felt she had nothing left to lose. Accordingly, she trotted out three more books of varying shades of bland, on Queen Mary, Princess Margaret and Princess Elizabeth. Her burgeoning career as a writer came to grief, however, when in June 1955 *Woman's Own* published her ebullient accounts of that year's Trooping the Colour and Royal Ascot. She had in fact written them in advance of the events they purported to describe. This meant that when both were cancelled at the last minute, poor old Crawfie turned into a national figure of fun.

Never again would she appear in print. George died in 1977, the year of Queen Elizabeth II's Silver Jubilee. At some point between his death and her own, Crawfie attempted suicide. She finally passed away in an Aberdeen nursing home, Hawkhill House, on 11 February 1988. At her poorly attended funeral, wreaths from the Royal Family were nowhere to be seen. Asked about her later in life, Princess Margaret replied simply, 'She sneaked.'

85

Princess Margaret attended a benefit concert at the Royal Albert Hall in 1979 for the Invalid Children's Aid Society. Introduced by the Princess's great admirer, the chat-show host Russell Harty, the star of the evening, Dusty Springfield, arrived onstage in a glittering white trouser-suit, and launched straight into her 1968 top ten hit, 'I Close My Eyes and Count to Ten'.

Later on, when she came to sing 'We are Family', Dusty placed a special emphasis on the line 'I got all my sisters with me'. Was this a nod to the high proportion of lesbians in her audience?

After singing 'All I See is You', she said, 'It's nice to see that all the royalty is not confined to the royal box,' a risqué remark that was received with whoops and cheers, though not from those in the Royal Box. Far from it: Princess Margaret was spotted leaving her seat for what a member of the Royal Albert Hall staff described as 'a fag and gin break', lending credence to the rumour that she had indeed taken offence.

Two-thirds of the way through, Dusty left the stage to execute a rapid change of costume, and returned dressed in a lilac trouser-and-tails suit. Glancing up at the Royal Box, she caught sight of the Princess chatting away to a lady-in-waiting. She then sang the opening lines to her next song – 'Quiet please, there's a lady on stage' – before pausing theatrically. Whether she intended it as a reprimand or not, it was followed by a loud round of applause.

At this point, she took the opportunity to address the audience. 'There wasn't much time to change,' she said. 'This song is really for those people who have been legends in their time. I'm sure you know who you are.' Once again, the crowd roared. 'Sometimes, the ladies I'm speaking of give too much of themselves, sometimes not enough. This song is for all those people, all those women, no matter who they are.'

After the concert, Princess Margaret was escorted backstage to meet those involved. When she came to Dusty Springfield she walked past her without a word, even though Dusty's manager had just handed her a cheque for £8,000, made out to the charity.

Had the Princess been offended by the suggestion that she should keep quiet? Did she disapprove of Dusty's crack about royalty and the Royal Box? Nobody knew for sure. But the next day, Dusty Springfield received an envelope through the post, containing a typed apology to the Queen, with a space left for her signature. The return address was Kensington Palace. Had the envelope been sent by Princess Margaret? Springfield certainly thought so. She signed it, and sent it back.

Decades later, Fred Perry, Dusty's lighting designer and stage director for twenty-five years, confessed that to his 'horror and regret' it was he who had caused the trouble.

'We were sitting in Dusty's house in Los Angeles, going over the upcoming show, and she was trying to come up with a funny line along the line that John Lennon had used at the Royal Show when the Beatles played in the sixties ... Knowing of Dusty's loyal gay following, I came up with the line, "It's nice to see that all the royalty is NOT confined to the Royal Box!" She was appalled, but laughed her head off and said, "They'll never let me get away with that" ... Anyway, Dusty used the line, pissed off Princess Margaret, and the rest, as they say, is history.'

Perry denied that the Princess had blanked Dusty, though he did remember her being extremely brusque. 'I have the full-length version of that tape and when going down the line, Princess Margaret spoke to everyone on the line. When she got to Auntie, she shook her hand, murmured thanks, and moved on. It's a definite snub, but at the time, none of us knew why. She had actually requested a couple of songs from albums of Dusty's that she had never sung as part of her regular shows, so we knew she was a fan ...

'I am still baffled all these years later when I recall that this was about the time that PM was under fire for spending far too much time with a failed pop singer named Roddy something or other, on the island of Mustique, which, as far as I am concerned, caused a lot more trouble for the Royal Family than one simple line said with affection at a fund-raising concert.'

Margaret and Dusty were photographed together only once, following a charity concert at the London Palladium ten years earlier. In the photograph, Dusty curtseys to a smiling Princess Margaret. The line of performers also includes the eccentric singer Tiny Tim, who for some reason is carrying a large Union Jack bag, Lou Christie, David Bowie and Eddy Grant of the pop group the Equals, then sporting dyed blond hair.

There are striking parallels between the two women. They both enjoyed a sixties heyday, and favoured vivid evening gowns, heavy mascara and bouffant hair. They had an indefinable air of camp, and attracted a strong gay following. They were waspish, demanding and dissatisfied. And, as time went by, they both came to personify loneliness. The image of them as disappointed women was fuelled by the public's keen sense of *schadenfreude*: once the talk of the town, they had taken wrong paths, and their best days were behind them. The title of one of Dusty's signature tunes was 'I Just Don't Know What to Do With Myself', but it may just as well have been Margaret's.

After many ups and downs in her career and in her personal life, Dusty Springfield was finally awarded the OBE in the 1999 New Year Honours List. 'Isn't that the one they give to cleaners?' she asked. By now she was dying of cancer, and confined to bed. Permission was given for her OBE to be collected by her manager Vicki Wickham, who presented it to her at the Royal Marsden Hospital, surrounded by a small group of friends.

Dusty Springfield died on 2 March 1999, the very day she had been due to go to Buckingham Palace. After her death, rumours circulated that she and Princess Margaret had once been an item. This seems improbable, but then again, improbability is no barrier to gossip.*

---

* Those with whom Princess Margaret was, at one time or another, rumoured to have had sexual relationships include, in alphabetical order: Barton, Anthony, wine producer; Beatty, Warren, actor and director; Bindon, John, actor and criminal; Douglas, Sharman, daughter of US Ambassador to the Court of St James; Douglas-Home, Robin, pianist and novelist; Edinburgh, Duke of, brother-in-law; Elliott, Dominic, son of the Earl of Minto; Fisher, Eddie, actor and singer; Hutchinson, Leslie 'Hutch', singer and pianist; Jagger, Mick, singer; Kaye, Danny, actor and singer; Lichfield, Lord (Patrick), photographer; Llewellyn, Roddy, singer and garden designer; Lonsdale, Norman, businessman; Niven, David, actor; O'Toole, Peter, actor; Sellers, Peter, actor and comedian; Spencer-Churchill, John, landowner; Springfield, Dusty, singer; Townsend, Group Captain Peter, royal equerry; Turner, John, Prime Minister of Canada; Wallace, Billy, son of the wartime Minister for Transport.

86

In 1983, Princess Margaret was invited by her lady-in-waiting, Lady Anne Tennant, to contribute to *The Picnic Papers*, a collection of reminiscences about memorable picnics. She called her contribution 'Picnic at Hampton Court'. Barely five hundred words long, it was the only piece of sustained prose she ever wrote for publication.

She began confidently, with a stab at contemporary sociology. 'Nearly all picnics in Britain,' she writes, 'end up in a layby by the road because, in desperation, no-one can decide where to stop.' When it came to choosing a location for her own picnic, she was determined to avoid this common trap. 'I felt that another sort of treat, slightly different and rather more comfortable, was indicated.'

'Indicated' is a curious word to have chosen, suggesting that someone else was in charge, hovering overhead, pointing her in this or that direction. Of course, when it comes to completing any sentence, it is easy to get boxed in by words that have gone before and to feel corralled into choosing a final word that is somehow not quite right. My guess is that the Princess had been nearing the end of her second sentence – 'I felt that another sort of treat, slightly different and rather more comfortable, was –' when she hesitated, not knowing which word to choose next.

Something rather more comfortable was … Was what? 'Needed'? 'Wanted'? 'Required'? Perhaps she finally chose 'indicated' through some subconscious link with the road and the layby in the previous sentence. But she soon got back into her stride. 'In my opinion,' she wrote, 'picnics should always be eaten at table and sitting on a chair.'

When is a picnic not a picnic? Many would consider the absence of a chair and table key to the definition of a picnic. A picnic is eaten sitting on the ground; the moment a chair or table appears, it turns into something else, something rather grander.

'Accordingly,' she continued, 'my picnic, in May 1981, took the form of an outing to Hampton Court.' There followed a potted history of Hampton Court Palace, after which she revealed that 'The Queen kindly let me take some friends. The best plan, it seemed to me, was to do some sightseeing and have lunch in the middle. So I got in touch with Sir Oliver Millar, Surveyor of the Queen's Pictures, who delighted in taking us round the recently restored Mantegnas which are housed in their own Orangery.'

But where would be the perfect spot for a picnic in Hampton Court? Again, she called in an expert. 'I asked Professor Jack Plumb, Master of Christ's College, Cambridge ... where we should have our cold collation. He suggested the little Banqueting House overlooking the Thames. This seemed an excellent place for a number of reasons. It wasn't open to the public then, it was a shelter in case of rain, and, as far as anyone knew, there hadn't been a jolly there since the time of Frederick, Prince of Wales.' With both the Surveyor of the Queen's Pictures and the Master of Christ's College, Cambridge, now on board, the Princess was determined to leave nothing to fate. And, just in case, 'I took my butler to ensure that everything would be all right.'

It was all a far cry from a cheese-and-pickle sandwich in the pouring rain. Margaret failed to specify exactly how many guests she entertained, but a series of fuzzy black-and-white photographs in the book shows the large hall equipped with two long tables, one groaning with dishes, the other laid for twenty people or so. One photograph shows the Princess gazing out of a window, her back towards the camera. Five besuited men are gathered around, clasping their hands behind their backs, as men do when they wish to appear worldly.

'We started with smoked salmon mousse, followed by that standby of the English, various cold meats and beautiful and delicious salads. Those with room then had cheeses.' At the end of their meal, the royal party drank a toast to Frederick, Prince of Wales, before continuing their tour of the palace, taking in the chapel and the royal tennis court, where they watched a game in progress.

'It was altogether a glorious day. The sun was shining on one of its brief appearances that summer, and everyone was happy.'

The Princess concluded her piece with a recipe for avocado soup. It involved throwing three or four avocado pears into a blender with some chicken consommé and 'a little dry sherry', then adding 'a little dab of double cream' before serving.

Her fellow contributors to *The Picnic Papers* all sprang from the well-to-do end of the world of letters. Harold Acton wrote of a picnic accompanied by Pouilly Fumé at the Ming tombs in Peking; Penelope Chetwode of eating suprème de volaille in Cappadocia; Patrick Leigh Fermor of sitting in the dales of Moldavia eating chicken croquettes, 'fragrant mititei' and, 'by the ladleful, wonderful Black Sea caviar from Valcov'; and the McGillycuddy of the Reeks supped on smoked salmon, lamb in puff pastry and 'a large supply of Guinness' in Kerry. Picnics in laybys were nowhere to be seen.

Shortly after the book's publication in the spring of 1983, Princess Margaret was the guest of honour at Sir Guy and Lady Holland's annual concert in their Gloucestershire barn. By chance, also present was one of her catty chroniclers, James Lees-Milne, who had broken ranks with the other contributors, refusing to participate in their spirit of bonhomie. His essay, called 'I Loathe Picnics', started with the words 'I loathe picnics,' and ended with the words 'I loathe picnics.' Lees-Milne was unabashed in his disapproval of the institution: 'It may be hereditary. My parents also loathed them as much as they disliked each other, and certainly as much as they disliked us.'

'Nearly dying of cold' in the Gloucestershire barn, Lees-Milne and his wife Alvilde found themselves swept up by their hostess and escorted to a tent. There they were presented to Princess Margaret, who was drinking whisky out of a large tumbler. Lees-Milne had never found her easy company; this occasion was to prove no exception.

'She, possibly distracted by meeting so many people within a small enclosed space, was not gracious and a little brash. Said to me, "Had I known you were a contributor to the Picnic Book, I would not have written my piece."'

Lees-Milne was nonplussed. 'How does one take this sort of remark? I smiled wryly and said, "Oh Ma'am, but I so enjoyed yours." "Do you like the book?" she asked. "I liked the jacket," I said untruthfully.

'"I hate picnics," she said, "but did you like the book?" – this time to A. as much to me. That was as far as our contact went. How I hate meeting royalty. One gets absolutely nowhere.'

87

The artist Maggi Hambling would probably agree with Lees-Milne's judgement. Her own meeting with Princess Margaret in the 1980s failed to achieve lift-off.

'In 1986, Aids was a fashionable charity to support and a small select evening reception for the well-heeled was held at the Royal Academy,' she recalls. 'The organiser, Colin Tweedie, was of lamp-post height and he appeared from nowhere, picked me up by the scruff of the neck and said, "You're the sort of person she [Princess Margaret] should meet." He then propelled a well-oiled me into a small gallery and introduced us. Ignorant, in those days, of the correct pronunciation of ma'am, I called her Marg – a cross between Margaret and Marm. Ignorant also of the protocol that one does not open the conversation, I immediately did, by asking her why she was surrounded by "all these feminists". Through scarcely parted lips, she replied that they were her ladies in waiting, who immediately looked alarmed.

'Prior to the encounter, reckoning that the event counted as a private party, I had lit a cigarette only to be instantly manhandled by several guards. However, once in The Presence, most satisfactorily they could only seethe in silence as I joined the Princess in chain-smoking. I realised that as long as I was with her, their hands were tied.

'I proceeded to ask Marg if she was watching *The Singing Detective* and she replied, "Is that the one about the man with the skin disease? We don't like it."

'I then told her, without drawing breath except to smoke, that she was making a huge mistake, that it was the best thing on television for years, that Michael Gambon was giving a sensational performance, and that Dennis Potter was a genius. My theme did not vary, as I described every detail of the series.

'The face remained as if carved in stone (rather like that of Tim Henman's father at Wimbledon) for the next twenty minutes before another subject replaced me, and I had to bid Marg good night.'

88

The story of the Royal Family in the 1990s involved a lot of going off the rails. The marriages of three of the Queen's four children – Charles, Anne and Andrew – hit the rocks, amidst a series of scandals reminiscent of a particularly fruity Carry On film. This had the effect of making Princess Margaret, now in her sixties, appear almost straitlaced by comparison. Moreover, her own two children, David and Sarah, had both embarked on enduring marriages; they were now widely regarded as more accomplished and personable than their Windsor cousins. The media spotlight had moved on. 'They all leave me alone these days,' she told a visitor. 'They've got other fish to fry.'

In 1994, when Margaret was sixty-four, a rackety journalist called Noel Botham published *Margaret: The Untold Story*, a book containing two love letters written by Margaret to her lover Robin Douglas-Home in the spring of 1967. Their authenticity was inarguable: the Princess's handwriting was reproduced in facsimile.

Douglas-Home, the nephew of the former prime minister, had committed suicide in October 1968, eighteen months after the brief affair had come to an end. A lounge lizard, he had first entered Princess Margaret's orbit while playing piano at fashionable nightclubs in the late 1950s. After a brief, unhappy marriage to the eighteen-year-old model Sandra Paul,* he had returned to the piano stool in 1966, this

---

* Who remains married to her fourth husband, Michael Howard, leader of the Conservative Party 2003–2005.

time at a restaurant called The Society, his modest salary supplemented by a fast-flowing stream of champagne cocktails.

He was one of the men Margaret would invite for dinner from time to time, partly to stave off the boredom and loneliness caused by Lord Snowdon's protracted absences, and partly to make him jealous. Their affair lasted barely a month before Snowdon got wind of it, and brought it to a halt.

'Darling Robin,' began her first letter, written on Valentine's Day 1967, when she was thirty-six:

Thank you for a perfect weekend …
    Thank you for the care and trouble you took to make everything delicious, which restored one's heart.
    Thank you for the concert, the pleasure of which will remain in the mind for ever, and in a way shocked one into sensibility again.
    Thank you for the music, which mended the nerve ends.
    Thank you for making me live again …

The second, written a fortnight later, was in response to an emotional outburst from Douglas-Home after Margaret had been forced by Snowdon to swear on the Bible that she had been faithful. It is a heart-felt mixture of love, fear and faith.

Darling,
    I have never had a letter like it. I don't suppose one like it has ever been written. The beauty in it, and the poetry lifted my heart again.
    Then came two nights of complete attack on – the affair of the heart – denied, as said, on the Bible, my only consolation being that that revered book was not there to lay my hand on.
    I think all the time of you. I was so happy when I heard your voice again … This is to be a bleak time for love. I am only encouraged by the knowledge that I am secure in yours and I would do anything, as you know, to make you happy and not hurt you.

I am hampered by thoughts and hearts being divided at this moment when a real effort must be made on my side to make the marriage work.

I feel I can do this, curiously enough, more convincingly with this happiness of security in you, and feeling of being upheld by you, than without

My brain wireless must have been tuned in quite well, for I felt your presence very strongly. I do hope that by being 'très sage' that we can keep the precious memories safe. They are more precious to me than perhaps you think. I, too, would love to unlimit the limitedness, but I see no possibility of this happening.

What I don't want us to do is to yearn and long, and eat our hearts out wanting something that is forbidden.

We must make the most of this wonder that has happened to us to do particularly wonderful things … so that people will marvel at them and they won't know why we are doing such excellent things in such a special way.

No one will know, only us with our secret source of inspiration. I shall try and speak to you as much as possible but I am in fear of him and I don't know what lengths he won't go to, jealous as he is, to find out what I am up to, and your movements, too.

… Our love has the passionate scent of new mown grass and lilies about it.

Not many people are lucky enough to have known any love like this. I feel so happy that it has happened to me.

… Promise you will never give up, that you will go on encouraging me to make the marriage a success, and that given a good and safe chance, I will try and come back to you one day.

I daren't at the moment.

You are good and loyal, think that I am, too, whatever I may seem to do or say.

All my love my darling,

M

Had these letters entered the public domain at the time they were penned, Margaret would have been vilified as the scarlet woman, and Tony sanctified as her poor, long-suffering victim. But over the course of twenty-seven years, the mood and mores of the country had moved on. In contrast to the more sordid philanderings of the younger generation, this seemed passionate and loving, and more like the stuff of true romance. Margaret, long seen by the British public as difficult and dissolute, would now be welcomed back into her former, youthful role as the Unhappy Princess, or the Princess Unlucky in Love.

89

On New Year's Day 1996, the novelist Robert Harris and his wife Gill went for lunch at a friend's house in Wiltshire. Princess Margaret was expected, but soon after the arrival of the Harrises, at 12.30 sharp, their host was telephoned with the news that the royal party was just setting off. It was an hour before they appeared. Harris made a note of the event.

> Eventually they arrived – HRH, Janie Stevens (with whom she was staying near Abingdon) and the rest of their house party: Jack Plumb, Kenneth Rose, an Irishman called Ned Ryan, and Lady Penn, who turned out to have once been Kim Philby's secretary in MI6. The Princess complained loudly about how far she had had to come. ('I thought the journey would never end. Where on earth are we?') The eleven of us were split between two tables with myself on HRH's right. She was friendlier but dimmer than I'd expected. It was a year after the publication of *Enigma*.* She said she'd been taken to Bletchley by a friend who had worked there ('a perfectly ghastly place'). I asked her what she was reading at the moment, and she replied, rather grandly, 'Hancock,' as one might say 'Joyce' or 'Proust'. I racked my brains as to who this might be – surely she couldn't be reading old Tony Hancock scripts? – but it turned out to be Graham, author of *Fingerprints of the*

---

* Harris's novel set at Bletchley Park.

Gods. We talked of the weather (they had had snow at Sandringham over Christmas the previous week), holidays ('by the end of July one is simply *gasping*'), and the Caribbean (she mentioned BWIA – British West Indian Airways – and claimed the initials stood for 'But Will It Arrive?'). She was perfectly civil to me but thoughtlessly rude to the waitresses: she drew back in theatrical horror at the sight of the main course of lamb and later waved the so-called 'autumn pudding' away saying 'Oh God, no, take it away – summer pudding is bad enough.' As we were leaving, our host gave her his copy of *Enigma* and I had to sign it to her. She watched me, beady-eyed. I have always had an awkward grip and she said: 'Oh, look, the poor man holds a pen exactly like I do.'

A couple of years later I met her at a party of Tom Stoppard's and said hello and mentioned the lunch; she looked right through me and walked away.

90

What happened in the shower? Nobody quite knows.

In February 1999, Princess Margaret was on Mustique. Her guests at Les Jolies Eaux were enjoying a relaxed breakfast, chatting about the day ahead. Suddenly, the cook rushed in. There was steam coming from under the bathroom door, she said: the Princess must be trapped inside. Unable to get a response from the bathroom, the Princess's personal detective broke down the door. The Princess was badly scalded, and in shock. He carried her out.

It seems the accident had occurred because Princess Margaret had made the easy mistake of mixing up the hand controls. There might also have been a faulty thermostat, which had heated the water to boiling point. Intending to have a lukewarm shower, the Princess turned the wrong knobs at the wrong time; jets of searingly hot water shot out straight onto her feet. She was unable to move until her rescue, perhaps five or ten minutes later. The extreme damage to her feet from scalding was probably exacerbated by a pre-existing condition called Raynaud's disease, which affects the circulation.

Princess Margaret had been brought up in the grin-and-bear-it school of medicine. She insisted there was nothing seriously wrong with her, no point in making a fuss, and absolutely no way in which she would be prepared to curtail her precious holiday. According to Tim Heald, 'The Princess's own stubbornness and famous hauteur now contributed to the severity of her illness.'

She struggled on for several weeks on Mustique, unable and unwilling to fly to a hospital. She had to move from Les Jolies Eaux because her son David, to whom she had transferred the house ten years before, had let it out, and the new tenants were due to arrive. Eventually an American neighbour agreed to let her move to his beach cottage. Once there, she never left her room, and would only let Anne Tennant come into it, summoning her by buzzer at all times of the day and night.

Eventually, Anne Tennant put a call through to the Queen at Balmoral, asking for help. Taking the matter in hand, the Queen organised a flight back to Britain on Concorde. Margaret then spent months convalescing at Balmoral, but still refusing the skin grafts recommended by the doctors. She did not appear in public for six months, when she opened a project for sexually abused children in Aberdeen. From now on, her walking would be restricted to just a few steps at a time.

She gradually recovered, but kept using a wheelchair, even though her elder sister considered it unnecessary. When Margaret and her mother visited Buckingham Palace together, an unseemly scene of wheelchair wars took place. The Queen had seen to it that a footman would have a wheelchair ready for her mother, but as the lift doors opened onto the first floor, Margaret made a dash for it. 'For God's sake, Margaret – get out! That's meant for Mummy!' remarked the Queen.

At a reception for the Queen Mother's centenary at Windsor Castle on 21 June 2000, Princess Margaret hopped into a wheelchair that had been brushed aside by her mother. Her action was said to have left the Queen 'fuming'. But in early January 2001, her health went rapidly downhill. A second stroke was followed by further strokes in the months to come: she lost her sight in one eye, and most of the left side of her body was paralysed. She was soon restricted to her wheelchair, and sank into a depression. Old grudges and resentments festered, and her paranoia increased. For a time she took to blaming her condition on her treatment at the hands of Lord Snowdon. Often she refused to

see anybody, including her mother. She spent most of her time in bed, with the curtains drawn. 'She often didn't know what time it was, mistaking lunch for breakfast and that sort of thing,' says a friend.

Roddy Llewellyn visited, but before long she decided that she would have no more male visitors. 'I look so awful now – I don't want them to remember me like this,' she told Anne Tennant. Many felt she had lost the will to live. 'It wasn't easy to feel sympathy,' her old friend Prue Penn told Tim Heald. 'She'd sit in the bedroom looking utterly miserable. The things she asked me to read … there was a Trollope. A frightfully dull book. No men came at all. She couldn't bear to be seen by men. When she went to sleep, I stopped reading. "I'll go, nurse," I'd say. "She's asleep."

'"I'm not," she'd say.'

91

At 8 a.m. on Saturday, 9 February 2002, Alastair Campbell, the prime minister's press secretary, was phoned by the duty clerk, Nick Matthews, to be told that Princess Margaret had died; Mr Blair was being informed, and the death would shortly be announced by Buckingham Palace. By way of conversation, Campbell reminded Matthews that it was he who had called Campbell back in 1997 to tell him of the death of Princess Diana.

'That was a bit more dramatic than this one,' replied Matthews bluntly.

Tony Blair, who was preparing to fly to Sierra Leone, called Campbell for advice. 'I said it was important he didn't try too hard, or appear emotional, just say she was basically a good thing, thoughts with the Queen, Queen Mum, rest of the family, etc.'

In his diary, Campbell recalls watching Blair on television a few hours later, broadcasting live from his plane on the way to Sierra Leone. Blair, he writes, 'did his doorstep on Margaret' – a doorstep, in this context, meaning a few words to the media, apparently delivered off-the-cuff.

'I'm deeply saddened to hear of the death of Princess Margaret,' said Blair. 'My thoughts are with the Queen, Queen Elizabeth the Queen Mother and the rest of the Royal Family at this time.'

Campbell was not wholly convinced by this doorstep. 'It was a bit actorish for my liking, but OK I guess. We had to watch any sense of the thing being anything like Diana.'

The Queen's private secretary, Robin Janvrin, called Campbell before the prime minister spoke to the Queen. Campbell agreed with Janvrin about the appropriate level of grief, and how to stage-manage it. 'I felt the simplest thing was to make clear this was different to Diana's death in part because it was expected. I also felt people would respond to the fact the Queen and Queen Mother would take this differently, and there was a case for them being seen fairly soon, showing she was still up and about and doing her duty, but also showing some emotion at the loss of a younger sister. She would clearly be thinking of her own mortality, not to mention her mother's.'

Campbell continued: '[Prince] Charles went to Sandringham "to comfort the Queen Mother"'. In his diaries, he put that last phrase in inverted commas, almost as though it were unreal. Campbell hadn't particularly liked the way Prince Charles had delivered his own tele-vision statement about the death of Princess Margaret: 'OK, but he was not a natural presenter and he shifted around too much, creating constant distractions from what he was saying.' Campbell seems to have seen it entirely in PR terms, the presentation of emotion being more important than the emotion itself.

Tributes to the Princess were also delivered by the other party leaders. Like Blair, the Conservative leader Iain Duncan Smith was deeply saddened: 'I am deeply saddened by this morning's announcement that Her Royal Highness Princess Margaret died in hospital. An active member of the royal family and a strong servant of her country, she will be sorely missed. Our deepest sympathy and condolences go to Her Majesty the Queen, the Queen Mother, and the rest of the royal family at this sad time.'

* * *

Her old friend Lord St John of Fawsley went much further. 'I have got wonderful memories of her,' he said. 'She was the most beautiful debutante of her generation and she kept that beauty right through her life. She was highly intelligent. In many ways, she was one of the most intelligent women, one of the cleverest women, I have ever met, and she never really had an outlet for that intelligence. She had a turbulent life, of course, but at the close of her life – in the last decade – she had somehow "come into port". She was not at all unhappy. She loved her royal duties and she did them tremendously professionally.'

Her lifelong friends, mainly women, remembered Princess Margaret with affection. They felt she had never been given her due, and recalled private acts of great kindness. When she had heard that an acquaintance from Mustique had lost his job, his wife, his money and his home, she had asked him where he was going to live when he got back to London. He said he didn't have a clue. She invited him to stay at Kensington Palace, and he lived there for several months, while she helped him back on his feet.

Lady Anne Tennant looked back to the time in the late 1980s when her son Henry was first diagnosed with Aids. 'A lot of people were frightened – they wouldn't bring their children to stay, but she always did. And she saw Henry and hugged him. And we used to go to the Lighthouse together, long before Princess Diana did – nobody knew that. We used to talk to the young men there whose partners had died and their families wanted nothing to do with them. And she was so kind, so good. And at some point I did sort of break down, and she said, "Now, do stop crying, Anne, no crying." She was a very, very good friend, and her kindness to Henry was extraordinary.'

Elizabeth Cavendish also paid tribute to her kindness. 'She was, I think, the most loyal person I have ever met and of course to me a wonderful friend. I know, or at least I think I know, that no matter what I had done she would have been there. The people who knew her best were devoted to her. It was the fringe friends who could be so unpleasant.'

Lady Elizabeth Anson spoke of the Princess on the BBC show *Breakfast with Frost*. She refused to accept the way her cousin had been portrayed as a 'troubled princess'. Far from it. 'Of course the latter years have not been at all easy and nobody would want anybody to go through that. She was such a talented person I think in certain ways she could have carved out a musical career for herself and possibly been on the stage … It always used to irritate me that whenever there was any kind of cartoon about her she was always somehow attached to a bottle of Famous Grouse and a cigarette holder and a packet of cigarettes when in fact for many years she neither smoked nor drank. It was a very unfair thing to do to someone who couldn't answer back in that way.'

She would remember her, she said, as she had been when they went out to a restaurant a year previously, just before she suffered another stroke. 'It was the first dinner she had had in many months and, I think, unfortunately the last … She looked so wonderfully beautiful. She was wearing a beautiful red-and-gold jacket and she had taken out her rubies and she did look as she did before she had her very first stroke. She was in fantastic form and that is how I would like to remember her.'

Prince Charles, too, spoke of his 'darling aunt' with affection. 'She had such a dreadful time in the last few years with her awful illness and it was hard, let alone for her to bear it, but for all of us as well. She had such a wonderfully free spirit and she absolutely loved life and lived it to the full and from that point of view it was even harder for everyone to witness this. She also had an incredible talent. I think one of the fondest memories I shall have of her was of her sitting at the piano playing away with a large, very elegant cigarette holder in her mouth.'

* * *

'She had more quality than she was given credit for,' says Hugo Vickers. 'I always thought Snowdon's friends were more loyal to him than hers were to her. She always came out badly. It is so easy to make her life look tragic. Perhaps on the big issues it was, but on the little issues it wasn't at all. She was nicer than she thought she was.'

Sir Roy Strong, a guest at so many of her dinner parties over three decades, issued no public statement, but chose to confide his misgivings to his diary, ready for publication at a later date. 'It is a curious fact that if she had died in the middle of the 1960s, the response would have been akin to that on the death of Diana.

'As it was, she lived long enough for the bitter truth about her to become general knowledge. In my case, as we passed into the 1990s, my attitude to the Royal Family changed. I was brought up in the age of deference. Now a member of the Royal Family has to earn my respect. I can't indulge in sycophancy any more.

'I decided in 1997 that I no longer cared whether I saw Princess Margaret again. A bridge had been crossed. The way she behaved by that date was so inconsiderate that I really couldn't stand any more of it.

'This was a Princess who never seemed to think of anything other than everyone's role to fulfil her slightest whim. All of this was so sad because, when young, she had been beautiful, vivacious and at times quick-witted. But the downside won and that's what the public in the end perceived. She was devoid of the common touch, attracting many to her circle who were sleazy glitterati and lived, it seemed, entirely for her own pleasure. The end was so tragic, a half-paralysed, bloated figure in a wheelchair but, I suppose, 50 years of cigarettes and whisky had effectively destroyed her system.' He then added, by way of explanation, or exculpation, 'It's terrible to write this but there has been a need to "clear the decks".'

* * *

There was, said the *Evening Standard*, 'a steady trickle' of members of the public wishing to sign the books of condolence for HRH the Princess Margaret the day after her death. These books had been placed in a red-carpeted tent at St James's Palace. One of the first in the queue was Barbara Girelli-Kent. 'Princess Margaret was my era in the 1960s,' she said. 'She was symbolic of correctness and strength of character. She had a mind of her own but great respect for Her Majesty the Queen and the royal institution. She was a trouper.'

Anthea Mander Lahr said, 'She was a colourful character not much older than myself. She added a bit of spice to life with her scandals. It's such a nationalistic thing to say but it gives you pride of being British.'

John Fellowes, an Australian on holiday in London, had popped by to pay his respects. 'To an older person it is a break with the past. I'm also reminded of what Mr Donne said many years ago – "No man is an island". It is a changed era from when she was young and vital, and I suppose there's not so much interest in royalty today, but I am.'

92

Within a week, the poet laureate, Andrew Motion, had composed a brand-new poem to mark the Princess's death. He called it 'The Younger Sister'. It reads much as though a taxi driver were holding forth to a grandee in the back of his cab: 'The luxuries, of course, and privilege – the money, houses, holidays, the lot: all these were real, and all these drove a wedge between your life and ours.' But when chopped up, it looks more like poetry:

> The luxuries, of course, and privilege –
> The money, houses, holidays, the lot:
> All these were real, and all these drove a wedge
> Between your life and ours.

Motion was suggesting, of course, that money, houses, holidays – 'the lot' – were absent from his own particular life, and from the lives of almost everyone other than the late Princess, and that this imbalance somehow 'drove a wedge/Between your life and ours'.

All very well; but then the poet laureate seemed to have second thoughts:

And yet the thought
Of how no privilege on earth can keep
A life from suffering in love and loss –
This means we turn to you and see how deep
The current runs between yourself and us.

Thus, Motion (or 'us', as he styled himself) had, over the course of a couple of lines, come to feel that, when push comes to shove, we are all akin to Her Royal Highness:

And now death spells it out again, and more,
As it becomes your final human act:
A daughter gone before her mother goes:
A younger sister heading on before;
A woman in possession of the fact
That love and duty speak two languages.

His effort was met with a widespread thumbs-down. A.N. Wilson, never one to mince his words, criticised the poem as 'extraordinarily impertinent', condemning Motion as 'a Royal Lickspittle', and adding, 'All he's done as Laureate … is to persuade me that this rather absurd position should be abolished.' A month later, in March 2002, the left-wing poet Adrian Mitchell protested at Motion's obsequiousness by declaring himself the 'anti-poet laureate', and vowing to have himself installed in the post at a ceremony in Trafalgar Square.

After hearing of the death of Princess Margaret, the Archbishop of Canterbury, the Rt Rev George Carey, went to pay his respects. He was a devotee of all members of the Royal Family, going so far as to wonder, in his autobiography, *Know the Truth*, 'if our nation [is] actually worthy of their devotion and unflagging sense of duty'. In the same work, he described Prince Andrew as 'outgoing, direct and entertaining', and the Duchess of York as 'a refreshing young woman'. He also paid tribute to

Prince Philip's 'inimitable sense of humour', and called the then Camilla Parker-Bowles 'a most attractive and charming person, warm-hearted and intelligent, with a down-to-earth attitude'. Above all, he claimed to have developed a 'special friendship' with Princess Margaret. 'She had very firm views about religious services, and would have no truck whatsoever with "new-fangled" services, so the Book of Common Prayer rite would always be used when she was present.'

The former archbishop recalled celebrating communion at the Princess's bedside. 'The effect of the steroids she had been prescribed showed in her swollen face and she was rather depressed that evening,' he revealed, 'but she noticeably brightened up during the simple and short service.' Afterwards, he had anointed the Princess with olive oil his wife Eileen had brought back from Bethlehem, before decanting it into a smaller flask. After suggesting that the Princess might like to anoint herself nightly, he presented her with the flask. 'Princess Margaret was thrilled with it.'

Popping his head around the door after her death, Carey was now gratified to note that the 'attractive little flask' of Eileen's olive oil lay between the two candles flickering in the semi-gloom above her coffin.

93

Had she died a decade earlier, Princess Margaret might have enjoyed a warmer send-off from the obituarists. But by now the days of dutiful celebration of the recently departed had come to an end. A steelier, less forgiving approach was in operation, even for members of the Royal Family.

'Princess Margaret, who has died in hospital after suffering a third stroke aged seventy-one, was the most striking illustration of the capricious and troubled relationship that beset the British and their monarchy in the second half of the twentieth century,' began the obituary in the *Guardian*.

> Not even the life of Diana, Princess of Wales concentrated quite so many questions about the role and style of the royal family as that of Margaret Rose, second daughter of George VI, only sibling of Elizabeth II; for while both were creatures of their time, Margaret lived beyond hers into a more critical, ever less deferential era; and her life, above all, posed that essential question which Diana, in her own way, was trying to answer: what, exactly, is a princess for?

The author, Charles Nevin, argued that while Margaret had been unconventional in her enjoyment of the arts, she was in other ways 'as conventional as any Victorian or Edwardian, particularly in her unquestioning assumption that her royal status commanded the utmost respect irrespective of circumstance or behaviour. Royalty was *toujours sans reproche*. To put it in a rather less high-flown way, she wanted to have her cake, and to eat it.'

Writing in the *Independent*, Hugo Vickers felt that 'The absence of a role was her tragedy. Whereas her father's life was fulfilled when he was called, reluctantly, to serve as King, the Princess never received such a call.' Vickers went on to suggest that her 'slightly forbidding exterior concealed a kind heart. She moved in that society which relished feuds and firm loyalties – her friends were, in principle, friends for life, but she was a naughty enemy.' She was capricious: 'Close friends learned to be wary of her ways. At the moment that everyone was relaxing, she would surreptitiously resume her royal rank and reduce some helpless guest to dust.' Nevertheless, 'the key to her character was a spirit of generosity to which even she might not have admitted'.

In the *Sunday Telegraph*, her old friend Kenneth Rose rallied to her defence. 'In a life devoted to public duties and private passions, Princess Margaret was cruelly exposed to the whims of popular opinion,' he began, berating his fellow journalists for their 'hurtful campaign of denigration and spite'. For Rose, the Princess was 'an icon of 20th century monarchy. She loved clothes and jewellery, wore them with panache, retained her dazzling complexion and trim figure of youth to the end of her life. Standing a shade over five feet, she made up for her lack of inches, about which she was needlessly sensitive, by her dignity and grace of bearing.'

As the article progressed, Rose's case for the defence transformed, as if by magic, into the case for the prosecution. 'It has been surmised that her imperious, even wayward, interpretation of her role sprang from dissatisfaction or envy; what colloquially could be called second-sisteritis. There is no truth in the assumption. For the person and pre-eminence of the sovereign she insisted on punctilious respect.' It was almost as though, having trumpeted his doughty loyalist credentials at the beginning of the article, Rose felt he had now earned the right to list her shortcomings. 'Even her closest friends were startled by the swiftness with which enticing intimacy could give way to a Hanoverian blue stare,' he continued. '"Hopping back on her twig", they called it.'

Many of the passages in his piece begin with a compliment before veering off towards an insult. 'Her private whims were of luxurious simplicity. She ate very little, rarely meat.' So far, so good. 'Although game and some fish were acceptable, she would wave away a dish of gleaming salmon trout, demand an omelette, ask if she could exchange it for a boiled egg which in its turn was rejected as too hard or too soft.' And then the U-turn: 'Hosts and hostesses never forgot the princess who came to dinner ... Princess Margaret could be an exacting house guest who thought nothing of re-arranging the furniture in her bedroom to her own satisfaction.'

Rose's glowing interpretation often seemed at odds with the evidence he offered. 'The Princess shone as a mimic. She would recall Dame Joan Sutherland greeting her backstage after her sleepwalking scene from *Lucia di Lammermoor*: "Oi'm always meeting yew in moi nightie."'

Insults were smuggled like contraband beneath the cover of wide-eyed questions. 'So who did she like in a world of real and imaginary slights magnified by her own insecurity?' In answer to his own question, Rose listed her mother and sister ('though both relationships were subject to occasional exasperation'), her children, and a handful of women friends, 'some of whom had served as ladies-in-waiting'.

The *New York Times* announced that 'Princess Margaret, the younger sister of Queen Elizabeth II, whose troubled private life aroused both worldwide sympathy and widespread reprobation, died yesterday morning in London. She was 71.' The tone of the obituary was even edgier than its British counterparts. 'She was often less than gracious when faced with the drudgery of public appearances – the ribbon-cuttings, diplomatic functions and endless other official occasions by which Britain's royals justify their position and the public money that finances it. Easily bored and often petulant, the princess was known for indulging her moods.'

In later years, the obituary continued, she had been criticised for 'demanding motorcycle escorts and government helicopters to travel around Britain'. To many people she appeared to be 'the black sheep of her generation of royals. But this reputation did not necessarily trouble her.' The obituarist went on to describe the Princess as 'haughty', with 'a penchant for saying the wrong thing'. She also had 'a traumatic private life', and 'as a houseguest she was notoriously demanding. At parties she often objected if other guests ignored royal protocol and left before her. Even her children were expected to refer to her as "Princess Margaret" in front of visitors. So did her husband, though he was said to have called her Ducky in private.'

The anonymous *Daily Telegraph* obituary seemed to be written more in sorrow than in anger. 'She had talents and qualities which might, perhaps, have blossomed more fully away from the constant blaze of publicity,' it began. 'She had defects which, precisely because she was completely honest, she neither would nor could conceal: wilfulness, a dislike of being crossed and an inability to reconcile her royal status with her love of the bohemian.'

Though witty, she was 'sometimes bitingly sharp to those who presumed too far'. On the other hand, for all her misfortunes, she 'always retained her sense of fun'. The obituarist then executed a neat little somersault: 'Whatever may have been foolishly and maliciously said at various times, the Princess was a remarkably beautiful and stylish woman who put duty first.' The obituarist ended by indulging in a game of 'What if …?'

'A complex figure, Princess Margaret seemed, despite her exalted position, more often than not to have been dealt a peculiarly bad hand for the game of life … It was Princess Margaret's misfortune to have narrowly missed being a Queen – a job at which she might have been rather good – while being saddled with the secondary task of being a Princess, for which she was temperamentally unsuited.' But what of the rest of us, dealt such a monstrously bad hand in the game of life that we missed the throne not by an inch, but a mile?

94

Perhaps wisely, the author didn't elaborate on his aside that Margaret might have made a rather good queen. Since then, others have begged to differ. 'The Almighty gets the right people to be born first,' her cousin Margaret Rhodes told Tim Heald. 'Thank heaven Margaret wasn't the eldest – it would have been disastrous the other way round.'

The Princess would at least have gone along with her cousin's theology. Her sister's position was, in her opinion, decreed by God. A.N. Wilson remembers one evening spent in her company. 'Someone mentioned the quasi-religious feelings excited in many bosoms by the thought of the Queen. Someone else spoke of the common phenomenon, in all ranks of society, of dreaming about the Queen, and said that in their case these dreams brought feelings of peace and benediction, as if they had been in the presence of God. "Quite right, too," said Princess Margaret firmly. "After all, the Queen is God's representative in this realm." Admittedly the Princess was in a condition which *Private Eye* would describe as "tired and emotional", but I got the impression that her words were meant entirely seriously.'

In fact, Margaret Rhodes's glowing interim report on the Almighty's gift for administrating the royal succession was a little selective: in 1502 He saw to it that the first-born, Prince Arthur, perished from sweating sickness at the age of fifteen, thus allowing his reckless younger brother Henry to be crowned King Henry VIII on their father's death seven years later. In 1894 He arranged for the flighty

Duke of Windsor to be born first, before the dependable King George VI. Had it been the other way round, would the Duke of Windsor's supporters now be saying that, if only he had been born first, he might have made a rather good king? Likewise, the Queen's grandfather, King George V, was born second, the early death of his flaky elder brother, Prince Albert Victor, described by the historian Philip Magnus as 'a merciful act of providence'.

But what if Margaret had been born first? Would she really have been better-suited to the role of Queen than the secondary role of Princess? John Updike once suggested that 'Margaret would have made a more striking and expressive queen', though he then went on to ask, 'but would she have worn as well, and presided as smoothly?'

What if Elizabeth had been the younger daughter? Would she have turned out all moody and demanding? Pursued any further, these idle speculations spiral to the very heart of human existence. Nature or nurture? If the egg that turned into Elizabeth had instead turned into Margaret – that is to say, had Margaret been born first – would Margaret have become the dutiful monarch, and Elizabeth the wayward bossyboots? Or would Queen Margaret I have been a chain-smoking, high-camp, acid-tongued, slugabed monarch, leaving her younger sister, HRH the Princess Elizabeth, in her tweed skirts and her sensible shoes, to pick up the pieces? Was Margaret's entire life overshadowed by the conviction that she had missed out on the throne? How odd, to emerge from the womb fourth in line, to go up a notch at the age of six, up another notch that same year, and then to find yourself hurtling down, down, down to fourth place at the birth of Prince Charles in 1948, fifth at the birth of Princess Anne in 1950, then downhill all the way, overtaken by a non-stop stream of riff-raff – Prince Andrew and Prince Edward and Peter Phillips and Princess Beatrice and the rest of them, down, down, down, until by the time of your death you have plummeted to number eleven, behind Zara Phillips, later to become Zara Tindall, mother of Mia Tindall, who, if you were still alive, would herself be one ahead of you, even when she was still in nappies. Not many women have to face the fact that their careers peaked at the age of six, or to live with the prospect of losing their place in the pecking order to a succession of newborn babies, and to face demotion every few years thereafter. Small wonder, then, if Princess Margaret felt short-changed by life.

But what if she had been the first-born? Would it have been any different? What if she had been Queen? Or if Elizabeth had died young? What if, somewhere along the line, Margaret and Elizabeth had switched characters?

What if? What if? What if?

95

HM Queen Margaret's Christmas Broadcast, 1977

As I go about this country and abroad, I meet many people who, all in their own ways, are making a very real contribution to their community.

Many of them find ways to give service in their spare time, through voluntary organisations or simply on their own individual initiative, contributing in a thousand ways to all that is best in our society.

Of course, some are conspicuous by their absence.

I am talking now of those who are happy to take a fancy title when they get married and boost their own tiresome little careers from all the publicity but won't lift a finger for anyone else.

And I am also talking of those who have devoted their lives to undermining the contributions of those more conscientious and infinitely better-born than themselves.

You know full well who you are. May that be an end to the matter.

Christmas is traditionally a time when we take the opportunity to look back on the year that is coming to an end, and to look ahead to the year that is shortly to commence.

My own year has been faintly tiresome, but that's only to be expected. I have been dragged here, there and everywhere as part of my Silver Jubilee celebrations. If I see one more plate of coronation chicken, I shall be left with no choice but to scream. The street parties and village fêtes, the presents, the flowers from the children, the mile upon mile of decorated streets and houses; these things suggest the real value and pleasure of the celebration for everyone, except, of course, for the one person whom they are meant to be celebrating, namely oneself. It's the same everywhere I go: yes, of course people are thrilled to see one, it makes their day, but are they prepared to give something back in return? Answer: no.

Of course, it wasn't always like that. Far from it. When my mother visited the East End of London during the Blitz, she was delighted by the marvellous spirit she found there: people resolutely cheerful, quite regardless of the awful mess they may have found themselves in. But sadly today they have all grown used to what I call the 'something for nothing' society, in which they expect the rest of us to do all the work, while they simply loaf about.

And, with this in mind, I'll wish you all a very happy Christmas, not because I really want to, but because I suppose I must.

96

Four hundred and fifty mourners attended the funeral of HRH the Princess Margaret at St George's Chapel, Windsor. Among them were her former husband, Lord Snowdon, who was heard to complain that the lord chamberlain had assured him there would be no steps. At one point he and Roddy Llewellyn exchanged glances, but they did not speak. The Queen Mother, dressed all in black, her face covered by a veil, entered by the North Door. Her biographer-to-be Hugo Vickers observed her close-up. She was, he thought, 'impressive and demonic'; he detected 'a kind of steely resolve that was more involved with her own attendance at the ceremony than any sympathy she might feel for her dead daughter. It was a mixture between her wonderful resolve and perhaps a tiny hint of triumphalism.'

The Princess had been planning her own funeral for a few years; it had become something of a pastime. 'I am always altering the arrangements for my funeral. I drive the Lord Chamberlain's Department mad,' she told Kenneth Rose.

She would chop and change as the mood took her. 'I rather think I should like to be buried at sea,' she once mused to a friend.

'With a Union flag wrapped round your coffin?' asked the friend.

'Certainly not. I have my own Standard.'

In the end, she had opted for dry land. Her choice of music included a bit of *Swan Lake*, a choral version of Psalm 23 and the Nunc Dimittis, as well as two stirring hymns: 'Immortal, Invisible, God Only Wise' and 'When I Survey the Wondrous Cross'.

The canon-in-residence, the Rev Canon Barry Thompson, said a prayer for the Princess: 'O eternal God … we remember before thee this day thy servant Margaret, rendering thanks to thee: for her loyalty and sense of duty; for her faithfulness towards her family and her friends; for her energy and enthusiasm; for her quick wit and sound advice; for her depth of knowledge and her love of life …'

The lesson, from Romans 8, was read by her son, Lord Linley. As the coffin was carried to the hearse by eight soldiers from the Princess's own Glasgow and Ayrshire Regiment, the 1st Battalion Royal Highland Fusiliers, a lament was played by a lone piper. Chosen by the Princess's daughter, Lady Sarah, it was called 'The Desperate Struggle of the Bird'. Another lament was played by a piper from the Royal Highland Fusiliers, and 'The Last Post' was sounded by the trumpeters of the Hussars and Light Dragoons. This was followed by 'Reveille'.

Despite all this, the Archbishop of Canterbury, the Rt Rev George Carey, felt the service 'sadly lacked the personal touch. I was dismayed that there was no homily to pay tribute to a woman who had put her loyalty to Crown and country before her personal happiness … Apart from my prayer at the end, when I mentioned the Princess by name, it could have been anybody's funeral service.' In an interview on the BBC the following day, he emphasised his own special significance in her life: 'I've prayed with her on several occasions,' he told the royal correspondent Nicholas Witchell. 'I remember one Christmas, going to her bedside at Sandringham and praying with her and she was deeply grateful for that.'

Afterwards, the mourners retired to Windsor Castle for tea and cake. Some were dissatisfied by the day's arrangements. Prince Rupert Loewenstein considered what he referred to as the 'tickets' for the funeral 'rather strange', as 'morning coat' or 'lounge suit' were recommended both for the men and the women. 'If taken literally it would have made an excellent cabaret scene in the Weimar Republic.' He was unimpressed, also, by 'a flimsy note' attached to each invitation saying, 'You can get a cup of tea in St George's Hall after the service.'

Standards had fallen, he felt. 'I did not think that David Ogilvy, the 12th Earl of Airlie, who was Lord Chamberlain to Queen Elizabeth the Queen Mother, would have allowed such wording to pass through under his white staff.' As the business manager of the Rolling Stones Prince Rupert Loewenstein had, for some decades, been used to dealing with these social niceties.

While the others were enjoying their tea, the Princess's corpse was driven three and a half miles to Slough crematorium for a municipal cremation. 'Police were on duty at each roundabout and junction on the short journey from Windsor,' reported the *Daily Telegraph*, 'but they were not needed. There were no crowds lining the route and the hearse was merely waved through the late-afternoon traffic without fanfare.'

The Princess wished to be buried with her father in the Royal Vault at St George's Chapel, and had opted for cremation as there was no room in the vault for a full coffin. The cost of cremation at Slough was £280, plus a surcharge of £20 for those, like the Princess, who lived beyond the borough. It is not known whether or not this fee was waived.

Princess Margaret had insisted that her children and her sister should not attend the cremation, so they joined the rest of the Royal Family for tea at the Castle while the coffin of English oak, accompanied by only three courtiers – the Dean of Windsor, the Princess's former private secretary, Viscount Ullswater, and the lord chamberlain, representing the Queen – headed off to Slough. In honour of the deceased, the gates of the crematorium had been given a fresh splash of paint.

A service of remembrance for the Princess was held at Westminster Abbey on 19 April. Before it began, an orchestra played a selection of the Princess's favourite music, including the 'Awakening' *pas de deux* from Tchaikovsky's *Sleeping Beauty*, and pieces by Bach. The service itself was set around Fauré's *Requiem*, with Felicity Lott and Bryn Terfel singing solos, and contributions from the choirs of Westminster Abbey, King's College, Cambridge, and St George's Chapel, Windsor. Lord Linley read from Corinthians ('O, grave, where is thy victory?'), and the actress Felicity Kendal read an extract by William Penn.

As the congregation of 1,900 milled out of the Abbey, Sir Roy Strong, as he now was, felt that the service had lacked a certain something. It was, he thought, 'a perfectly choreographed, unemotional ritual gone through like clockwork but lacking any spirit. How could it have been otherwise? She was such a capricious, arrogant and thoughtless woman. And yet she was a loyal, practising Christian with flashes of generosity along with wit.'

His final verdict on his old friend was brief and to the point: 'The common touch she had not.'

97

On 13 and 14 June 2006, Christie's auctioned 896 items from the collection of Her Royal Highness The Princess Margaret: cigarette lighters, silver salvers, fans and pepperpots; candlesticks, umbrellas, tiaras and chairs; paintings, playing cards, trophies, menu-card holders; portraits, mirrors, brooches, bowls, toys, books and occasional tables; snuffboxes and pillboxes, fish knives and forks, photo frames, tea sets and sugar bowls; gifts from her mother, gifts from her father, gifts from her grandmother, gifts from her aunts; gifts from musicians and movie stars, gifts from artists and authors; gifts from the rich, gifts from the poor; gifts from countries, royal families, corporations, regiments, town councils and housing associations; gifts from the crew of the royal yacht *Britannia*; gifts from the pensioners of Balmoral, Birkhall and Sandringham.

Remember, man, that thou art dust, and unto dust thou shalt return: a life in 896 objects, ready for dispersal to the four corners of the earth. Where had she kept it, this great mountain of bric-à-brac? The jewellery alone – brooches, necklaces, hairpins, earrings, wristwatches, earclips, bracelets, key-chains, bangles, rings, pendants, lockets – amounted to 185 different items, which sold, in all, for £9,598,160. While she was alive, those who chose to pity her would point out that the only property she had ever owned was her modest villa on Mustique, a gift from an old friend. Yet she had always had the wherewithal to buy something infinitely more splendid. One single piece – Queen Mary's antique diamond rivière, consisting of thirty-four diamonds, weighing eighty-five carats – sold for just under £1 million.

Over the course of two days, the remnants of Princess Margaret went under the hammer. They say that when you drown, your whole life flashes before you. Do the wealthy see it hoisted aloft by men in brown coats?

Watch it go down! The silver teaspoon given to the five-year-old Margaret for Christmas 1935 by Queen Maud of Norway, complete with a Santa Claus label on it, bearing the handwritten message, 'for dear little Margaret from Aunt Maud' – gone, for £3,840! A set of three white-and-gilt-painted pelmets that once masked the tops of the curtains in Apartment 1a in Kensington Palace – gone, for £1,200! A French gold toothpick box, circa 1800 – gone, for £1,600! A gem-set gold Cartier cigarette case,* engraved 'To Margaret from her very devoted Papa GR Christmas 1949' – gone, for £102,000, twenty times its highest estimate! A cigarette box, 'Presented to Her Royal Highness The Princess Margaret by The Government and People of the West Indies as a token of their abiding loyalty and affection on the occasion of her visit to Port of Spain in April 1958 when on behalf of Her Majesty the Queen she graciously inaugurated the Parliament of The West Indies' – gone, for £8,400!

The Baroque bed that once belonged to the Princess's grandparents, the Earl and Countess of Strathmore – gone, for £48,000! A pair of George III silver-mounted ivory lemon-squeezers – gone, for £2,800!

---

* The thirty-seven cigarette-based items in the auction, including fifteen ashtrays, one of them a wedding present from the 3rd King's Hussars, stand as testament to the Princess's prodigious devotion to tobacco. Her reputation as a dedicated smoker clearly preceded her on trips abroad: gifts of cigarette lighters, cigarette boxes and cigarette cases came from France, Russia, Austria, Belgium, Italy, the West Indies, Canada, Hungary and the Channel Islands. Lot 363 was 'A filigree cigarette-case and cigarette-holder, perhaps Yugoslavian. The cigarette-case of book form with filigree scroll and flower front and back and reeded side, the inside applied with a plaque engraved with a signature, the cigarette holder with a composition mouthpiece, contained in a fitted green leather case, with a note inscribed in an unknown hand "*From Tito 1952 or 3*". It fetched £6,600.

A George V silver cup, a trophy from the Royal Windsor Horse Show, bearing two inscriptions, the first 'WON BY H.R.H. THE PRINCESS MARGARET', the second 'ROYAL WINDSOR HORSE SHOW 1944 FIRST PRIZE THE BEST WAR-TIME UTILITY SINGLE DRIVING CLASS PRESENTED BY ODEON THEATRES LTD' – gone, for £16,800! The original artwork of the eighteen-year-old Margaret's picture on the cover of *Time* magazine, June 1949 – gone, for £11,400! An antique Victorian diamond and gem-set bee bar brooch, originally a christening gift to the Queen Mother, accompanied by a note in Princess Margaret's own hand: 'Almost the first bit of jewellery given to Mum … given to me 10 Feb 1945' – gone, for £33,600!

A Virgin and Child travelling icon, in a frame of rubies, together with a card inscribed 'from Pope Pius XII 1949' – gone, for £14,400! A presentation copy of *Liberace: An Autobiography* in its original dustjacket, signed on the title page 'To the Princess Margaret, Countess of Snowdon, With fond remembrance of the Royal Variety Performance in 1972. Liberace 1973', accompanied by a doodle by the famous pianist of a grand piano and candelabra – gone, for £540! An eighteenth-century side table, a twenty-first birthday present from the St John Ambulance Brigade Cadets – gone, for £10,800!

A thousand potential customers filled five sales rooms; another five hundred were in touch by telephone. Within the first thirty seconds, Lot No.1, a ruby, cultured pearl and diamond necklace, valued somewhere between £1,200 and £1,500, had shot past the £6,000 mark, eventually selling for £27,600. Lot 2, a pair of child's ivory bangles, worthless without provenance, sold for £3,840, almost twenty times the estimate. By its close, the sale had raised £14 million, with a number of lots going for up to a hundred times their estimate. The Princess's Fabergé cigarette holder, guide price £2,000, sold for £209,600; the oak chair Queen Mary sat upon for the 1937 coronation of King George VI and Queen Elizabeth, guide price £300–500, sold for £38,400. Four sets of playing cards with King George VI's cypher, circa 1940, guide price £200–300, sold for £13,200.

A Russian jewelled two-colour gold-mounted guilloche-enamelled Fabergé clock, once the property of Queen Mary, sold for £1,240,000. The Princess would have heard its discreet tick-tock as she woke each morning: it had lived above the fireplace in her bedroom.

To some, including a few members of her own family, it seemed as though a price had been attached to virtually everything the Princess ever owned. There had, though, been one or two hasty last-minute withdrawals. On the first day of the sale, Christie's announced that an ornate 1930s cast-iron railing acquired by the Princess from Ascot racecourse and transferred by her to the rose garden at Kensington Palace would be withdrawn from sale: it emerged that fixtures and fittings from any royal residence are protected by law, their removal punishable by a custodial sentence of up to seven years. 'The client has decided to give it to the nation,' explained a spokesman for Christie's. The railings were returned to Kensington Palace without further ado.

The two people responsible for this almighty clear-out were Princess Margaret's two children, Viscount Linley and Lady Sarah Chatto. 'I had the sale for a very simple reason, which was an inheritance tax situation, and wanting to build for my family's future and my children's education – normal family requirements,' explained Viscount Linley. 'We are a modern family who need to live in a certain way.' In fact, his mother had already left him and his sister £7 million in her will; death duties came to just over £3 million.

Out went objects accrued by the Princess over the course of seven decades: the twelve silver birthday-candle holders that had been placed in her first and second birthday cakes, each engraved with the initials 'MR'; her *Snow White and the Seven Dwarfs* Walt Disney breakfast set (circa 1937), comprising an electroplated nickel silver cup, plate and bowl, with knife, fork and spoon featuring Mickey Mouse and Donald Duck; three umbrellas employed by the Princess on rainy days in the 1960s and 1970s; the Poltimore Tiara, its thirty-four diamonds mounted in silver and gold, bought by the Queen Mother and given to Princess Margaret to wear at her wedding. The candle-holders had raised £6,600, the Disney breakfast set £7,200, the three umbrellas £2,400, the Poltimore Tiara £926,400, sold to an anonymous buyer from Asia.

Several items in the sale had been gifts from staff and subjects, the fruit of whip-rounds: a silver snuffbox for her twenty-first birthday, 'Presented to Her Royal Highness Princess Margaret by The employees at Sandringham 21st August 1951'; a bronze statuette of a man and child, with a presentation plaque, 'To HRH Princess Margaret from the people of Uganda, 6 May 1960'; a rose bowl from the Government and People of Victoria, Australia; a mahogany and tulipwood dining table, 'Presented to Her Royal Highness on the occasion of her marriage to Mr Armstrong-Jones by members of the Army, 6 May 1960'; a Wedgwood mug 'Presented to HRH Princess Margaret Countess of Snowdon on 1st July 1980 by the Beth Johnson Housing Association on the Occasion of the Opening of Compton Close, Lichfield Road, Stafford'. Before the auction went ahead, the Queen issued an instruction that the proceeds from any item given to her late sister in her official capacity should be donated to charity.

Asparagus tongs, binoculars, hymnbooks, bell-pushes, lemon-squeezers, menu-card holders, dice, trunks, table ornaments, scissors; a toothpick box, a mustard pot, an academic gown, a travelling stationery box, a child's rattle, *The Tale of Peter Rabbit*. The auction revealed quite how much stuff the Princess had accumulated over her seventy-one years: had it been worth hundreds rather than millions she might well be remembered not as a collector, but as a hoarder.

The auction catalogues also suggest that one of her suspicions was ill-founded: for years she complained that her grandmother, Queen Mary, had nursed a grudge against her. Yet the sheer abundance of Queen Mary's gifts to Margaret told a different story. As well as the Fabergé clock, Queen Mary also gave her an art deco pearl and diamond necklace for her eighteenth birthday; a pair of Fabergé jewelled glass scent bottles; an art deco sapphire and diamond bar brooch ('For darling Margaret on her confirmation day from her loving Grannie Mary R, God Bless You, April 15th 1946'); another confirmation present of a set of mother-of-pearl fruit knives and forks ('for darling Margaret from her loving Grannie Mary April 15th 1946'); a silver-gilt dressing-table service in a brass-bound rosewood case; a needlework fire screen, a present for Christmas 1947; a French painted fan with a note in Queen Mary's hand: 'Fan which belonged to Queen Alexandra given her by her sister Marie Empress of Russia – given to Princess Margaret of York by her grandmother Queen Mary, 1932'; a silver-gilt dressing table decorated with flowers containing a complete service along with a card inscribed in Queen Mary's hand, 'Queen Mary bought this dressing service for Princess Margaret some day'; an Irish oak linen chest; a silver nine-piece tea and coffee service; a fan of Honiton lace ('made to order of Victoria Mary, Princess of Wales, for the St. Louis Exhibition, USA in 1904, given to Princess Margaret by her grandmother Queen Mary in 1939'); and *The Letters of Queen Victoria*, the first volume marked 'For darling Margaret from Grannie Mary 1944. These 3 volumes were given to your Great Aunt Victoria by her father King Edward VII.' Given so much, and so regularly, by their grandmother, few other grandchildren would have nursed a grievance about being unloved.

There were gifts from many others besides, including books signed by writers from the more comfortable end of society, among them Patrick Leigh Fermor ('For Her Royal Highness Princess Margaret, with the author's humble duty … Feb. 1959') and Harold Acton ('For HRH the Princess Margaret, with humble duty and affection, from the old aesthete, Haroldo'). A book called *Pavlova Impressions* was inscribed by Margot Fonteyn, 'Ma'am who is such a great inspiration to the Royal Ballet, affectionately, Margot.' Five volumes of the plays of Noël Coward were signed 'To Her Royal Highness the Princess Margaret. Dear Ma'am, This brings you my affectionate best wishes for your happiness always, Noël Coward.'

Like many family sales, possibly most, this one caused a certain amount of friction. Some muttered that her children should not have sold her wedding tiara, for instance. 'The tiara was obviously a very strong image,' countered Viscount Linley, 'but, being realistic, we have a young family that needs educating, and education does not seem to be getting any cheaper, going by recent figures … We looked very long and hard about whether to include it or not, but I think my mother would have felt it was a good idea. It was an iconic piece, but who in the family would be in a position to wear it very often, versus the opportunity it gave? So it was a very rational decision.'*

Both his father and his sister were also said to be upset by Viscount Linley's inclusion of Pietro Annigoni's 1957 portrait of Princess Margaret, a sister piece to the portrait of the Queen hanging in the National Portrait Gallery. After some discussion, Viscount Linley bought it back for £680,000, over three times its original estimate; any remaining misgivings about the auction were buried beneath an avalanche of hyperbole.

'The extraordinary results of this important and unparalleled sale are a wonderful tribute to a beautiful and stylish princess,' concluded François Curiel, chairman of Christie's Europe. 'HRH The Princess Margaret's widespread appeal was reflected in the exceptional prices.'

---

* The cost of privately educating a child at a boarding school for a fourteen-year period was then estimated at £468,000 for a boarder and £286,000 for a day pupil, so the sum needed for Princess Margaret's four grandchildren's education would not have exceeded £2 million.

98

From the Mustique-island.com website, 2017

For generations, those who have visited Mustique have been captivated by the unique sense of island life; where you can enjoy the ultimate in luxury villa living with the privilege of being on your own private tropical island.

There are not many rules on Mustique, no protocol or expectations. Guests can simply do as they wish.

Enjoy the privacy of your own villa, or the legendary house party atmosphere at The Cotton House, when fellow guests get together to enjoy anything from a gastronomic dinner, a cocktail party, to a beach barbeque, or Jump Up at Basil's. On Mustique, anything goes.

Explore the island at your own speed, where a whole host of experiences await; from swimming and scuba diving in the jewel coloured waters, to sailing and snorkeling with the turtles at nearby Tobago Cays. Onshore choose from riding horses along the beaches to honing your tennis skills at the renowned Mustique Tennis Club, or indulge in a world-class spa treatment.

Les Jolies Eaux

Standing dramatically on a private peninsula at Mustique's southern tip, this legendary villa, previously featured in *Architectural Digest*, was designed for HRH The Princess Margaret, Countess of Snowdon.

Accommodation

Living

Les Jolies Eaux has been extensively refurbished and expanded to incorporate a new master bedroom, dining pavilion, media room and office as well as offering spacious and comfortable indoor and outdoor dining areas.

Bedroom

Bedroom 1: King, AC, En-suite with Dressing, Shower, Double Basins & WC

Bedroom 2: King, AC, En-suite with Dressing, Shower, Tub, Double Basins, bidet, WC & private porch

Bedroom 3: Queen, AC, En-suite with Shower, Double Basin, WC and private porch

Bedroom 4: Twin, AC, En-suite with Shower, Double Basin, WC and private porch

Bedroom 5: King, AC, En-suite with Dressing, Shower, Double Basin, WC and private porch

Villa Features

AC

Media/Entertainment Room

iPod docking station

DVD/TV

Wi-Fi and Broadband

Mosquito nets

Hairdryers

Safes

Bathrobes

Office

Power 220/110 V UK Plugs

Outdoor Features
    40 Ft Pool
    16 Ft Pool
    2 Kawasaki Mules

Villa Staff
    1 Chef
    1 Butler
    1 Housekeeper
    1 Maid
    1 Gardener

Price per Week
    15th December 2016 to 30th April 2017 $34,000
    1st May 2017 to 22nd July 2017 $20,500
    23rd July 2017 to 23rd August 2017 $26,000
    24th August 2017 to 14th December 2017 $20,500

All rates subject to 10% government tax and a 10% island fee. Certain holiday dates may be subject to rate supplements. A discretionary tip of 5% minimum is recommended.

ENQUIRE NOW

99

14 May 1995

Princess Margaret attends David Hare's play *Skylight*.

It is set in a first-floor flat in north-west London.

'Patterned carpets which have worn to a thread and a long wall of books' is how the playwright sets the scene. 'The kitchen area at the back of the room looks cluttered and much used.'

The only female character, Kyra Hollis, 'is just past thirty. She is returning to her flat, blue with cold. She has a heavy overcoat wrapped round her, and is wearing thick woollen gloves. She is carrying three large plastic bags.'

After it is over, Princess Margaret is asked if she found the play depressing.

'It was a bit like one's own life,' she replies.

ACKNOWLEDGEMENTS

My thanks to Frances Wilson and Terence Blacker for reading early drafts, to Anna Morrison for the wonderful cover, to Naomi Mantin for handling the publicity so deftly, to A.N. Wilson, Selina Hastings, Maggi Hambling, Polly Devlin, Robert Harris, Susanna Johnston, Hugo Vickers, Christopher Sykes, Eleanor Bron, Mary James, Johnny James, Lucy Lambton, Francis Wheen and David Jenkins for their help, and to my editors at 4th Estate, Nicholas Pearson, Lettice Franklin and Robert Lacey, for their skill and encouragement.

My darling wife Frances has been amazingly sympathetic through-out, especially considering that she has had her own Russian royals to worry about. Our children, Tallulah and Silas, are both now professional writers, and very proud of them we are, too.

SOURCES

To keep things as brief as possible, I am mentioning each source only once, so as to avoid the froggy choruses of ibid-ibid-ibid that so often clog up the notes at the back of books.

Wherever possible, I have concentrated on individual accounts of personal encounters with Princess Margaret, as described in a range of letters and diaries. These include: *The Letters of Kingsley Amis*; *The Diaries of Cecil Beaton: The Unexpurgated Beaton* and *Beaton in the Sixties*; *Writing Home* by Alan Bennett; *Enlightening: Letters 1946–1960* and *Affirming: Letters 1975–1997*, both by Isaiah Berlin; *John Betjeman Letters* Vols I and II; *The Richard Burton Diaries*; *The Blair Years: Extracts from the Alastair Campbell Diaries*; *Chips: The Diaries of Sir Henry Channon*; *The Alan Clark Diaries*; *Darling Monster: The Letters of Lady Diana Cooper to her son John Julius Norwich 1939–1952*; *The Noël Coward Diaries*; *The Letters of Noel Coward*; *The Crossman Diaries*; *In Tearing Haste: Letters Between Deborah Devonshire and Patrick Leigh Fermor*; *National Service: Diary of a Decade at the National Theatre* by Richard Eyre; *The Letters of Anne Fleming*; *John Fowles: The Journals* Vols I and II; *The Diaries of Donald Friend* Vol. IV; *The Diaries of Cynthia Gladwyn*; *My Name Escapes Me: The Diary of a Retiring Actor* and *A Positively Final Appearance*, both by Alec Guinness; *Peter Hall's Diaries*; *Mandarin: The Diaries of Nicholas Henderson*; *The Letters of Ted Hughes*; *The Christopher Isherwood Diaries* Vols I, II and III; *Selected Letters of Philip Larkin 1940–1985*; *Letters to Monica* by Philip

Larkin; *King's Counsellor: The Diaries of Sir Alan Lascelles; The Diaries of James Lees-Milne: Ancestral Voices, 1942–43, Prophesying Peace, 1944–45, Caves of Ice, 1946–47, Midway on the Waves, 1948–49, A Mingled Measure, 1953–72, Ancient as the Hills, 1973–74, Through Wood and Dale, 1975–78, Deep Romantic Chasm, 1979–81, Holy Dread, 1982–84, Beneath a Waning Moon, 1983–85, Ceaseless Turmoil, 1988–92,* and *The Milk of Paradise, 1993–97; The Lyttelton Hart-Davis Letters* Vol. III, *1958; The Macmillan Diaries* Vol. I: *The Cabinet Years* and Vol. II: *Prime Minister and After; Decca: The Letters of Jessica Mitford; Love from Nancy: The Letters of Nancy Mitford; The Diaries and Letters of Harold Nicolson* Vol. III; *Halfway to Hollywood: Diaries 1980–1988* by Michael Palin; *Visiting Picasso: The Notebooks and Letters of Roland Penrose* (which contains invaluable documents relating to the artist's crush on the Princess); *The Diaries of A.L. Rowse; Tears Before Bedtime* by Barbara Skelton; *New Selected Journals 1939–1995* by Stephen Spender; *Splendours and Miseries: The Roy Strong Diaries 1967–1987* and *Scenes and Apparitions: The Roy Strong Diaries 1988–2003; Burnt Diaries* by Emma Tennant; *The Diaries of Kenneth Tynan; The Kenneth Tynan Letters; The Andy Warhol Diaries; The Diaries of Auberon Waugh: Four Crowded Years 1972–1976* and *A Turbulent Decade 1976–1985; The Diaries of Evelyn Waugh; The Letters of Evelyn Waugh; Mr Wu & Mrs Stitch: The Letters of Evelyn Waugh and Diana Cooper; The Kenneth Williams Diaries;* and *The Kenneth Williams Letters.*

For background material, I have plundered all the biographies of Princess Margaret. Of these, I found particularly useful *Princess Margaret: A Life Unravelled* by Tim Heald and *Princess Margaret: A Biography* by Theo Aronson. Nigel Dempster's *HRH The Princess Margaret: A Life Unfulfilled* is strong on the Roddy Llewellyn years. Noel Botham's *Margaret: The Last Real Princess* is unreliable, but sometimes strays into the realms of accuracy, notably when dealing with the Princess's brief romance with Robin Douglas-Home. It also contains her letters to him, on which I have drawn. Being semi-authorised,

Christopher Warwick's stiffer *A Life of Contrasts* is more upright and forgiving. The use of the negative in the subtitles of Princess Margaret biographies – 'Unfulfilled', 'Unravelled', and so forth – seems to have been pioneered by Willi Frischauer in his *Margaret: Princess Without a Cause*, published in 1977.

Snowdon: The Biography by Anne de Courcy is a treasure trove of information about the Snowdons' stormy marriage. In *Time and Chance: An Autobiography*, Peter Townsend plays his cards pretty close to his chest, but his reticence gives the book a certain magnetic quality. I have made extensive use of Townsend's recollections of his relationship with Princess Margaret.

The view from below stairs is often pooh-poohed by royal biographers, but I tend to find servants' memoirs more candid and therefore more interesting than those of grandees. Consequently, I have made good use of Marion Crawford's scorned but charming *The Little Princesses* and David John Payne's fascinating, though rather more sinister, *My Life with Princess Margaret*. Both *Adventures of a Gentleman's Gentleman* by Guy Hunting and *Backstairs Billy: The Life of William Tallon* by Tom Quinn are full of amusing high-camp stories about life at court. *Lord of the Isle: The Extravagant Life and Times of Colin Tennant* (2012) by Nicholas Courtney, the former general manager of Mustique, is straightforward and level-headed.

Hugo Vickers' *Elizabeth: The Queen Mother* offers by far the fullest account of the rise and fall of poor old Marion Crawford. For things Crawfie, including her letters to and from the Queen Mother, I am also indebted to the Manuscripts Division of the Department of Rare Books and Special Collections at Princeton University. Vickers' biography also sheds new light on Princess Margaret's uneasy relationship with her mother. *Queen Elizabeth the Queen Mother: The Official Biography* by William Shawcross, and its companion volume, *Counting One's Blessings: The Selected Letters of Queen Elizabeth the Queen Mother*, both present the twinkly, authorised version, but remain an invaluable source. Those in need of something madder and a good deal more sour may prefer to opt for *Queen Elizabeth: A Life of the Queen Mother* by Penelope Mortimer.

There are countless dogged and dutiful biographies of HM the Queen, most of them ploughing through the same dreary old material in the same dreary old way. A cut above the rest is Gyles Brandreth's witty and unabashed *Philip and Elizabeth: Portrait of a Marriage*, but I have also plucked bits and pieces from *Elizabeth the Queen* by Sally Bedell Smith; *Royal: Her Majesty Queen Elizabeth II* by Robert Lacey; *Queen Elizabeth II: Her Life in Our Times* by Sarah Bradford; *Sovereign: Elizabeth II and the Windsor Dynasty* by Roland Flamini; *The Diamond Queen: Elizabeth II and Her People* by Andrew Marr; and *The Queen: A Biography of Elizabeth II* by Ben Pimlott. *The Duke: A Portrait of Prince Philip* by Tim Heald is good-humoured and fair-minded.

More general works of reference include *Princess Margaret's Wedding Book* (1960); *Debrett's Book of the Royal Wedding* (1981); *Debrett's Book of the Royal Engagement* (1986); *The BBC Book of Royal Memories*; *The Book of Royal Lists* by Craig Brown and Lesley Cunliffe; *Voices Out of the Air: The Royal Christmas Broadcasts 1932–1981*; and *The Royal Encyclopedia*, edited by Ronald Allison and Sarah Riddell. Background on the Royal Family can be found in *King George VI: His Life and Reign* by John Wheeler Bennett; *King George V* by Kenneth Rose; and *King Edward VIII* by Philip Ziegler. *Thatched with Gold: The Memoirs of Mabell, Countess of Airlie*, has lots on the Princess's birth. Margaret Rhodes's otherwise kindly memoir, *The Final Curtsey*, reveals unexpected shards of cattiness whenever Princess Margaret puts her head round the door.

Princess Diana is in danger of attracting almost as many biographies as HM the Queen. The most reliable of those I have read are Sarah Bradford's *Diana*, and *Diana: Story of a Princess* by Tim Clayton and Phil Craig. Those in search of something brassier might enjoy *The Diana Chronicles* by Tina Brown. *Diana: Her True Story – In Her Words* by Andrew Morton (1998) includes transcripts omitted from his original *Diana: Her True Story* (1992), which is now rightly regarded as the Dead Sea Scrolls of Diana Studies.

My appetite for royal kitsch makes me a devoted reader of Sarah, Duchess of York's unstoppable outpourings, not least her original autobiography, *My Story* (1997), and its infinite follow-ups, some of them, such as *What I Know Now: Simple Lessons Learned the Hard Way* (2003), sadly available only in America, where there is more of a taste for these things. *Finding Sarah: A Duchess's Journey to Find Herself* (2011) is, as its title suggests, a classic of the genre. *Sarah* by Ingrid Seward offers a portrait of the Duchess before her repeated falls from grace. Those looking for something less wordy and more picture-based would do well to dig out *Knockout: The Grand Charity Tournament*, subtitled *A Behind-the-Scenes Look at the Event of the Year*, with an introduction by HRH the Prince Edward. It is a colourful memento of the pivotal royal event of 1987, sometimes wrongly referred to as *It's a Royal Knockout*. Kitsch galore may also be found in *The Royals* by Kitty Kelley.

James Pope-Hennessy's 'The King over the Millstream', posthumously published in *A Lonely Business: A Self-Portrait of James Pope-Hennessy* is a delightfully beady sketch of the Duke and Duchess of Windsor in exile. *Behind Closed Doors: The Tragic, Untold Story of the Duchess of Windsor* by Hugo Vickers is similarly compelling. *The Last of the Duchess* by Caroline Blackwood is, like many mad books, full of piercing insights.

Princess Margaret is set in her times in David Kynaston's wonderful panoramic history of post-war Britain, collectively titled *Tales of a New Jerusalem*, which also contains particularly rich pickings from the Mass-Observation archive. *Gossip 1920–1970* and *International Gossip 1970–1980*, by Andrew Barrow, are both full of tiny little details that graver authors tend to overlook.

Ma'am Darling is peppered with allusions to other works. Glimpse 2 is a pastiche of the final paragraph of *Queen Victoria* by Lytton Strachey. Glimpse 32 was inspired by Raymond Queneau's *Exercises in Style*. Glimpse 61 has echoes of Susan Sontag's *Notes on 'Camp'*.

For information about the many fruity and/or dodgy characters whose lives intersected with Princess Margaret's, I raided *Brewer's Dictionary of Rogues, Villains and Eccentrics* by my old friend William Donaldson; also *Bindon* by Wensley Clarkson; *Confessions of a King's Road Cowboy* by Johnny Cigarini; *By Appointment* by Andy Dempsey; *The Truth at Last: My Story* by Christine Keeler; *High on Arrival* by Mackenzie Phillips; *Papa John* by John Phillips; *Jeremy Thorpe* by Michael Bloch; and *A Very English Scandal* by John Preston.

Princess Margaret was drawn to inhabitants of the worlds of art and show business, as they were to her. Stories about these often bizarre alliances and confrontations may be found in *True Britt* by Britt Ekland; *The Life and Death of Peter Sellers* by Roger Lewis; *The Music Man: The Autobiography of Leslie Bricusse*; *Dream Girl: My Life as a Supreme* by Mary Wilson; *The Supremes: A Saga of Motown Dreams, Success and Betrayal* by Mark Ribowsky; *An Affectionate Punch* by Justin de Villeneuve; *The Sorcerer's Apprentice: Picasso, Provence and Douglas Cooper* by John Richardson; *A Prince Among Stones: That Business with the Rolling Stones and Other Adventures* by Prince Rupert Lowenstein; *The Kid Stays in the Picture* by Robert Evans; *What's it All About?* by Michael Caine; *Watch Me* by Anjelica Huston; *Take it Like a Man: The Autobiography of Boy George*; *Can I Go Now?: The Life of Sue Mengers, Hollywood's First Superagent* by Brian Kellow; *Dancing with Demons: The Authorised Biography of Dusty Springfield* by Penny Valentine and Vicki Wickham; *Dusty: An Intimate Portrait* by Karen Bartlett; *As Luck Would Have It* by Derek Jacobi; *Tainted by Experience: A Life in the Arts* by John Drummond; *Elizabeth Taylor* by C. David Heymann; *Furious Love: Elizabeth Taylor, Richard Burton – The Marriage of the Century* by Sam Kashner and Nancy Schoenberger; and *Wear and Tear: The Threads of My Life* by Tracy Tynan.

For glimpses of Princess Margaret's meetings with the Beatles, I drew on *The Beatles Anthology*; *The John Lennon Letters*; *A Twist of Lennon* and *John*, both by Cynthia Lennon; *The Love You Make: An Insider's Story of the Beatles* by Peter Brown and Steven Gaines; *John*

Lennon: The Life by Philip Norman; and *Wonderful Today: The Autobiography of Pattie Boyd*.

Other books that have come in handy include, in no particular order: *Know the Truth* by George Carey; *The Rise and Fall of the House of Windsor* by A.N. Wilson; *Dreams about HM the Queen and Other Members of the Royal Family* by Brian Masters; *Twentieth Century Words* by John Ayto; *The Picnic Papers* edited by Susanna Johnston and Anne Tennant; *Memoirs* by Kingsley Amis; *Redeeming Features* by Nicholas Haslam; *John Betjeman: New Fame, New Love* and *Betjeman: The Bonus of Laughter*, both by Bevis Hillier; *Betjeman* by A.N. Wilson; *The Life of Noël Coward* by Cole Lesley; *James Lees-Milne: The Life* by Michael Bloch; *Cyril Connolly: A Life* by Jeremy Lewis; *Speaking for Myself: The Autobiography* by Cherie Blair; *Maurice Bowra: A Life* by Leslie Mitchell; *New Bats in Old Belfries* by Maurice Bowra; *Life on Air: A History of Radio Four* by David Hendy; *Double Act: A Life of Tom Stoppard* by Ira Nadel; *Hugh Trevor-Roper: The Biography* by Adam Sisman; *The Life of Kenneth Tynan* by Kathleen Tynan; *Every Time a Friend Succeeds Something Inside Me Dies: The Life of Gore Vidal* by Jay Parini; *Palimpsest: A Memoir* by Gore Vidal; *Snapshots in History's Glare* by Gore Vidal; *Point to Point Navigation: A Memoir* by Gore Vidal; *Kings, Queens and Courtiers* by Kenneth Rose; *Angus Wilson* by Margaret Drabble; *Chance Witness* by Matthew Parris; *Of Kings and Cabbages* by Peter Coats; *Nigel Dempster and the Death of Discretion* by Tim Willis; Christie's catalogues for the sale of *Property from the Collection of Her Royal Highness The Princess Margaret, Countess of Snowdon* Vol. I: *Jewellery and Fabergé* and Vol. II: *Silver, Furniture and Works of Art*; *The Queen* and *The Audience*, both by Peter Morgan; *Skylight* by David Hare; *Some Hope* by Edward St Aubyn; *The Collector* by John Fowles; and *More Matter* by John Updike.

News reports and articles from hundreds of newspapers and magazines have been extremely useful, prime among them: 'How We Loved Her' by David Jenkins, *Tatler*, December 2014; John Fortune's *New Statesman* diary, 25 February 2002; A.N. Wilson's *Spectator* diary, 11

May 1990; 'For Better or for Verse' by Craig Raine, *Daily Telegraph*, 3 April 2005; interview with Terence Stamp by John Preston, *Sunday Telegraph*, 4 February 2013; Frank Kermode on Stephen Spender, *London Review of Books*, December 1985; obituary of Cyril Connolly by Stephen Spender, *TLS*, 6 December 1974; interview with Jonathan Aitken by Geoffrey Levy, *Daily Mail*, 22 October 2016; 'The Princess Who Never Knew Her Place' by Selina Hastings, *Sunday Telegraph*, 16 November 1986; obituary of Betty Kenward, *Daily Telegraph*, 26 January 2001; obituary of Betty Kenward, *New York Times*, 1 February 2001; 'The Years with Jennifer' by Vicki Woods, *Spectator*, 23 March 1991; 'The Beatles and Royalty' by Bill Harry, *Mersey Beat*, 28 October 1964; 'Letters from Gore Vidal to Louis Auchincloss', *New Yorker*, 24 June 1996; article on Princess Margaret by A.N. Wilson, *Evening Standard*, 11 February 2002; interview with the Beatles, *Playboy*, 28 October 1964; interviews with David Griffin in *Guardian*, 3 December 2002, *Daily Mail*, 14 March 2016, and *Isle of Wight County Press*, 30 December 2002; article on *Lysistrata* by Germaine Greer, *TLS*, 16 July 1999; interview with Robert Brown, *Guardian*, 19 December 2013; interview with Lord Charteris, *Spectator*, 5 January 1995; 'The Princess and the Peabrain' by Alastair Forbes, *Spectator*, 18 February 1978; and obituary of Lord Snowdon by Philip Hoare, *Independent*, 13 January 2017.

Internet sites such as YouTube are a treasure chest, allowing one to watch any amount of news footage of Princess Margaret. Those interested in the curious tale of Robert Brown may wish to see him putting forth his claim there. From the Anglican Communion News Service website I retrieved Nicholas Witchell's interview with George Carey, 15 February 2002. Mustique-island.com provides prospective tenants with important information about renting Les Jolies Eaux. The Let's Talk Dusty website is a mine of information about Dusty Springfield. On Spotify, I listened to *Dusty Springfield Live at the Albert Hall*.

ILLUSTRATIONS CREDITS